200 SCIEN
INVESTIGATIONS FOR
YOUNG STUDENTS

Practical Activities for Science 5–11

Martin Wenham

University of Leicester

P·C·P

Paul Chapman
Publishing Ltd

Paul Chapman Publishing Ltd
A SAGE Publications Company
6 Bonhill Street
London EC2A 4PU

SAGE Publications Inc
2455 Teller Road
Thousand Oaks, California 91320

SAGE Publications India Pvt Ltd
32, M-Block Market
Greater Kailash-I
New Delhi 110 048

British Library Cataloguing in Publication data

A catalogue record for this book is available from the British Library

ISBN 0 7619 6348 0
ISBN 0 7619 6349 9 (pbk)

Library of Congress catalog record available

Typeset by Dorwyn Ltd, Rowlands Castle, Hampshire
Printed in Great Britain by The Cromwell Press Ltd., Trowbridge, Wiltshire

Contents

Preface

The aim of this book is to help teachers develop a basic repertoire of science activities for children: first-hand experiences of the world through which they can learn to observe, investigate and interpret in a scientific way. Two basic assumptions have guided the selection, invention and presentation of activities. The first is that children are most likely to develop scientific knowledge if they can use concepts, theories and ways of working to investigate, predict, interpret and communicate their own, first-hand experience.

The second assumption is that only a teacher who knows a class well can decide how a particular activity can be used most effectively to meet the needs and develop the abilities of the children. With this in mind, activities have been presented, even when quite highly-structured, in a 'generic' form. This means that they have not been devised or written for a particular age-group, though indications of aspects particularly suited to younger or older children are given on occasion. The intention is that teachers should select, adapt and modify these activities to meet the needs of their particular classes, in the context of their ongoing programme of science education.

The overall plan and numbering of sections follows that of my *Understanding Primary Science* (Paul Chapman Publishing, 1995), which provides more extended discussion of the scientific background to the activities in each section. References with an asterisk, thus: (*12.2) are to that book; other references, to particular chapters, sections and activities, are cross-references within this volume.

The structure and presentation of the activities are varied. Where standardized materials and equipment can be specified and a particular sequence of activity and questioning is helpful, a detailed and structured approach is adopted. Where resources are likely to vary widely according to locality or availability, or where a more highly-structured approach is not needed, the activity is discussed more generally rather than being set out as a detailed procedure (compare, for example, Activities 6.1.2 and 6.1.3). Where a particular procedure is suggested, things to do are shown by bullet-points (●) and questions by bold question-marks (?). Short answers to questions, including the expected results of observations or measurements, follow each question in brackets. Where a more extended discussion is needed, this is given in a separate paragraph.

Particular attention has been paid to devising activities which use commonly-available materials, and to reducing the need for expensive and specialized equipment to a minimum. There are two reasons for this. The first is to increase access to science education: to ensure, as far as possible, that teachers and classes are not held back for lack of resources. The second is less obvious, but no less important: to help children and teachers see the role that scientific knowledge and modes of enquiry can play in their everyday lives and activities. Science does not have to be high-tech to be relevant, interesting and significant: the most fundamental ideas are often shown very clearly by objects and events so familiar that usually we do not think much about them. Children have as much to learn from a loaf of bread, a bicycle or the feeding of birds in a garden as from the Hubble space telescope or genetic engineering.

In researching and writing this book it has been my hope that teachers will (as I have done) work through the activities for themselves before attempting to decide how they might be used in the classroom. Only in this way can the potential of any activity to promote children's learning in science be properly assessed and any necessary modifications be made. This kind of hands-on preparatory work has the added advantage that potential problems of execution, management or understanding are much more likely to become evident, so that they can be resolved in advance.

Acknowledgements

There is a theory that works of art and science are produced not by individuals but by communities. This book is a good example of that theory in practice. It is a pleasure to record here my gratitude to Dr. Alan Garlick, and to Dr. Doug Skehan, Mr. Tom Spyt and their cardiological, surgical and nursing teams at Glenfield General Hospital, Leicester, without whose skill, dedication and professionalism I probably would not have survived long enough to complete it.

Throughout the project I have also been grateful for the support of my colleagues at the School of Education in the University of Leicester, and particularly to the Director, Tom Whiteside; to Paula Buck and Jonathan Westgate who have been more than helpful in providing resources and technical support; and to Laurence Rogers, who is always ready to share ideas and has saved me from many errors of fact and interpretation.

My thanks are also due to Sally Pudney for invaluable advice on early years practice; to David Brown for expert help in understanding sundials and for Fig.18.3; to Neil Millington for information on dental hygiene; to Janet and David Stevenson for generous help with photocopying and to Marianne Lagrange of Paul Chapman Publishing, who encourages, guides and motivates in equal measures.

Finally, my greatest thanks must go to my own 'community': to my wife Christine and our family, without whom nothing could be begun, sustained, or completed.

Martin Wenham
Leicester, 2000

1

The Role of Activities and Investigations in Science Education

Science is one way in which humans seek to understand and learn more about the world, both natural and man-made. Science is not simply a body of knowledge and a way of knowing: it is also a way of doing, which may involve a wide range of activities, including interpretation, communication, prediction, experimentation and observation, aimed at understanding the world better and finding out more about it. Children's learning in science, as in any part of the curriculum, is most effective when knowledge and experience interact; knowledge being used to interpret experience, and experience making it possible for knowledge and understanding to be extended.

Scientific facts, concepts and theories stored up in books, CD-ROMs and other resources (including the memories of teachers!) are essential to the learning process, but so is first-hand experience. Effective learning is the product of intentional, skilfully-managed interaction between the two. Without knowledge, activities such as observation and experimentation lack direction and the means to understand what is experienced. Without first-hand experience to which it can be related, scientific knowledge has no active part to play in a child's life and will never become significant. The role of activities and investigations in science education is to provide part of the first-hand, personal experience which children need if they are to acquire and use scientific knowledge in ways which are relevant, useful and enjoyable.

Variety and style in learning

To be effective, a science education programme has to include a wide range of activity by both pupils and teachers. This includes activities which are teacher-centred, such as instruction and demonstration, together with others which are child-centred, such as experimentation and exploratory play. There are two main reasons why this range of activities is necessary. First, because individuals have different learning-styles and secondly, because different topics in science present different ranges of opportunities and problems.

The two extremes of learning-style can be represented by the 'knowledge first' and 'experience first' models:

- *Knowledge first:* facts, concepts and theories are learned and integrated with remembered experience and existing knowledge. They are then made meaningful by being applied to observation, interpretation or prediction of real-life situations.
- *Experience first:* hands-on experience, coupled with existing knowledge, is used to develop a new idea. This is then verbalized, communicated and made meaningful by modifying or extending existing knowledge.

In practice, no one seems to rely solely on either of these models. Any person's learning is likely to be a complex, interactive activity within which elements of both can be identified, but individuals may show a marked preference for one of these styles of learning and avoid the other.

Some learning situations in science may also lend themselves more readily to one style of learning rather than the other. For example, when learning about basic plant structure (Section 4.2), the 'knowledge first' approach is likely to be helpful. Basic and partly familiar concepts such as stem, leaf and bud can be introduced and related using a diagrammatic plan as an 'advance organizer' before children try to observe and interpret varied forms of plants in the classroom or outdoor environment (Fig.4.1–4.6). In contrast, children can often arrive at concepts of magnetic and non-magnetic materials, and magnetic poles, through exploratory play (Sections 15.3, 15.4). Their ideas can then be verbalized and shared in discussion, brought into line with accepted scientific terminology and consolidated by being used in further investigations.

Science education as a process of discovery

It is often said that science education should be, in part at least, a process of discovery. This is true; but the idea can be effective only if we as teachers are quite clear about what we expect children to discover. What they *cannot* be expected to discover for themselves are complex scientific ideas and theories, such as the idea of adaptation or knowledge of the way in which plants take up and transport water. Scientific facts and ideas like these cannot be 'discovered' by children. They have already been discovered, through years of patient research and debate, and are shared by the whole scientific community.

What children can and must discover if their learning in science is to be effective is what the ideas, facts and theories which make up scientific knowledge mean to them personally. They can do this only by using shared scientific knowledge to interpret their particular experience in a scientific way, which at the same time will enable them to learn and understand more. No scientific knowledge has been truly learned until the learner has assimilated it by using it in this personal way, and at least begun to perceive its relevance to her or him as an individual. The central role of activities and investigations in science education is to provide starting-points for this process: experiences designed to be approached, worked on and interpreted scientifically, enabling children to increase their knowledge and understanding, while discovering more about themselves, the world and their place in it.

2

Life and Living Processes

2.1: The concept of 'living'

Whether at the beginning of their learning in science or later, children need to develop a concept of what it means to be alive. Like most complex concepts, the ideas of 'life' and 'living' are likely to be acquired gradually, as they are used to build knowledge and understanding in the context of widening experience.

Conventional ways of distinguishing living things by their life-processes (the so-called 'signs of life' such as feeding, respiration, response, movement, growth and reproduction) are not, on their own, effective at primary level. This is because in many of the organisms which children encounter, some of these processes either do not occur at all, or are not detectable by any means which young children can readily understand and use. The solution is to abandon the idea that we can always tell here and now whether or not something is alive (though sometimes we may be able to) and adopt a more flexible approach to the problem.

2.2: A wider concept of 'living'

The most fundamental difference between things which are alive and those which are not is the way in which they change over time. If left to themselves and not eaten or afflicted by disease, all living things grow, take in material from their environment, become more complex, capable of more activities and usually make more living things like themselves. Familiar examples which children can observe include eggs growing into animals, seeds growing into plants and plants colonizing their surroundings. In contrast, things which are not alive tend to break down, become simpler and less organized, with their material increasingly spread out into the environment. Familiar examples include the disintegration of abandoned buildings and machines, the decay of dead bodies and (given long enough) the erosion of whole landscapes.

The idea of using patterns of change over time to distinguish living things is particularly useful in the case of plants, which do not show immediately visible 'signs of life' such as moving around, feeding and responding to changes in the environment. The wider concept of 'living' suggested here is not in opposition to more traditional views, but complementary to them. What it does is point to a kind of behaviour shown only by living things, in addition to the traditional 'signs of life', which children can observe through quite simple and straightforward practical activities. An effective first stage is to find out what children think is meant by 'being alive', by way of a simple exercise of classifying a set of carefully-selected items into three groups:

  i) *living* (is alive now);
 ii) *dead* (was once alive but is no longer);
iii) *non-living* (never was alive).

Activity 2.2.1

Living and non-living things
The actual selection of items used in this activity will depend on the resources available to individual schools and teachers, but could usefully include the following, which will also be needed for Activity 2.2.2:

Living things

Animals: soil- and ground-dwelling invertebrates (*5.1) including earthworms, woodlice (sow-bugs), slugs and snails. These should all be kept separately in cool, damp conditions so that they can be seen by the children without being disturbed, e.g. in clear plastic tanks or boxes with lids on and with damp paper towel in the bottom.

Plants: Any potted plants, preferably some with flowers and/or seeds (see introduction to Chapter 4). If possible also include small non-flowering plants, such as mosses (*5.2) growing on soil, bark or stones, kept cool and damp.

Dead things
Bones, feathers, leather, wool, cotton, wood, paper, bark (including cork), dead leaves, seed-pods and cones (*without* seeds), fossils.

Non-living things
Rocks and minerals (not fossils, chalk or limestone); man-made materials such as brick, ceramics, glass, plastics, metals.

It may be helpful to begin, particularly with younger children, with a small selection of items (say two in each category, six in all) which seem likely to be easily classifiable, and see what their response is. For example, do the children clearly understand that wood comes from the inside of trees, and do they regard trees as being alive? If animals (e.g. snails) do not appear to be active, do the children think of them as being alive? Distinguishing between dead and non-living items usually requires them to be identified and their origin known. For example, brick and paper are both man-made materials, but paper is made mostly of pulped plant fibre and brick of fired clay (a mineral), so paper is dead whereas brick is non-living.

To extend this activity it is useful to have a wide selection of items available which are likely to provoke discussion, the most obvious example being dry, dormant plant seeds, which can well form the subject of a separate small enquiry (Activity 2.2.3).

Developing a wider concept of 'living'
Once agreement has been reached on the origins and classification of the dead and non-living objects, the activity can usefully concentrate on the living things and those about which there is doubt or dispute. Most groups of children have little difficulty in classifying animals as alive, even if they are not active at the time they are observed, because at some time similar animals will have been seen moving, responding and feeding, in ways which machines and other non-living things do not do. Most often the outstanding question is, are plants alive; and if so, are they as much alive as animals are? There is quite likely to be dispute over this. The most satisfactory (and scientifically competent) outcome is for the children to decide either that they do not know, or that they cannot agree, and that *they need to know more before they can answer the question.*

If, on the other hand, the children confidently and with no dissent classify both plants and animals as living, it can be useful for the *teacher* to adopt a sceptical position: most animals are 'obviously' alive, but plants do not seem to do anything, so how can they be thought of as being alive? This should stimulate the children to argue their case and show whether their belief that plants are alive has any basis in knowledge, or is simply a repetition of what they have heard elsewhere.

By one route or another the discussion needs to be brought round to the point at which the children realize either that their own ideas are questionable (e.g. the belief that plants are not alive); or that their ideas do not seem to be wrong, but need to be tested. It is at this point that the teacher can usefully introduce the idea of looking at the way living things change over time and the wider concept of 'living' outlined above.

Activity 2.2.2

Finding out if things are alive
If living things are to be distinguished from dead or non-living things by the way they change over time, as well as by more obvious activities, how can we find out if any particular object is in fact alive? The answer is, to put the object in conditions which might be expected to favour its activity and development, then observe it, over a long period of time if necessary, carefully recording any changes. Examples of changes and recording methods could include:

Soil-dwelling animals

Equipment and materials: Soil-dwelling animals in a terrarium (see Section 5.1).

- Put the animals in the terrarium in a cool, shady and quiet place.
- Leave the animals completely undisturbed for at least 30 minutes, then start watching them and recording what they do.
? Are all the animals visible? (Slugs and snails will be; woodlice [sow-bugs] may have moved down between dead leaves.)
? Are the animals you can see active and moving around? Are any of them feeding?
? Have the animals you *cannot* see moved around? (Yes, because they have burrowed into the soil.)

? Do any of the animals respond if they are *gently* touched or if a light is shone on them? (Slugs and snails will draw in their 'horns' (eye-stalks) if touched; woodlice will usually move and hide if a light is shone on them.)
● Return all animals to their natural habitat as soon as possible.

These observations show that all the animals are alive: no non-living or dead things move around and respond in this way.

Flowering plants

Equipment and materials: House-plants in pots, preferably in bud or flowering; white correcting-fluid or paint and small brush; ruler; paper and pencil; camera if available.

● Measure and record the height of upright plants.
● Mark the smallest leaf visible at the tip of one or more shoots with a small dot of white correcting-fluid or white paint. Record the plant and the marked leaf by photographing or drawing it.
● Leave the plant growing in good conditions (light, adequate water, suitable temperature) for at least a week. Examine and measure it; compare your results with the earlier records. If the plant is growing by a window (with light mainly from one side) look at it carefully to see if it has turned and grown towards the light.
● If the plants have flower-buds or flowers, these are likely to develop more quickly than leaves. Watch them carefully and record growth daily if necessary, by drawing or photographs.
? Has the plant grown in size? Have more leaves grown? Has it turned and grown towards the light? (Growing towards the light is an important response by the plant, Activity 4.3.6.)

Activity 2.2.3

Dormant organisms: living or not?
Having established the principle that we often cannot decide whether something is alive or not until we have had the opportunity to observe it for quite a long time, it may be useful to assess children's learning and the extent to which their ideas have advanced by introducing quite a difficult category of object: something which is regarded scientifically as being alive, but which is apparently completely inactive. The most obvious and readily-available examples are the dry seeds of plants.

Equipment and materials: Large, dry seeds which will germinate readily (e.g. pea, bean, sun-flower); plant-pots (e.g. cut-down plastic bottles); sowing compost.

● Look at the seeds carefully.
? Are they doing anything or changing in any way that you can detect? (No; they seem completely inert.) If you left them as they are for a few weeks, would they be likely to change? (No.)
? Can the seeds change naturally, and if so, how? (Yes: by putting them into damp soil in fairly warm conditions they will germinate and grow.)
? When a young plant is growing from a seed, is it alive? (Yes: it changes in the ways we expect living things to do.)

? Is the seed alive now? (The scientific view is, yes.)
● Plant the seeds and keep them in conditions which you think will allow them to germinate and grow (Activity 4.3.2). This should prove whether they are alive or not.

Some children (and adults!) are likely to argue that the seeds are not alive now, but will become alive when they germinate. This is not the scientific view. Even if something appears to be inactive, it may not be (seeds do actually carry on very slow respiration) and if it has the potential for active growth and development it is regarded scientifically as being alive, but dormant.

Many living things show dormancy at some time in their lives, often to survive unfavourable conditions such as cold or drought. Perhaps the least obvious, though certainly the largest, examples of this are deciduous trees which become almost completely inactive in winter (north-temperate regions) or the dry season (sub-tropics and tropics). Other examples include adult animals in cold (hibernation) or drought (aestivation) and the eggs of many animals, particularly insects. The most widespread dormant living things are bacteria and the spores of fungi which are almost everywhere on Earth, able to re-activate and decompose dead material whenever it becomes available (see Activities 5.3.1; 5.8.1).

3

Humans as Organisms

The overall aim of the activities described and discussed in this chapter is to help children build up their knowledge and understanding of the structure of their own bodies and the way they work and behave. The broad relevance of this is two-fold. First is the simply scientific: using ourselves as an example of an animal and investigating ourselves because our own bodies and responses are the ones we know most about and which are most important to us. Secondly, enabling children to study and investigate themselves has a significant contribution to make in the wider area of health and social education in which it assumed that, at least in adulthood, primary health care is the responsibility of the individual.

3.1: Basic human anatomy

Learning about how the body functions and how it may be cared for requires at least an outline knowledge of its structure and the activities of its main parts. Some of this knowledge can be gained only from information resources such as books, CD-ROMs, charts and so on, but unless this information is linked to first-hand investigations by children of their own bodies they are unlikely fully to realize its relevance and importance to them personally.

Activity 3.1.1

Finding body landmarks
Body landmarks are places where internal structure, most often the skeleton, can be felt beneath the skin, which can help children to locate parts of their bodies accurately and so introduce investigations into the ways in which they work and behave.

A useful procedure is to identify a landmark on a model, chart or other illustration, find it on one's own body and then begin to consider what its significance is. This work should be undertaken when the children are lightly clothed, ideally in shorts or swimming costumes only. It is assumed throughout that each child will feel only his or her own body; but it can be very useful, if the children are willing, for them to work in pairs so that they can *see* each other's movement, for example from the back when looking for the shoulder-blade or spine, and from the front when breathing in to feel the rib-cage.

Equipment: Any or all of the following: model or chart of human skeleton; model or chart of human body; CD-ROM on human anatomy with equipment for interactive use by children.

The main body landmarks are:

- *Head*: the top of the head or cranium (young children must feel this gently); eyebrow ridges, cheek-bone and eye-socket; lower jaw, its joint and the angle below the ear.
- *Arm and hand*: shoulder and elbow-joints (feel movement); lower arm (twist and feel that there are two parallel bones); wrist, knuckle joints.
- *Neck*: Collar-bones between the hollow at the base of the neck and the shoulder on either side.
- *Chest*: ribs; breast-bone; base of breast-bone and bottom of rib-cage.
- *Spine*: bend forward, feel bones (vertebrae) on mid-line below neck and in the small of the back.
- *Hip region*: upper edges of the hip-bone (pelvis), from the side of the body round to the back.
- *Leg*: top of thigh-bone and joint with hip (feel movement); knee-cap and joint (feel movement); shin-bone; ankle and heel-bones; joints of toes.

Activity 3.1.2

Relating body landmarks to major internal organs
If children are to begin developing an understanding of how the body works, they need to know the location of its major parts, including internal organs. Again this learning is likely to be most effective if they can compare information from resource material with observation of their own bodies, using landmarks for guidance.

Equipment: Any or all of the following: model or chart of human skeleton; model or chart of human body; CD-ROM on human anatomy with equipment for interactive use by children.

The first step is to understand the shape and position of the diaphragm, which divides the trunk into two parts: upper (thorax) and lower (abdomen), whose main organs can then be located.

Diaphragm
The diaphragm is a sheet of tough, inelastic fibre-tissue (tendon), with muscle all round its edges. It is an important part of our breathing mechanism (Activity 3.6.1), moving up and down as we breathe out and in.

- Find the lower end of your breast-bone. The main part of the diaphragm is a rather flat dome shape with its top at about this level (Fig. 3.1). The edge of the diaphragm, which is a muscle, is attached to the inside of the bottom edge of the rib-cage, all the way round.

Thorax
The main organs of the thorax or chest region are the heart and lungs.

- *Heart*: to see roughly where and how big your heart is, make a fist with your left hand. Place your fist, thumb uppermost, over your left nipple. The fist is about the

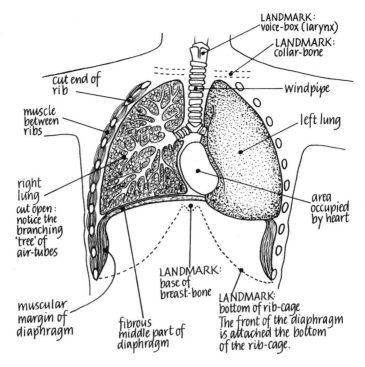

LANDMARK:
voice-box (larynx)

LANDMARK:
collar-bone

cut end of
rib

windpipe

muscle
between
ribs

left lung

right
lung
cut open:
notice the
branching
'tree' of
air-tubes

area
occupied
by heart

muscular
margin of
diaphragm

fibrous
middle part of
diaphragm

LANDMARK:
base of
breast-bone

LANDMARK:
bottom of rib-cage
The front of the diaphragm
is attached the bottom
of the rib-cage.

Figure 3.1   The position of the diaphragm in relation to body landmarks and the main organs of the chest region, seen from the front

same size as your heart and directly over its position inside your chest (see also Fig. 3.1 and Activity 3.8.1).

Lungs: Apart from the heart and the very large blood-vessels, the remainder of the thorax is filled with the lungs and the main air-tubes (Fig. 3.1).

Abdomen
The main organs in the abdomen which children may need to know about and locate are the stomach, liver, intestines and kidneys.

Stomach: The stomach takes the food we swallow and carries on its digestion, so its size and shape vary a lot, depending on how much we have eaten.

● Find the bottom of your breast-bone. Fold your left thumb into the palm of the hand, then lay the hand on the front of your body so that the folded thumb is just below the breast-bone, in the notch where your rib-cage divides. Your hand will then show the approximate size and shape of your stomach (Fig. 3.2), which is much higher than is commonly imagined (see also Activity 3.3.2).

Liver: The liver is a very large organ and is the body's main biochemical factory, carrying out a very wide range of chemical changes on food and other body products.

● Find the bottom of your breast-bone: this is the level of the top of your di-aphragm. Run your fingers at this level to the right, over your ribs: the top of your

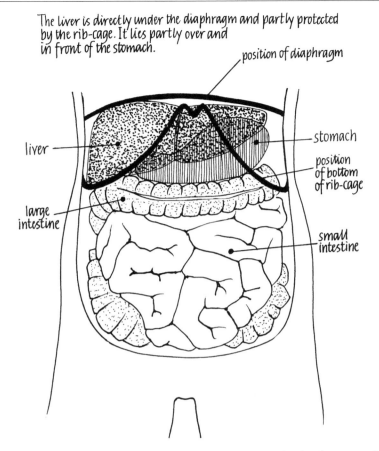

The liver is directly under the diaphragm and partly protected by the rib-cage. It lies partly over and in front of the stomach.

position of diaphragm

liver

stomach

position of bottom of rib-cage

large intestine

small intestine

Figure 3.2 Position of main abdominal organs in relation to the diaphragm and rib-cage, seen from the front

liver is inside your ribs at about this level (Fig. 3.2). Both the stomach and the liver are partly protected by the ribs, and more at the back than at the front.

Intestines: These fill most of the remainder of the abdomen from below the stomach and liver to the pelvis (Fig. 3.2). They complete digestion of food and enable the useful products to be absorbed into the blood.

Kidneys: We have two kidneys: they filter waste products, excess salt and excess water from the blood.

- Your kidneys lie inside the back of the abdomen, on either side of the spine, about level with the gap you can feel between the bottom of the ribs and the top of the pelvis.

3.2: Nutrition: teeth and dental care

Apart from sugars, our main food-chemicals (starch, proteins and fats) have to be broken down chemically (digested) before the body can absorb and use them. The first stage of digestion is chewing: the breaking-up and pulping of food before it is swallowed, carried out by the jaws and teeth but also requiring saliva (see Activity 3.3.1).

Practical activities on teeth at primary level can profitably be linked closely with dental care as part of health education. If children are to avoid serious tooth decay and diseased gums, they need to practise a simple, regular routine of dental hygiene. The greatest danger is the buildup of a sticky bacterial film (plaque) on the teeth, especially between teeth and near the gum-line where it may be difficult and, if oral hygiene is neglected, uncomfortable to remove.

Activity 3.2.1

Dental plaque and the effect of brushing

Equipment and materials: Dental disclosing (erythrosine) tablets; new toothbrushes; toothpaste (all usually available from manufacturers in promotional packs); drinking water and disposable cups; sink or bucket; mirror.

- Disclosing tablets have a bright red dye in them which stains the plaque on your teeth. Chew a disclosing tablet; use your tongue to move the solution of dye in your mouth all over your teeth. After 1 minute, rinse out your mouth with water.
- Look at your teeth and gums in a mirror, pulling your lips aside to look at your back teeth.
- ? Are your teeth stained red? Which parts are stained?

Few children (or adults) are likely to have completely unstained teeth. Areas of plaque are coloured *bright* red: clean tooth enamel is at most very pale pink. The greatest amount of staining is usually near the gum-line and between teeth.

- Draw your teeth to show where the staining is. The stain shows where plaque has built up on the teeth.
- Now brush your teeth using toothpaste until you have removed all the stain.
- ? Which is the most difficult plaque to remove, and why? (First, that between teeth, because it takes more skill to brush up and down than from side to side. Secondly, that near the gum-line, because brushing to remove it may make gums sore and bleeding.)
- To see how fast plaque can build up on teeth, clean your teeth so that they have no plaque on them, then don't clean them at all for 48 hours. (This may require parental consent, but will not cause harm to teeth if done only once.)
- Now re-test your teeth with a disclosing tablet.
- ? How much plaque has built up in 48 hours? (The answer is usually, quite a lot.)
- Clean your teeth thoroughly until you have removed all the plaque.

3.3: Nutrition: digestion

Digestion is a process of chemical change (*9.1), by which complex foods are broken down into simpler products which the body can use. For example, starch is a basic food for most humans, but can neither be absorbed nor used by the body until it has been digested to sugars. The only parts of the digestive process which children can investigate at primary level are those at the start: what happens as food is taken into the mouth, chewed and swallowed.

Activity 3.3.1

What happens as food is chewed

Materials: Starchy, sugar-free foods, e.g. dry bread, cream crackers.

Normally the inside of the mouth is moist but there is not a lot of liquid in it.

- Start to eat a piece of bread or a cream cracker slowly, until you have an amount in your mouth which is comfortable to chew. Chew carefully and do not swallow at all.
- Chew the food for about a minute to break up the lumps. At the same time observe how it is changing.
- ? How does the food change as it is chewed? (It becomes moist, and chewing turns it into a paste.)
- Keep the paste of food in your mouth but do not chew it any more once you have broken up the lumps.
- ? What is the liquid which wets the food as you chew it? (It is saliva, made [secreted] by glands inside the mouth.)
- ? What is the flow of saliva commonly called? ('Watering at the mouth'.) What starts it? (Food in the mouth or, if you are hungry, simply the smell of food you like.)

Salivating is a good example of a stimulus (food in the mouth) leading to an almost immediate response (making saliva; see introduction to Section 3.10).

- Leave the ball of food-paste in your mouth for 3 minutes.
- ? How has the taste of the food changed since you first chewed it? (It has become sweet. If this cannot be detected, swallow the chewed and partly digested food, then immediately eat another piece of bread or cracker. The difference is then easier to detect.)

The sweetness develops because saliva contains a chemical agent (an enzyme, salivary amylase) which digests starch to a sugar (malt-sugar, maltose). The change in taste is evidence that this is a chemical change (see also Activity 9.2.3; contrast Activity 6.5.2).

- ? Could you easily swallow dry bread or crackers without chewing them? (No: it would be difficult, and even dangerous, because you might choke on the crumbs.)
- ? How does chewing with saliva make swallowing possible? (It softens and moistens the food so that it forms a paste and clings together in a soft lump which can be swallowed. Saliva is also a little slimy, which helps the food slide down to the stomach.)

Chewing food thoroughly is an important part of digestion because it helps the stomach to continue breaking the food down quickly and efficiently. If food is insufficiently crushed and therefore swallowed in lumps, the stomach has to do the work which should have been done by chewing and may become painful as a result: one cause of 'indigestion'.

Activity 3.3.2

Where does food go when it is swallowed?

Equipment and materials: Disposable cups; hot water; acidic fruit-juice (e.g. orange or grapefruit).

Safety note: This activity must be done under supervision to make sure that the children do not drink liquid which is too hot.

- Mix some fruit juice with hot water in a cup. Sip a little of the mixture to feel how hot it is. Add more water or juice until the mixture feels hot in your mouth **but not uncomfortable.**
- Swallow a mouthful of the mixture and sit still. You will feel the liquid go down through your chest. The liquid (and your food) goes down a tube inside the back of the chest, just in front of the spine.
- ? Where does the tube take the liquid and the food you eat? (To the stomach; see Activity 3.1.2 and Fig. 3.2).
- Put your hand over the part of your body where the liquid went: this shows you where your stomach is.

The tube through which food and drink reach the stomach is the gullet (oesophagus). Sensors in the gullet and stomach respond to the warm, slightly acidic liquid so the children will be able to feel where they are. This observation shows that the stomach is much higher in the body than most people imagine (see Fig. 3.2).

3.4: Nutrition: food and diet

The overall range of foods which any animal eats is its diet. An adequate or correctly-balanced diet is a combination of foods which will enable a particular animal to remain healthy in the long term. For humans, a correctly-balanced diet includes a variety of foods, together with the vitamins they contain, minerals and water.

Practical investigations into diet and eating habits at primary level is, potentially at least, a very sensitive issue. Conclusions about the value of particular dietary items, or the adequacy of any person's diet, should be drawn (if at all) by pupils for themselves and not by the teacher. Up-to-date dietary advice, based on the ongoing research into human nutrition and adapted to local conditions, is readily available from health promotion agencies. By making lists of what they eat day by day, children can compare this advice with their own individual diets. This can be done in a simple way by comparing ranges of food eaten, or more precisely by studying nutrition information given on food packaging and comparing the content of different foods.

3.5: Skeleton, joints, muscles and movement

Humans are vertebrates: animals with backbones (*5.1). Our bodies have a bony skeleton inside them, some parts of which can be investigated by feeling them through overlying tissues and the skin (Activity 3.1.1). Most of our skeleton is made of bone, which is either rigid or only slightly flexible (Section 7.5): properties which enable it both to support the body and to protect vulnerable organs such as the brain, heart and lungs.

In spite of the rigidity of its parts, the skeleton also enables us to move about. Two things make this possible. First, most of the bones of the skeleton are joined so that they can move in relation to one another. Secondly, the bones have muscles attached to them. Muscle is a specialized tissue which can move and exert a force, but on its own it would not enable the body to move. Only when the force is applied to the skeleton, which acts as a lever system, can part or all of the body move about. Neither muscle nor skeleton could move the body on its own, so although they may be investigated separately to begin with, it is helpful to work towards thinking of them as a single, *skeleto-muscular* system.

Activity 3.5.1

The skeleton: support and protection
Instructions for finding parts of the skeleton by way of body landmarks will be found in Activity 3.1.1. At each stage of this activity, children should be encouraged to relate what they do and observe to body landmarks and available resource material on human anatomy.

Equipment: Any or all of the following: model or chart of human skeleton; model or chart of human body; CD-ROM on human anatomy with equipment for interactive use by children.

The skeleton as support

● Work in pairs. Ask your partner to lie flat on the floor, then get up on to hands and feet, as shown in Fig. 3.3. Watch carefully as she or he does this, then change places and do it yourself while your partner watches.

Turn hands in, spread fingers and straighten elbow-joints.

Bend feet to rest on toes; keep knees as straight as possible.

Figure 3.3 Making a body-bridge

? Which parts of your body did you use to lift yourself up? (Mainly, the arms and legs. More precisely, the muscles and bones of the arms and legs.)
? When you had lifted your body from the ground (Fig. 3.3), what structure was your body like? (A bridge.)

? What was supporting the 'bridge'? (Again, the muscles and bones of the arms and legs.)

? How can the arms and legs keep straight and hold the body up? (The bones are rigid and the muscles stop the arms and legs from folding up.)

● If you are strong enough, do a few press-ups. Notice that once your elbow-joints are straight ('locked-out'), it is easier to keep them straight and support your body than it is to push your body up, because the bones are then able to act like pillars. For the same reason, you can stand upright with your knees straight with much less effort than is needed to lift your body from a squatting position.

The skeleton is like a frame to which the other body parts are attached and which supports the whole body. The role of the skeleton in movement will be further investigated in Activities 3.5.2–3.5.4.

The skeleton as protection

By looking at resource materials and feeling the cranium and rib-cage, children can see and feel how the hard bone of the skeleton protects the brain, heart, lungs and liver. These observations can then be related to safety issues such as the wearing of crash-hats by cyclists and seat-belts by drivers and passengers in cars. Activity 14.2.3, investigating forces involved in impacts, is relevant here.

Activity 3.5.2

The skeleton and movement: joints

Throughout this activity, children should be encouraged to relate what they do and observe to body landmarks (Activity 3.1.1) and available resource material on human anatomy.

Equipment: Models or charts of the human skeleton; CD-ROM on human anatomy with equipment for interactive use by children.

There are three main kinds of joints in the skeleton, two of which children can investigate.

The first kind of joint is fully movable, though the extent and direction of movement varies a lot between different joints. This is the kind of joint with which children will be most familiar. Examples include the joints of the jaw, shoulder, elbow, wrist, fingers, hip, knee, ankle and toes.

The second kind of joint moves only in a limited way, the main examples being the joints between the bones of the spine (vertebrae).

Children cannot investigate the third kind of joint, because it does not move at all. The main examples are the joints between the bones of the brain-case (cranium).

Joints in the arms, legs and hands

● Sit down facing a table and put your hand on the table, palm down and with the table-edge under your wrist. With the other hand, press down on the bones of the forearm.

? Did the bones bend, or are they rigid? (They are rigid.)

You could repeat this observation all over your body. Nearly all your bones are rigid, though some (e.g. the ribs) are slightly flexible.

? If bones are rigid, how can we move parts of our bodies about? (Because the bones have movable joints between them.)
● Move and feel the different parts of your arm.
? How many joints are there, and what do they join together? (Three: the shoulder joins the upper arm to the body, the elbow joins the upper arm to the forearm and the wrist joins the forearm to the hand.)
● Move your shoulder-joint in as many ways as you can. Feel the joint moving with the fingers of the other hand.
? Does your shoulder-joint allow your arm to move in many directions, or only in one? (Many directions.)
● Sit at a table and put one elbow on it. Keeping your upper arm and shoulder quite still, move your forearm at the elbow in as many different ways as you can.
? Does your elbow-joint allow movement in many directions, or only in one? (Only in one direction, out-and-back, in line with the upper arm. This can be confirmed by lifting the arm, turning it in any direction and then moving the elbow-joint. The forearm can move only in line with the upper arm.)
● Repeat these observations with the hip, knee and finger-joints, to see if they allow movement in many directions, or only in-and-out.

Although differently-shaped joints move in different directions, all the joints you have investigated so far work in much the same way: the ends of the bones can slide smoothly over one another. If the joints cannot move easily and smoothly, for example if they are damaged or inflamed as in the disease arthritis, movement is restricted and may be very painful.

Joints in the spine
The joints in your spine are different from those in your arms and legs: there are 24 of them.

● Stand upright, then move your body to make your spine bend in as many ways as you can, e.g. forward, back and in circles. Notice that although it can move in many directions, the amount of movement is limited. Also, with so many joints, each one must only be moving a little.

Except the top two which are specialized to let the head move, the vertebrae are joined by thick discs of tough, flexible tissue which hold them in place. As the spine is bent, each disc is squashed and stretched a little so that the spine as a whole can bend, but not so much that the spinal cord is damaged. Lifting heavy weights in the wrong way (e.g. with the back bent) can result in permanent damage to the joints of the spine, disability and a lot of pain.

Activity 3.5.3

Finding tendons
Muscles can pull on bones because they are connected by tendons. Tendon is a fibre-tissue which is almost totally inextensible (i.e. it has high stiffness in tension, see

Activity 7.5.1), though it is soft and flexible when not under load. Tendons have different forms, but with one exception (the diaphragm, see Activities 3.1.2 and 3.6.2) all the tendons children can locate and investigate easily are cord-like.

Throughout this activity, children should be encouraged to relate what they do and observe to body landmarks (Activity 3.1.1) and available resource material on human anatomy.

Equipment: Charts and models of the human body (particularly muscles); CD-ROM on human anatomy with equipment for interactive use by children.

• Sit at a table with one hand under the edge (Fig. 3.4).

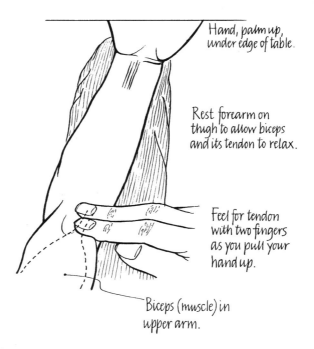

Hand, palm up, under edge of table.

Rest forearm on thigh to allow biceps and its tendon to relax.

Feel for tendon with two fingers as you pull your hand up.

Biceps (muscle) in upper arm.

Figure 3.4 Finding a tendon in the elbow

• Place two fingers of the other hand in the crook (angle) of your elbow (Fig. 3.4). Keeping the fingers there and your upper arm still, pull your forearm and hand up so that you lift (or try to lift) the table. A tight ridge appears under your fingers: this is a tendon under the skin.
• Still pulling up, press down on the tendon with your fingers.
? Is the tendon flexible? (Only very slightly: it is very stiff and feels quite hard.)
• Keeping your fingers on the tendon, lower your arm and rest it on your thigh again.
? How does the tendon change when the arm is supported? (It becomes soft and much more difficult to feel.)
? When the tendon is stiff and hard, a force is acting on it. Is it a pulling or a pushing force? (A pulling force. This is an important point and worth emphasizing: tendons feel stiff and hard *only* under tension [pulling forces]: if not under tension they feel soft and flexible.)

The tendon you have felt is the cord which pulls on one of the forearm bones (radius), lifting up the forearm and bending the elbow-joint. Of the many other places in the body where tendons can be felt, two are particularly easy to find and investigate: tendons behind the knee (hamstring tendons) and at the base of the neck, felt when turning the head left and right.

Activity 3.5.4

Muscles and their action
Muscle is the tissue whose action makes bones of the skeleton move. The muscles of cattle and sheep are the red meat we see in butchers' shops and our muscles are very similar. This activity continues and builds on Activity 3.5.3. It aims at establishing three points which are important to children's understanding of how the skeleton, muscles and tendons enable us to move. The first point is that when muscles work, they pull; secondly, muscles can *only* pull: they cannot push; and thirdly, that bending and straightening of any joint requires action by at least two muscles.

Equipment: Any or all of the following: charts or models of the human skeleton; charts or models of human anatomy; CD-ROM with equipment for interactive use by children.

In Activity 3.5.3 we found the tendon which pulls the forearm up; in this activity we find and investigate the action of the muscle (biceps) which does the pulling.

The pulling action of muscle

- Sit as in Fig. 3.4, but resting one forearm on your thigh. Gently squeeze the flesh in front of the upper arm, about half-way between elbow and shoulder: it is soft and quite floppy (relaxed). What you are feeling is muscle under the skin, but the muscle is not working: it is at rest.
- Now pull up your hand and forearm to raise the table, as in Fig.3.4, feeling the muscle all the time.
- ? What change do you feel in the muscle as it becomes active and starts to pull? (It becomes much firmer and a more obviously round shape.)
- ? What do these observations tell you about changes in the 'feel' and shape of muscle as it starts to pull? (When a muscle is working [pulling] it is firm; but when it is relaxed it is much softer and not such a definite shape.)
- Feel the tendon in the crook of your elbow, as in Activity 3.5.3: this joins the muscle to the forearm bone.
- ? When the muscle lifts the forearm, is it exerting a pulling force or a pushing force? (A pulling force.)
- ? How can you tell? (Because the tendon at the elbow is tight. When tendons are not under tension they are soft and pliable. They become tight and feel hard only when under tension; that is, a pulling force.)

Muscles can only pull: they cannot push
We have seen that a muscle pulls up the forearm, bending the elbow-joint. We now need to find what can straighten it again.

- Stand facing a wall with your hand flat on the wall as in Fig. 3.5. Relax your whole arm and hand. Feel at the back of your upper-arm bone: you will feel relaxed muscle.

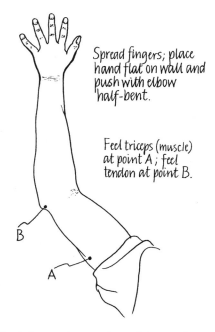

Spread fingers; place hand flat on wall and push with elbow half-bent.

Feel triceps (muscle) at point A; feel tendon at point B.

Figure 3.5   Feeling muscle action as the arm is straightenend

- Still feeling this muscle, push hard on the wall, as if trying to straighten your arm.
- ? What change do you feel in this muscle? (It becomes firm and tight.)
- ? What does this tell you about the muscle's activity? (It is working; exerting a force.)
- Stand as before with your hand flat on the wall. Keeping the whole arm relaxed, feel the bony point of your elbow with your finger-tips, then move your fingers about 1cm towards your upper arm. Now push on the wall and relax a few times: you will feel a tendon tighten and slacken.
- ? When you straighten your arm with a pushing action, is the tendon pushing or pulling? (It is *pulling*.)

These observations show that both the bending (pulling) and straightening (pushing) actions of the arm are brought about by the pulling action of muscles. This is true of movements generally because *muscles can only pull: they cannot push*. This means that any action of moving a joint one way and then moving it back again must involve at least two muscles, attached *on opposite sides of the joint*. In joints such as the elbow, the muscle on the inside bends the joint and another on the outside, pulling 'round the corner' as it were, straightens it. Another example of a similar action which can easily be felt is the bending and straightening of the foot by muscles in the lower leg.

3.6: Breathing and respiration

Respiration is a complex chemical process by which living things transfer energy derived from their food (chemical-potential energy, *12.2) for activities such as growth and movement. Breathing is the activity of animals which enables them to take oxygen into their bodies. Breathing involves an *exchange* of gases: oxygen needed for respiration is taken in, while carbon dioxide, the main waste product, is removed from the body and breathed out.

   Humans and other mammals (*5.1) breathe using two lungs which are complex air-sacs in the chest (see Activity 3.1.2), supplied with air by the wind-pipe which runs down the neck in front of the spine and the gullet. When investigating our own breathing it is important to realize at the outset that the lungs cannot move them-selves: air can be made to flow in and out of them only by changing the shape and volume of the chest. This can be shown in a simple way by making a model of the chest, lungs and diaphragm, which is also a useful introduction to an investigation of one of our two ways of breathing.

Activity 3.6.1

Modelling the chest and breathing

Equipment and materials: 2-litre transparent plastic bottle; thin polythene sheet (e.g. cut from plastic bag); round balloon; two elastic bands; adhesive tape about 2cm wide; craft knife; scissors.

- Make a model of the chest as shown in Fig. 3.6. In this model the balloon represents the lungs, the bottle the chest and the polythene sheet, the diaphragm.

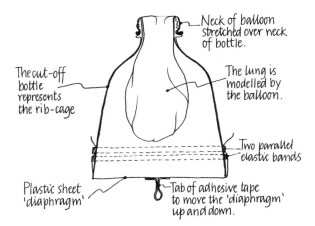

Figure 3.6   Modelling the thorax

- Hold the bottle neck and the tab in the middle of the 'diaphragm'; push the tab up and down, watching what happens to the 'lung'.

- Put your face just above the neck of the balloon. As the 'diaphragm' is pushed up, you will feel air flow out of the 'lung'.
? What happens to the 'lung' as the 'diaphragm' is moved up and down? (As the 'diaphragm' is pushed up the 'lung' deflates. As the 'diaphragm' is pulled down, it partly inflates again.)

This model is useful in that it:

- emphasizes that the lungs are passive in breathing: they are moved but do not move themselves;
- shows the in-and-out (tidal) flow of air as we breathe (the air does not circulate);
- correctly shows that the diaphragm is pushed up when breathing out and pulled down when breathing in.

It is, however, potentially misleading in that:

- there is only one lung whereas we have two;
- the 'lung' does not fill the 'chest' whereas (apart from the heart) ours do;
- the shape of the diaphragm is too flat: in our bodies it is dome-shaped (Fig. 3.1).

These are not serious drawbacks, but they need to be pointed out to children, preferably in the context of a chart, model or CD-ROM on the anatomy of the chest.

Activity 3.6.2

Movement of the diaphragm and ribs in breathing
As an introduction, children should be reminded beforehand of the basic anatomy of the chest in relation to body landmarks they can feel (see the first part of Activity 3.1.2 and Fig. 3.1) and any available resources.

Equipment: Any or all of the following: charts and models of the human body; CD-ROM on human anatomy with equipment for interactive use by children.

Safety note: Although single deep breaths need to be taken during this activity, at no time should children repeat these or breathe much more rapidly than usual. The objective is to find out about breathing movements. The effect of exercise on breathing will be investigated in Activity 3.9.2.

When we breathe, the volume of the chest is increased and decreased by the action of muscles and the skeleton. This is done in two different ways, which most people use together for most of the time: breathing with the rib-cage and with the diaphragm.

Breathing with the diaphragm
The model made in Activity 3.6.1 is a useful visual aid in this activity.

- Sit down and find the lower end of your breast-bone and the bottom of your rib-cage. The diaphragm is joined to the bottom edge of the rib-cage all the way round and below it is the abdomen.
- Interlock your fingers so that your hands are firmly joined together, place them over the lower end of your breast-bone and pull your elbows in on either side of your rib-cage.

- Press the hands and arms inwards on to the rib-cage to stop it moving and breathe in as if you were yawning. The abdomen will be pushed outwards.
- Still holding the rib-cage, breathe out again by pulling the abdomen in.

With a little practice you will probably be able to breathe this way without holding your ribs, which is something singers have to learn as part of their breath control.

The model made in Activity 3.6.1 is a model of this kind of breathing. When you breathe in, the diaphragm is pulled down and made flatter by the muscle round its edge (joined to the bottom of the rib-cage). This pushes the stomach, liver and intestines downwards, making the abdomen bulge out. At the same time the chest is made bigger, so air flows into the lungs. When you breathe out, the muscles in front of the abdomen pull inwards, pushing the intestines, liver, stomach and diaphragm back up again. This makes the chest smaller, so air flows out of the lungs again.

Breathing with the ribs

- Join your hands together as before, but put them lower down, over your abdomen. Pull your hands and elbows in, to prevent your abdomen from bulging.
- Breathe in and out by raising and lowering your ribs. Try not to move your diaphragm and abdomen at all, though this may be difficult. (It does not matter if they move a little.)
- ? How do your ribs move when you breathe? (When breathing in they move upwards and outwards; when breathing out, downwards and inwards.)
- ? When you breathe in and your ribs move up and out, does your chest change size? (Yes: it gets bigger.)
- ? What is the result? (Air flows into the lungs: you breathe in.)
- ? What happens when your ribs move down and in? (The chest gets smaller and air flows out of the lungs: you breathe out.)

This breathing action is brought about mainly by the muscles between the ribs themselves. One set pulls the ribs up and out; another set pulls them down and in again.

Both the ribs and the diaphragm are used in normal breathing by most people, though one may at times be more obvious than the other. When a person is lying relaxed or asleep, most of their breathing will be done by the diaphragm and abdominal muscles, but when engaged in vigorous exercise both kinds of breathing action will usually be more rapid and deeper (more air taken in with each breath) so that breathing with the ribs will be much more obvious (see Activity 3.9.2).

Activity 3.6.3

Respiration and body temperature

Respiration is the process by which energy is transferred in living things. It is a chemical process, but quite unlike burning (*9.4) because it is carried out in a very controlled way and at low temperatures, usually below 40°C. Finding evidence for respiration at primary level involves us in measuring body temperature. If an object is at a higher temperature than its surroundings, for example a hot drink in a cup, we expect it to cool down: to transfer thermal energy to whatever is around it (Activity 12.3.6) until it is at the same temperature as its surroundings. If an object consistently maintains a higher temperature than its environment, it must have some kind of internal heating process. In our bodies this process is respiration and the most easily-observed evidence for it is our body temperature.

Thermometers for measuring body temperature
Glass thermometers pose too many risks to be acceptable for children measuring their own body temperature and liquid-crystal (strip) thermometers are not accurate enough, so neither should be used for this activity. The best choice is a wide-range (–10°C to +110°C) digital thermometer, which shows the temperature at the end of a metal probe, in figures on an LCD display. This will also be exceedingly useful in many investigations, being reasonably robust, reliable and accurate, as well as much easier to read than the traditional graduated scale.

Body temperature and its significance

Equipment: Wide-range thermometer (any type) to measure room temperature; digital thermometer to measure under-arm skin temperature.

- If your classroom does not have a thermometer to measure room temperature, set one up in a safe place, away from direct sunlight and room heaters. Leave it for 20 minutes, then record the room temperature.
- Make sure that anyone whose body temperature is to be measured has not been eating, drinking, exercising or out in hot sunshine for the last 30 minutes.
- Place the thermometer probe in the armpit, close the arm over it and wait for at least 2 minutes. Read the thermometer (do not remove it unless you have to), replace and take a second reading to check: it should be the same as the first.
? Compare results from different people obtained using the same thermometer. Does everyone have the same body temperature? (Usually not; but the range of variation is normally narrow.)
? What is the difference between human body temperature and room temperature? (The body temperature is much higher, unless the room is very hot indeed!)
? What do you expect to happen to a hot object (e.g. a hot drink in a cup) if it is left in a cool room? (It will cool down to room temperature.)
? Why does the body not cool down to room temperature? (Because it keeps itself warm, i.e. it has an internal heating process.)

The internal heating of the body shows that energy is being transferred: the process by which this is done is respiration. Maintaining the body-core temperature is very important: if it varies by more than a few degrees, for example in fever (high temperature) or hypothermia (low temperature), this can be life-threatening. During exercise, over-heating of the body is avoided by cooling (see Activity 3.9.3).

3.7 and 3.8: Blood and its circulation

Blood is the fluid whose circulation is the main transport system of the body. Detailed investigation of blood itself is beyond the scope of primary science, but children can add significantly to their knowledge and understanding of how their bodies work by investigating its circulation. As in other areas of work on the human body, the most effective approach is likely to be a combination of first-hand investigation backed-up by resource materials such as charts, models and CD-ROMs on human anatomy.

Blood is pumped round the body by the heart, through branching blood-vessels (arteries, veins and capillaries). Since direct observation of the heart is not possible, children necessarily have to learn most of the facts about its structure and working from resource material; but they can listen to the action of their own hearts, find their pulse and count it: skills which can then be used when investigating the effects of exercise (Activity 3.9.1). They can also carry out simple observations on their arteries, veins and capillaries.

Activity 3.8.1

Listening to the action of the heart

Equipment and materials: Plastic funnel about 8cm diameter; 80cm plastic garden hose, outside diameter about 2.5cm; tapered pen-top whose wide end will fit into the hose; adhesive tape; craft-knife; fine sandpaper.

- Make a simple stethoscope as shown in Fig. 3.7, unless a clinical one is available. Push the spout of the funnel firmly into one end of the hose. To make an ear-piece, insert the wider end of the pen-top into the other end of the hose and fasten it firmly with adhesive tape. Trim the tip off the pen-top until the stub is about 6mm in diameter; smooth this down with fine sandpaper.

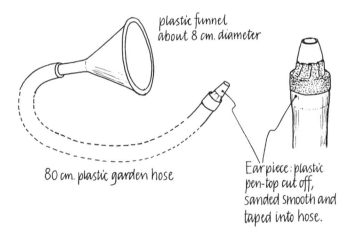

plastic funnel
about 8 cm. diameter

80 cm. plastic garden hose

Ear piece: plastic
pen-top cut off,
sanded smooth and
taped into hose.

Figure 3.7   Making a simple stethoscope

This simple stethoscope will enable children to hear the action of their own hearts (or someone else's). For the clearest sound, only a thin shirt or tee-shirt should be worn.

- Hold the funnel by its stem and the other end of the hose near the ear-piece; put the ear-piece into one ear.
- Sit down and place the rim of the funnel firmly on the chest, level with the nipples and a little left of the mid-line. Keep quite still (especially, do not move your fingers on the funnel or hose) and listen.

The sound which children will hear with a stethoscope is the sound of the heart-valves closing. Listening to the sound of the valves shutting and to any abnormal blood-flow is for doctors still a very important way of finding out how well the heart is working.

Activity 3.8.2

Circulation of the blood: arteries

Blood leaves the heart in arteries: tubular, branching vessels with thick, elastic and muscular walls. Only in few places do they run close enough under the skin to be easily detected. These are the places where we can 'feel our pulse' (see Activity 3.8.3). In one of these places, the wrist, it is also possible to show how arteries supply blood to one part of the body, the hand.

Safety note: At no time should pressure be applied to a child's wrist by anyone else, and excessive pressure must be avoided: this observation should not cause pain. The compression of arteries should not be maintained longer than 10s (ten seconds), or be repeated unnecessarily.

- Sit at a table and rest one elbow on it, holding the hand up with the palm facing you. Bend the wrist, pulling the hand towards you, and look for two tendons in the middle of the wrist (Fig. 3.8).

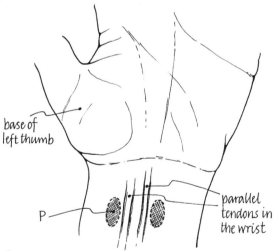

base of left thumb

parallel tendons in the wrist

P

Pressure-points are shown by cross-hatched areas. The pulse can be felt at pressure-point P.

Figure 3.8   Finding pressure-points in the left wrist

- Place the index and middle fingers of the other hand on either side of these tendons; the fingers will then be over two arteries which carry blood to the hand.
- Bend the hand away from you, make a **tight** fist and at the same time press firmly on the wrist with the fingers. This will cut off most of the blood supply to the hand.

- Keep the fist closed with the pressure on the wrist for a slow count of five, then open the hand **while keeping the pressure on the wrist**.
- ? What do you notice about the hand? (Most of it is very pale.)
- ? Why is the hand pale? (It has very little blood in it.)
- ? How has this come about? (Blood which was in the hand has drained back towards the heart through veins. Pressure on the arteries in the wrist has prevented more blood flowing in to replace it.)
- Release the pressure on the wrist.
- ? What do you see and feel? (The hand returns to its normal colour and a slight tingling is felt.)

The slight tingling usually felt is a mild version of 'pins and needles': a sensation caused by blood flowing into and refilling capillaries in tissues which had been deprived of their normal supply, for example when lying on one arm while asleep.

Activity 3.8.3

The pulse and how to find it
Finding and counting the pulse depends on being able to locate arteries using body landmarks, and is the quickest and easiest way of finding the *frequency* of heart-beat, measured in beats per minute.

The flow of blood from the heart is not constant. Every time the heart 'beats', a surge of blood is forced out into the arteries, making them bulge. It is this dilation which can be felt as the pulse in a few places in the body where arteries run close under the skin. The safest and most convenient place for children to feel and count their pulse is in the wrist.

Finding and counting the pulse in the wrist
The pulse in the wrist can be felt at one of the two pressure-points used to cut off blood supply to the hand in Activity 3.8.2.

Equipment: Stop-watch or clock; or classroom clock with a second-hand.

- Find the tendons on the inside of the wrist (Fig. 3.8). Feel for the pulse with the index and middle fingers of the other hand (*not* the thumb) in the hollow beside the tendons, on the same side as the thumb.

The pulse can often be felt more distinctly if the hand is moved to bend the wrist back, so stretching the skin over the artery.

- Practise taking your pulse. Sit down, find your wrist pulse and, keeping as still as possible, count how many beats there are in 30s, then multiply this by 2 to find your heart rate in beats per minute.
- Take your pulse four times, with a 30s interval between counts (i.e. pulse taken every minute).
- ? Does your pulse vary when you are sitting down? (The answer usually is, yes; because in most people taking the pulse itself causes an increase in heart-rate. After a minute or two this usually decreases again to a steady 'resting' rate.)

Making a pulse-pointer
This is an interesting and memorable alternative to conventional pulse-taking.

Materials: Drinking straw; drawing-pin (thumb-tack); Blu-tack.

- Put a small plug of Blu-tack into one end of a drinking straw, then push a drawing-pin (thumb-tack) into it. The straw and pin will then stand upright; this is the 'pulse-pointer'.
- Rest your forearm on a table, palm of the hand up. Pull the hand slightly up and tilt the wrist so that the place where the pulse can be felt is level or even a slight hollow.
- Check where your pulse can be felt, then place the 'pulse-pointer' on the same spot and sit very still, watching the straw. The end of the straw will move rhythmically, in time with your pulse, and can be used to count it.

The movement of the 'pulse pointer' is caused by the change in shape of the artery as pressure-surges pass through it. This tilts the drawing-pin slightly and the movement is magnified by the straw so that it is visible.

Activity 3.8.4

Circulation of the blood: veins
Veins are the vessels which carry blood back to the heart. Overall, veins are thinner-walled than arteries, the blood in them is at lower pressures and they are found near the surface of the body much more frequently than arteries are. This activity will succeed best in warm conditions because more blood will be flowing through the skin and superficial veins in order to keep the body temperature constant (see Activity 3.9.3).

- Sit at a table. If you are wearing a long-sleeved garment, roll one sleeve up to well above the elbow. Rest the forearm on the table with the palm of the hand up and relax the whole of the arm as much as you can.
- Hold your elbow-joint with the other hand; thumb behind, fingers in front.
- Slowly tighten your grip on the inside of the elbow (it doesn't have to be very tight), keeping the muscles and tendons of the arm relaxed. Watch your forearm and wrist.

Gripping the elbow in this way should constrict some of the veins draining blood from the forearm and make them more conspicuous than they are normally. They will appear as a branching system of slightly bluish lines, darker than the skin on either side.

- Keeping up the pressure on the inside of the elbow, turn your hand over to see the veins on the back of the hand.
- Release the grip on your elbow: the veins will 'fade' and return to their normal appearance.

Activity 3.8.5

Circulation of the blood: capillaries
Capillaries are the tiny blood-vessels into which blood from the arteries is pumped, and from which blood flows into the veins and eventually back to the heart. Every active part of the body has a dense network of blood capillaries running through it.

Capillaries in the skin cannot normally be seen because the outer layers of the skin are too thick, but their presence can be shown because the blood in them gives unpigmented skin much of its colour. This can clearly be seen in the palms of the hands and fingers (Activity 3.8.2).

Capillaries are very small; only a few thousandths of a millimetere (μm) across, so that even in the most favourable circumstances they can be seen only with a good microscope. However, it is possible to observe branching networks of very small blood-vessels where the skin is very thin. Though these are not as small as capillaries, they can serve to reinforce the idea of tiny blood-vessels forming the ultimate distribution and exchange system of the body.

Looking at very small blood-vessels in the eye

Equipment: Magnifying glasses of the highest magnification available; ×10 hand-lenses are ideal.

- Work in pairs in a very well-lit place but away from direct sunlight. Ask your partner to sit in a chair, tilt her or his head back and look up. If you use a magnifying-glass with your left eye, look at your partner's left eye or *vice versa*. Stand or sit so that you can look down into the eye.
- Put the magnifying glass close to your own eye and *keep it there at all times*. Move yourself and the magnifying-glass in towards your partner's eye until you can see it clearly.
- Ask your partner to open the eye wide. Look at the white part: you will see a network of very fine blood-vessels; some so small you can hardly see them.

These are the smallest blood-vessels which can be seen without a microscope but they are still bigger than capillaries! They illustrate clearly the way in which all blood-vessels branch repeatedly, but are unusual in that there are so few of them in such a large area: nearly all capillary networks are much denser and more crowded.

3.9: Exercise and its effects

Safety note: No exercise more strenuous than a normal PE or games session is required by any of the activities discussed. If any child participating in an investigation shows signs of distress they should **stop exercising immediately** and rest under observation by a responsible adult. At no time should children or adults attempt to measure the volume of air breathed in or out in any way. Measurements of this kind, especially with young children, require medical supervision.

When we engage in physical activity we increase the rate at which our muscles are working, and so the rate of respiration (*3.6). This has readily observable effects on pulse-rate, the sound made by the heart beating, breathing, skin temperature and cooling responses.

Activity 3.9.1

Exercise and the action of the heart

Equipment: Stop-clock or watch, or clock with second-hand; simple stethoscope (Fig. 3.7); large block (e.g. stage-block) about 20cm high, for step-ups.

- Work with a partner. Before you start, make sure that each of you can find and count the other's pulse (see Activity 3.8.3) and that the block for your step-ups is safe and stable.
- In turn, take and record each other's resting pulse. Take at least three counts of 30s each, with a 30s interval between them for recording (i.e. start counting each minute); multiply each result by two to find the resting pulse-rate in beats per minute.
- While your pulse is being counted, listen to your heart-beat using the simple stethoscope (Activity 3.8.1). Try to remember how loud the sound is.
- You should now exercise for about 3 minutes. A suitable exercise is to do step-ups; aim to do between 20 and 30 each minute. (One step-up is a complete movement on and off the block.)
- As soon as the exercise period is finished, sit down. Your partner should now begin taking your pulse again, as before, and continue until your pulse-rate returns to its resting level for three counts.
- At the same time, listen to your heart again with the stethoscope and compare what you hear with the sound it made when you were at rest.
? How did the sound of your heart change when you exercised? (It is 'quicker', i.e. a higher frequency, and usually the sound is both louder and sharper. The difference in the sound results from the heart-valves closing more violently.)
? How do you think the amount of blood being pumped by the heart changed during exercise? (It increased.)
- When your pulse-rate has returned to normal, repeat the measurements with your partner.
- When you have finished all your counts and observations, convert your counts to beats per minute (multiply each by two) and record these in a table, showing how long after exercise each count was begun.
- If you can, show your results in a graph of pulse-rate (vertical axis) against time (horizontal axis). Do not forget to include your heart-rate at rest and the interval during which you exercised.
? What differences were there? (E.g. resting heart-rates; heart-rates after exercise; time taken to recover to resting heart-rate.)

Resting heart-rates in different people are likely to be variable. Heart-rates will always be increased by exercise, but the amount of increase will again vary widely between subjects. The time taken to recover from exertion to resting heart-rate is one measure of physical fitness: the fitter the person, the shorter the recovery time.

? Try to explain your results. In particular, why does the heart beat more frequently and more vigorously after exercise? Why does the heart-rate take some time to return to normal?

Encourage children to explain the changes they have observed in terms of increased work and respiration rates, leading to increased demand for oxygen and increased blood-flow. Heart-rate can return to normal only when all the waste-products from the increased respiration (e.g. carbon dioxide) have been removed from the body.

Activity 3.9.2

Exercise and breathing
Exercise affects both the frequency of breathing and the volume of air taken with each breath. Because it is not possible to measure the volume of air breathed safely, children's observations must be restricted to breathing movements; but even with this limitation there is plenty to observe and discuss.

Equipment: Stop-watch or clock; or clock with second-hand.

- If possible, carry out observations before and after quite a long period of exercise, such as a PE or games session.
- Work in pairs: each partner can observe the other's breathing at the same time.
- Before beginning exercise, observe each other's breathing while you are relaxed and at rest. Count the number of breaths per minute, record this and look at the way your partner is breathing.
- Immediately after exercise, again count the number of breaths per minute and look at how your partner is breathing.
- ? How have the breathing movements changed? (All breathing movements are usually much more frequent and vigorous.)

Even without any measurement it is usually obvious that after exercise a far greater volume of air is being inhaled and exhaled with each breath. If the exertion has been severe, e.g. after running a race, deep movements of the rib-cage will be much more obvious than when at rest. The diaphragm will be moving much more as well, but the corresponding movement of the abdomen (see Activity 3.6.2) is less easy to see.

- ? Try to explain your observations. (Increased rate of work and respiration requires a greater rate of oxygen supply and carbon dioxide removal so the frequency and volume of breathing have to increase.)

Activity 3.9.3

Exercise, skin and body temperature
The normal heating of the body, by which a high and constant body-core temperature is maintained, is the result of respiration (Activity 3.6.3). If the rate of respiration increases, so does the rate at which the body is heated. The function of the body's 'cooling system' is to keep the core temperature constant when respiration increases. This is achieved by increasing blood flow to the skin and by sweating, whose effects are observed in this activity.

Equipment: A wide-range digital thermometer.

- These observations should be carried out when the person whose temperature is to be measured ('the subject') is lightly clothed: shorts and tee-shirt are ideal. If possible, carry out the observations before and after a PE or games session and in a cool rather than a hot environment.
- Use the digital thermometer to find the subject's under-arm temperature. Place the end of the probe in the arm-pit and close the arm over it. Wait for 2 minutes, take

a reading and then repeat this to check that the temperature shown is constant. (The under-arm temperature is usually a little lower than body-core temperature, but a useful approximation to it.)

- Take and record the subject's skin temperature on the upper arm, forearm and tip of the middle finger. Place the end of the probe firmly on the skin but do not press in hard. Make sure you wait until the reading on the thermometer is constant before recording the temperature.
? What differences are there in underarm and skin temperatures before and after exercise? (The *expected* differences are that the underarm temperature changes little, if at all, while the skin temperatures increase. The increase in skin temperature is usually more marked the further away one goes from the body core, i.e. least on the upper arm; greatest on the finger.)
- At the same time, look carefully at the subject's skin on the face and upper arms. Notice its colour and whether there is any sweat on the surface.
- After exercise, repeat and record all the measurements, looking also for differences in the appearance of the skin.
? What differences are there in the appearance of the skin before and after exercise? (The common differences are flushing of the skin, which may not be readily visible in children of racial groups with highly-pigmented skin; and sweating.)

Exercise results in an increased rate of heating of the body, which responds by flushing and sweating. Flushing is the visible effect of increased blood flow to the skin, which results in faster transfer of thermal energy, mainly by convection (*12.3). Sweat evaporates from the skin and this has a direct cooling effect (see Activity 6.3.4).

3.10: Senses and response

One of the most distinctive characteristics of living things is the way in which they respond to changes so that their chances of survival are increased. A change, whether within its own body or in the environment, which brings about an alteration in an animal's behaviour or the way its body works is a stimulus. The alteration in behaviour or body activity is a response. Like other animals, humans respond to changes both internal and external. Stimuli are detected by specialized sense organs and our response to them is integrated with overall control of the body by the brain and nervous system. Responses investigated elsewhere include the production of saliva (Activity 3.3.1) and cooling of the body (Activity 3.9.3). Other very important stimuli and sense-systems which children can investigate are: light (vision); sound (hearing); chemicals in solution and vapour (taste and flavour); change of temperature ('touch'); contact with solid objects ('touch').

Vision
The eye focuses light entering it (*17.1) into an image on the light-sensitive lining (retina) at the back of the eyeball. Children can easily investigate three aspects of vision which are very important in their everyday lives: the way in which the eye adjusts to varying light levels; the fact that we see in detail only a very small part of our overall field of vision; and the way in which we use both eyes together to judge distance.

Activity 3.10.1

Responding to changing light levels

We know from everyday experience that we cannot see clearly if the light is too bright or too dim, for example if we move suddenly from bright sunlight to deep shadow, or switch on a light in the middle of the night. On the other hand, we also know that people with normal vision can see well under a very wide range of light conditions. The connection between these two observations is the way in which the eye responds to the brightness of the light falling on it.

Equipment: Room with curtains or blinds (complete blackout is not required); table lamp.

- Draw the curtains or blinds so that the light in the room is dim, but you can still see well.
- Work with a partner, sitting at a table. Look at your partner's eyes. Notice the 'coloured' part of the eye (iris) around a central black hole (pupil).
- Place the lamp on the table to face your partner, about 50cm away, and ask him or her to look to one side of it. Go round to the other side of the table and, looking at one of your partner's eyes all the time, switch the lamp on.
? How does the eye change as the lamp is switched on? (The pupil becomes smaller; or, to be more accurate, the iris expands inwards leaving a smaller hole in the middle.)
? If the pupil is made smaller, what effect does this have on the amount of light entering the eye? (It is reduced.)
? When is it useful to reduce the amount of light entering the eye? (When the light is very bright. If too much light is allowed in, the eye will be 'dazzled'.)

One example of this, relevant to road safety at night, is that drivers or cyclists should not look directly at the headlights of oncoming vehicles, even if they are properly dipped. Instead they should look at the nearside of the road or lane they are on, to avoid being dazzled.

- Still watching the eye, switch the lamp off again.
? How did the eye change? (The pupil gets bigger again; i.e. the iris contracts outwards, leaving a larger hole in the middle.)
? If the pupil is made bigger, what difference will it make? (More light will enter the eye.)
? When would this be an advantage? (In dim light conditions: if too little light enters the eye, we cannot see clearly.)

As these observations show, the iris expands and contracts in response to the stimulus of decreasing and increasing levels of light falling on the eye, which has obvious survival value.

Activity 3.10.2

How much do we see clearly?

To most people it appears that they see the whole of what is in front of them clearly; but this is not so. In fact we see clearly and in detail only what is in the middle of our field of vision at any moment; in common language, the particular thing we are 'looking at'. The simplest way of showing this depends on children's ability to recognize words (or letters).

A letter and word-window

Equipment: Books with large print for letter-recognition or small print for fluent readers; sheet of A4 white paper; scissors; pencil.

- Fold the paper and cut a small rectangular 'window' about 1 × 2cm in the centre.
- Unfold the paper and put it over the open book; do not look at the 'window'.
- Use the pencil as a pointer. Put it at one edge of the paper and, *looking at its point all the time*, move it in towards the 'window'.
- ? When can you recognize any letters or read any of the words in the 'window'? (Only when the pencil-point, and so the centre of the reader's field of view, is at or even over the edge of the 'window'.)

This test shows very clearly how little of our field of view at any moment is seen in detail. How then do we see the whole of the scene in front of us? By making very rapid scanning movements of the eyes and building up in the memory a mental 'picture' or map of what we are looking at. This can be observed very easily by sitting in front of a person, giving them a large, interesting picture to look at and watching how their eyes move as they explore it visually. The eye-movements characteristic of reading are a highly-specialized example of the same kind of scanning.

Activity 3.10.3

Judging distances

In common with those of other hunting mammals (Activity 5.6.1), the eyes of humans are at the front of the head so that their fields of vision overlap to a great extent, giving us what is known as binocular or stereoscopic vision. In practical terms this means that we can judge very accurately how far away from us an object is in relation to other things around it.

Equipment: Two pencils with sharp points.

- Hold a pencil horizontally in each hand, points towards each other.
- With arms half-bent and both eyes open, bring the pencil-points together and try to make them touch. (Most people can do this easily.)
- Stretch and bend your arms a few times, then try to make the pencil-points touch *with one eye shut.*
- Carry out the test with both eyes open and one eye shut, ten times. Compare your success rates.
- ? What is it that we can do with both eyes open that we cannot do with one eye shut? (Tell accurately how far things are away from us *in relation to one another*.)
- ? In what kinds of situation is the ability to judge distances an advantage?

You might think of its advantages to stone-age man, modern man, and both.

Stone-age man: any kind of hunting or combat.
Modern man: riding a bicycle, driving a car, piloting an aeroplane, playing any kind of ball game.

Both: manipulating tools and materials, e.g. building or making artefacts; walking or running through a landscape with obstructions such as bushes, trees, rocks or other people.

Hearing

Apart from the external ear (pinna), the ear is wholly internal, so no direct observations of it can be made. Children can, however, carry out simple observations on the way humans hear, particularly in terms of loudness and direction. Humans hear sound from all round them and can learn to judge the direction from which a sound comes, but many other mammals have much larger and more mobile external ears. These act as funnels, directing sound-waves into the tunnel leading to the ear-drum. Modelling these large external ears by making a simple ear-trumpet shows not only what they do, but also shows something of the way in which our hearing differs from that of the mammals which have them.

Activity 3.10.4

Using an ear-trumpet to direct sound-waves

Equipment and materials: Large (80 × 60cm) sheet of stiff paper or thin card; elastic bands.

- Roll the paper into a cone at least 20cm wide, tapering to 1cm wide at the narrow end; hold it in shape with one or more elastic bands.
- Start observations in an ordinary classroom environment. With one hand, hold the narrow end of the cone in your ear (adjust its width so that it fits snugly).
- Close the other ear with a finger and listen to the sounds of the classroom. Turn slowly and keep taking the cone from your ear and then replacing it, listening to find out how using it affects your hearing.
? What differences does the cone make to your hearing?

Children may find this difficult to put into words. The most obvious effect is that when there is background noise the hearing becomes more acute, so that particular sounds are much easier to distinguish. This is partly because these sounds are louder, but also because the cone makes hearing much more directional: sounds can be heard, but only when the cone is pointed directly at their source.

The difference made to our hearing by the cone indicates that, in common with most of our senses, human hearing is rather unspecialized. As tribal hunters with elaborate means of communication through speech and gesture, it is more of an advantage to humans to be able to hear well all round them. This is in contrast to the highly-directional hearing of many animals which have large, mobile external ears, e.g. horses, cattle, deer, bats and some dogs such as foxes.

Activity 3.10.5

Hearing: judging direction

Although humans lack the ability to locate sounds by moving their external ears in the way that many animals can, we learn to locate the sources of sounds quite accurately by using both ears at once (binaural hearing), an ability analogous to binocular vision (see Activity 3.10.3).

A simple test is for a subject, blindfolded or with both eyes shut, to try to locate a repeated sound in a quiet room with both ears open and then with one ear shut, using a finger pressing on the flap just in front of the ear opening. A suitable sound-source is a small electric buzzer, passed *silently* round to people in different parts of the room.

Although the results are not likely to be as clear-cut as those for judging distance visually (Activity 3.10.3), they are usually definite enough to make clear the advantages of binaural hearing.

Smell and taste

Smell and taste are our two main responses to chemicals in our environment. Our sense of smell results from the response of the lining inside the top of the nose to vapours, while taste depends on the response of the tongue to chemicals in solution, but the two are linked in all but the most basic taste sensations. Our sense of smell enables us to distinguish a very wide variety of chemical vapours, which we can learn to identify and remember. On its own our sense of taste is, in contrast, very simple: the tongue alone can distinguish only four tastes: sweet, sour, salt and bitter. In normal tasting, however, the two senses combine, vapour from solutions in the mouth reaching the sensitive membranes inside the top of the nose, so that we can detect a very wide variety of flavours in addition to the four basic tastes.

Activity 3.10.6

Detecting tastes and flavours

Solutions giving three of the basic tastes (sweet, sour and salt) are easily obtained. The fourth (bitter) is more problematic. The classic bitter-tasting chemical is quinine, and though a dilute solution of quinine sulphate could be used, it has to be obtained from a pharmacist and many children find it very distasteful. A useful though less bitter substitute is a concentrated solution of instant coffee.

Equipment and materials: Lemon juice; solutions of salt (dilute), sugar and coffee (concentrated); small containers for samples of these; drinking straws cut into 3cm lengths; small, strongly-flavoured sweets (e.g. peppermints).

Safety note: Sections of drinking-straw should be used once only and then discarded. If a straw which has touched anyone's tongue is dipped into a solution again, that solution should be discarded and a fresh supply used.

- Work with a partner and test each other. Put a small amount of the four solutions into labelled containers.
- For each trial, one partner (the subject) should sit with eyes closed. The other partner (the experimenter) dips a piece of drinking-straw into one of the solutions and touches it in four or five places on the subject's tongue. The subject then tells the experimenter what the taste is.
- After each trial, change roles so that for each of you there is an interval between attempts to identify different solutions. Continue testing until you have tried all four solutions at least once.

- Now do a second set of trials in the same way, but with the subject holding their nose each time, as well as shutting their eyes.
? Is there any difference between your sense of the four tastes with your nose open and shut? (In the basic tastes, no; but the lemon juice and instant coffee solution have flavour as well as basic sour and bitter tastes, and these flavours should be detectable. If they have not been noticed, some re-testing would be useful to make the point.)
- Now suck a small sweet with a strong flavour (peppermint is good). As you suck it, hold your nose for a few seconds, then let it go again.
? What difference does holding your nose make? (When the nostrils are closed the *flavour* of the sweet [e.g. peppermint] cannot be detected, though the *basic taste* [sweet] can.)

When this happens naturally, for example when the nose is blocked because of a head-cold, it is often said that food seems tasteless. More accurately, it is flavourless: the basic four tastes can still be distinguished, but the flavours which make food enjoyable cannot. This shows clearly how both taste and smell are involved in our overall sense of 'taste'.

This activity can easily be extended by trying to identify a variety of raw fruit and vegetables, chewing small pieces with the eyes shut.

Touch
'Sense of touch' is a collective term for the response of the skin to three different kinds of stimulus: change in temperature (Activity 3.10.7), contact with solid objects (Activity 3.10.8) and pressure, each of which is detected by different sense-organs.
   The response of the skin to temperature is a particularly clear example of a more general trend which is encountered in other kinds of response: that we detect and respond to *changes* in our environment rather than measuring them in any absolute way as a thermometer does. Investigating the response of the skin to temperature not only demonstrates our positive ability to detect change: it also makes the equally important point that without a thermometer we can never make an accurate estimate of the temperature of our surroundings.

Activity 3.10.7

Detecting changes in temperature

Equipment: Three plastic basins, large enough to put a hand in; thermometer; supply of hot water; ice cubes for cooling water if necessary.

Safety note: At no time during this activity should children experience any discomfort. The water temperatures suggested should ensure this; but in no case should children put their hands into water above 45°C.

- Set out three basins in a row. Each needs to be filled with enough water to put all the fingers and thumb of one hand in without overflowing. By mixing and stirring tap-water with hot water (and ice cubes if necessary), adjust the water temperatures in the three basins: left-hand basin: 40°C; middle basin: 25°C; right-hand basin: 15°C.

- Put one hand in each of the left-hand and right-hand basins. Wait for one minute, stirring the water gently with your fingers.
- Move your right hand into the middle basin, wait for a few seconds, then return it to the cold water.
? How does your right hand feel in the middle basin? (It feels warm.)
- Move your left hand into the middle basin, wait for a few seconds, then return it to the hot water.
? How does your left hand feel in the middle basin? (It feels cool.)
- Now put both hands together into the middle basin.
? How do they feel? (The right hand feels warm; the left hand feels cool.)
? How do you explain the fact that your hands feel differently in water of the same temperature? (What the skin of the hands detects is *change* in temperature, i.e. that conditions are cooler or warmer than they were before.)

This activity makes a very clear and direct contrast between the ways in which human skin and a thermometer respond to temperature: our skin does not *measure* temperature at all. This has important practical consequences. For example, great care is needed not to overheat water being used for a bath, especially for babies. To someone who has already had their hands in warm water, bath-water which does not feel especially hot may in reality be hot enough to cause pain or even scald an infant. One way to avoid this is to test the temperature of a baby's bath by dipping an elbow in the water, rather than a hand.

Activity 3.10.8

Sensitivity to touch
Human skin responds both to contact with solid objects and to pressure from them. Pressure sensitivity tells us how hard an object is pressing on the skin. Touch, which children can more easily investigate, tells us which parts of the body are in contact with objects and, in some parts of the skin, something about their surface texture. The following investigation is simple but requires quite a lot of concentration.

Detecting texture

Equipment: Pieces of very coarse (60 grit) abrasive paper or cloth, about 2 × 5cm. Finer abrasives will not be effective. (Cutting this material will blunt any blade: use a craft-knife with an old blade which can then be discarded.)

- Press the skin of your forearm with the smooth side of the abrasive sheet, then with the rough side.
- Carry out the same test on the skin of your upper lip.
- Which area of skin is more sensitive? (The lip, because it detected the roughness of the sheet much more distinctly.)
- Test other areas of skin in the same way. You could try: the palm of the hand; the calf of the leg; a finger-tip; cheek and forehead. In each case, ask yourself if you can feel the difference between the rough and smooth sides of the sheet, and how distinctly.
? Which was the *most* sensitive area of skin you tested? (Usually, the lips.)

? Which was the *least* sensitive area you tested? (Of those listed, usually the calf of the leg.)

? Are your finger-tips more or less sensitive than your forehead or cheek? (Usually, more sensitive.)

? How do very sensitive lips and fingers help us to survive?

Sensitive lips help us to feed and detect the texture of our food because, as food enters the mouth, it cannot be seen. The sensitivity of our lips and tongue to touch and texture helps us to avoid eating harmful materials such as grit which could damage our teeth, or small bones which could cause choking. Sensitive fingers enable us to manipulate tools and materials effectively.

4

Green Plants as Organisms

Almost all animals on Earth are dependent, either directly or indirectly, on green plants for their food, because green plants are the producers at the base of nearly all food-chains (Activities 5.7.1, 5.7.2). In developing children's understanding of plants and their importance two problems have to be overcome. First, convincing first-hand evidence that plants are alive must be produced, which requires both time and the systematic recording of changes (Activity 2.2.2). Secondly, the variety of form in plants is enormous, which makes it difficult for the non-specialist to approach them with confidence.

The most practical approach is to select a small range of plants for basic study and investigation. No one plant is likely to be satisfactory for the whole range of investigations into plants undertaken at primary level, but three which have proved particularly successful are discussed below. Suggestions are made in each section as to which other species are likely to be suitable.

Conservation note
In Britain and some other states it is illegal to dig up wild plants and to pick some wild-flowers. In practice this ruling does not apply to common weeds such as creeping buttercup, shepherd's purse or willowherbs, but if in doubt do not remove any plant without first confirming its identity and status. Removing *any* plant or part of a plant without the landowner's permission is illegal.

General points about cultivating plants in classrooms
The most convenient way to grow plants is to place pots on gravel in plastic troughs, available in a range of sizes from garden centres. Surplus water drains into the gravel and then evaporates, helping to keep the air round the plants a little more humid, and roots a little cooler, than they would be otherwise. The biggest single problem for classroom plants in temperate or cold climates is likely to be currents of dry, hot air from room heaters. These tend to be more damaging to roots than to shoots, so if plants have to be placed above heaters, for example on window-sills, deflect the upward air-currents away from the plants with card held down by pots or troughs.

Three plants for primary classrooms
Two generally-successful perennial plants, which will continue growing for much if not all of the year next to well-lit windows, are 'geraniums' (pelargoniums, Fig. 4.1)

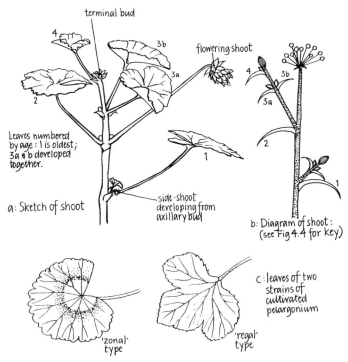

Figure 4.1   Shoot of Pelargonium ('geranium')

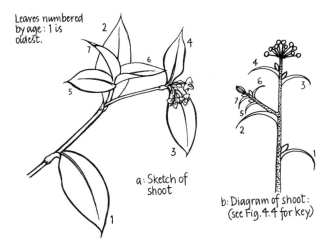

Figure 4.2   Shoot of Tradescantia

and various species of 'wandering sailor' (*Tradescantia* and its relatives, Fig. 4.2). The most useful pelargoniums are those with 'single', five-petalled flowers (Fig. 4.8). All pelargoniums require high light levels, will grow well in direct sunlight and flower for most of the year. Tradescantias will tolerate much lower light levels and prefer less or no direct sunlight; otherwise they have similar needs. Both tolerate drought well and are much more likely to be damaged by over-watering than the reverse.

An annual which can be very useful in the classroom is white mustard (*Sinapis alba*), a member of the cress-cabbage family. It has small, round seeds which are used in cooking and are widely available. These keep very well, germinate exceptionally quickly at any time of the year and can be used to observe not only germination (Activity 4.3.2), but also shoot structure, root-structure and root-hairs, the growth of roots and the response to light and gravity (Activities 4.2.1, 4.2.2, 4.3.1, 4.3.6–4.3.8). For general observation of plant structure, plants more than five weeks old are likely to be most useful. Keep the soil damp but not wet and in winter give the plants as much light as possible. In summer they may grow outdoors better than in the classroom.

4.1: Plants as living things

Some basic observations aimed at showing that plants are alive, by recording how they grow and change over time, are discussed as part of Activity 2.2.2. Older and more able pupils can profitably extend these activities by observing growth in more detail, in particular by measurement of stem and leaf growth. The most suitable plants are those which are robust and whose leaves are simple in shape and held well apart on the stem when fully-grown; round-leaved 'geraniums' (zonal pelargoniums) and tradescantias are both suitable.

Activity 4.1.1

Measuring stem and leaf growth

Basic observations on growth are most effective when this is rapid. Marking young leaves on each shoot with dots of quick-drying paint or correcting-fluid provides landmarks for measurements which will usually yield clear results if carried out weekly. Children need to understand clearly that stem growth is measured by *length*, whereas leaf growth is measured by *area*.

Equipment and materials: Plants; quick-drying white paint or correcting-fluid; pair of compasses or dividers; ruler measuring in mm; graph paper with 1mm squares, cut into strips about 10cm wide; stiff card or thin board the same size and shape as the graph paper; soft pencil with sharp point; paper clips or elastic bands; small paper labels.

Measuring stem growth (length)

- On each shoot to be measured, mark the base of the youngest leaf which has a distinct and measurable length of stem between it and the next leaf down. Put a small spot of white paint or correcting-fluid near the bases of both leaves or their stalks; label each shoot with a code number on a paper label.
- Using compasses or dividers, measure between the marks at the bases of the leaves. Make sure that you can measure to the same places each time.

- Find the distance between the leaf-bases in mm and record it in a table, with the date.
- Repeat this measurement for all shoots being measured, and again each week until the stem has stopped growing. If you can, present your results as a graph of stem-length (vertical axis) against time (horizontal axis).

Measuring leaf growth (area)

- Work in pairs. Fasten a piece of graph paper on to a board with clips or elastic bands. Measure the younger of the two marked leaves; ask your partner to hold the board and paper under the leaf as you draw round it.
- *Gently* press the leaf flat on to the paper and draw round it carefully.
- Measure the leaf area (in square millimetres) by counting the squares and estimating the part-squares within the outline you have drawn. Do not count the leaf-stalk, if there is one. Write the date and area inside the outline.
- Each week, draw the same leaf and again measure its area, so that you end the observation with a row of outlines on each sheet. If you can, present the results as a graph of leaf area against time.

When presented as a graph, the complete growth in both stem length and leaf area usually shows a distinct pattern, speeding up to a maximum and then slowing as full size is attained.

4.2: Basic structure and function in flowering plants

In each activity, children should have the opportunity of examining closely a variety of plants with contrasting forms. The primary aim is to enable them to identify the various parts of plants and to learn what role each plays in the life of the plant as a whole. These activities can be integrated into work on growth, photosynthesis and reproduction (Sections 4.3–4.5) but experience suggests that it is helpful if children can become acquainted with the structure of plants, and the scientific language used to communicate about it, before investigating their lives more closely.

Activity 4.2.1

Shoot systems

The aims of studying a variety of shoots are, first, that the children learn to identify the basic parts of a shoot system; secondly, that they learn the relationships between the parts; thirdly, that they at least begin to appreciate that the forms of most of the plants they see develop by relatively simple variations on a basic 'construction plan', shown in Fig. 4.3. No actual plant is exactly like this, but the sketch can usefully be thought of as a basic 'theme' on which a very large number of 'variations' is possible. It is then a useful starting-point when trying to understand the forms of particular plants and to identify their parts.

In most plants the part above ground is the shoot system and the part below ground, the root system. Flowers (Activity 4.2.3) are highly-specialized shoots; but all leafy shoot systems have only three major components. The relationship between these parts is constant, and from the outset it is helpful to couple identification and observation of them with outline information on the role each plays in the life of the plant. The leaf makes food for the plant by photosynthesis (Activities 4.4.1–4.4.2);

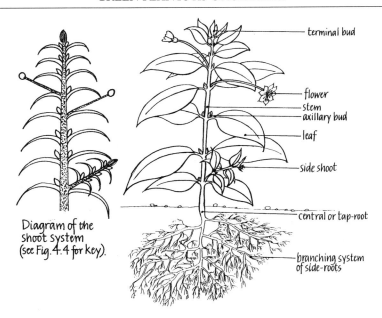

Figure 4.3   The main parts of a flowering plant

the stem supports the leaves and is also part of the plant's transport system (Activity 4.3.5). Buds are undeveloped shoots. They enable a shoot system to keep growing, to branch naturally, to continue growing if it is damaged (Activity 4.3.1) and may also produce flowers, which are shoots specialized for sexual reproduction (Activities 4.2.3 and 4.5.2–4.5.5).

A useful way to represent shoot structure is by way of diagrams (Fig. 4.4), which concentrate attention on what different shoot systems have in common (the relationship between their parts) rather than on their diverse appearance, so making it easier to identify the various parts and compare them, as in Figs. 4.1–4.3, where diagrams are given alongside more detailed sketches.

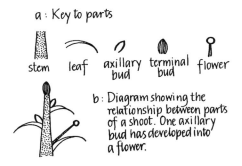

Figure 4.4   Diagrams of shoots

The easiest way to begin understanding the variety of shoot forms is to consider two kinds of variation on the 'basic plan' (Fig. 4.3a,b). The first is different degrees of branching (Fig. 4.5a,b). The second kind of variation is in the degree to which the leaves are separated by length growth in the stem between them (Fig. 4.6a,b).

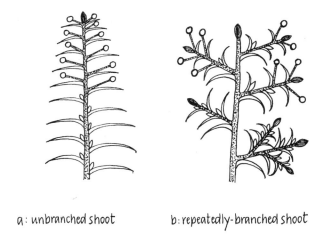

a: unbranched shoot   b: repeatedly-branched shoot

Figure 4.5   Variation in shoots: amount of branching

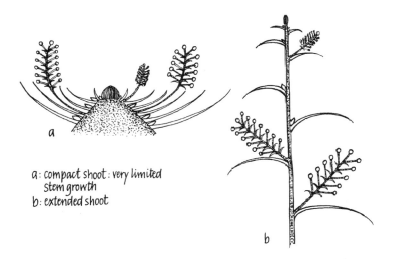

a: compact shoot : very limited
   stem growth
b: extended shoot

Figure 4.6   Variation in shoots: amount of length growth

Selecting plants for examining shoots
Among plants that can be grown in the classroom, round leaved 'geraniums' (Fig. 4.1) and white mustard show all parts of the shoot system very clearly. Tradescantias and their relatives (Fig. 4.2) are also useful, though their axillary buds are small and can be seen only if the leaf and its sheathing base are stripped from the stem. These should be compared and contrasted with other plant forms available locally. Weeds are particularly useful because they can be potted up and kept outdoors until they are needed. Twigs of shrubs and trees enable children to observe in a more general way the development of more complex shoot systems.

Activity 4.2.2

Root systems

In most plants, though not all, the part below ground is the root system, which sustains the plant as a whole in two ways. First, it anchors the plant to whatever material it is growing on or in, usually soil. Secondly, it absorbs water and other chemicals which the plant needs in order to live healthily and grow normally (see Activity 4.3.3). Children can usefully investigate and observe three aspects of root systems: their strength and the way they anchor the plant; their overall branching form; and the root-hairs which grow from them and which absorb water and chemicals from the soil.

Strength and anchorage
Children's own knowledge and experience, exploited by structured questioning from the teacher, can provide an introduction to this aspect of root systems. At one end of the scale, consider trees: they are very large, tall, heavy structures, but they do not usually fall down because they are anchored to the earth by their roots. At the other end of the scale, think about weeds. If we have to weed the garden, the weeds do not just fall out of the ground: they have to be pulled up. If possible, children should try pulling up weeds in the school grounds or garden to find out how difficult it is.

Looking at root systems
To look at root systems in more detail it is necessary to dig up plants carefully, with a ball of undisturbed soil round their roots.

Materials and equipment: Weeds or other small plants dug up carefully with balls of soil round their roots; plastic bowls; water, small clear plastic bottles.

- Put the uprooted plants into water in a bowl for a few minutes, then shake the root system, gently at first, to dislodge the soil.
- Fill a small, clear plastic bottle with water. Put the washed roots into the water; shake the plant gently to make them spread out. Look at the overall form of the root system and compare it with that of the shoot system.
? Is the root system more or less branched than the shoot system? (Usually, much more branched.)
? Imagine these branched roots growing out into the soil. Why are roots of this kind especially suitable for plants? (They grow out into cracks and between grains of soil, so they grip the soil very firmly and anchor the plant. As water moves through the soil, the roots can take it up, together with the chemicals the plant needs.)

Root-hairs
Root-hairs grow from single cells of the outer skin (epidermis) of roots, usually when they are quite young. Root-hairs vary a lot in length, but are always very slender. They can sometimes be seen with the unaided eye as a 'fuzz' around a root, but to see them clearly a good hand-lens is needed.

If actively-growing plants such as pelargoniums and tradescantias are turned upside-down and gently knocked out of their pots, slender, white, young roots will usually be visible at the sides and bottom of the root-ball. Plants of white mustard four weeks or more old also have easily-visible young roots and root-hairs. Using a hand-lens, root-hairs are easily seen behind the tips of these young roots. They are the main absorbing part of the root system. Each one is very small, but because there are so many of them and they can grow into the tiny spaces between soil particles, they are very efficient at obtaining the water and other chemicals the plant needs.

Activity 4.2.3

Flowers

Flowers are highly-specialized shoots which enable the plant to reproduce sexually by producing seeds. Attention should be confined to the flowers whose structures are easiest to understand. All of those discussed here are pollinated (*4.5) by insects and have an open structure with large, separate petals. It is worth arranging the year's science programme so that flowers of this kind will be available when they are needed.

The structure of two very common kinds of flower is shown in Fig. 4.7. From the outset it is important to link the different parts of the flower, if only in outline, with the role which each plays in the sexual reproduction of the plant (Activities 4.5.2–4.5.5):

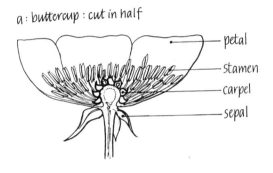

a : buttercup : cut in half

petal
stamen
carpel
sepal

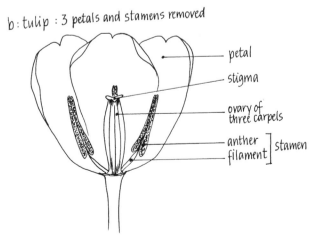

b : tulip : 3 petals and stamens removed

petal
stigma
ovary of three carpels
anther] stamen
filament

Figure 4.7   Parts of flowers

– *Sepals*, where present, help to protect the flower in bud;
– *petals*, and sometimes sepals too, attract insects with some combination of colour, scent and nectar;
– *stamens* make pollen and hold it in position so that it will brush off on to the bodies of visiting insects;
– *carpels* (which may be joined to form an *ovary*) receive pollen on a special area, the
– *stigma*, during pollination (see Activity 4.5.3). The carpels or ovary contain un-developed seeds (*ovules*) which, if fertilized following pollination, develop into
– *seeds* within the
– *fruit* (Activity 4.5.4), from which, in most plants, they are dispersed to begin the plant's life-cycle again (Activity 4.5.5).

Selecting flowers for observation
Almost any large, open, separate-petalled flowers are useful in helping children to become acquainted with basic structure, but a few may be suggested. Carpels sepa-rate: buttercups and anemones; magnolias may be available from gardens and have much larger flowers with very easily-seen parts. Carpels joined into an ovary: wall-flowers, cabbages and their relatives large and small; tulips, hyacinths including (English) bluebells, and other lilies. Among weeds, all the cress (cabbage) family and the willowherbs have flowers which are easily seen, though mostly rather small. Among house-plants, 'single' pelargoniums have easily-seen flowers (Fig. 4.8). Tradescantia flowers are small and basically like those of the tulip except that they have three petals and three small sepals. Viewed with a hand-lens, they can be seen to have beautiful 'hairy' stamens.

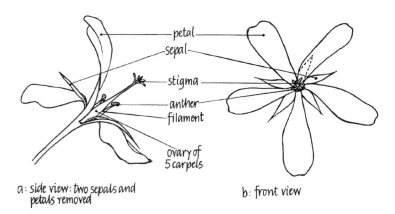

a: side view: two sepals and petals removed

b: front view

Figure 4.8   Flower of pelargonium

Looking at flowers
When looking at basic flower structure it is helpful to adopt a simple procedure so that different flowers can be more easily compared and resources used to the best advantage.

Equipment and materials: Flowers on plants in pots or in water if cut; magnifying glass; Blu-tack; bottle-corks; tweezers; pencil.

Safety note: Children with asthma or allergies may need to exercise caution when working with flowers, especially when smelling them. None of the flowers recommended has very light pollen (as for example grasses do) but pollen, scent or both may still cause problems to a small minority of susceptible children and adults.

● Look at a flower from all angles. Unless the flower is very large, use a magnifying-glass to examine it closely.
● If the flowers are quite small (e.g. buttercup or hyacinth), remove a single flower with its stalk. Put a piece of Blu-tack on to a bottle-cork; make a hole in the Blu-tack with a pencil-point and gently push the flower-stalk into it. Mould the Blu-tack round the flower-stalk so that it is held firmly. The flower can then be held up on the cork and is much easier to examine.
● Try to identify all the flower parts. Start with the flower-stalk and look at the 'back' of the flower.
? Does the flower have any sepals? If you cannot see any, look at a bud. Before the bud opens, are the petals protected by anything outside them? (Some flowers [e.g. tulips, hyacinths] have no sepals; in others the sepals drop off as the flower opens and in yet others [e.g. fuchsias] they look like petals.)
● Look at the outside and inside of the petals and smell them.
● Look just inside the petals: this is where the stamens develop. In some flowers (e.g. hyacinths) the stamens are attached to the petals; in others (e.g. pelargoniums) they are partly attached to each other.

Each stamen has a stalk (filament) with a small bag of pollen (anther) on its end, which may be quite brightly coloured. If you cannot see the anthers, look at a younger flower. Anthers often wither and drop off quite early in the life of the flower, after they have shed their pollen.

● Remove two or three petals from the flower (tweezers are useful if the flower is small).
● Look right in the middle of the flower for the ovary where the seeds will develop.

Buttercups, anemones and magnolias have an ovary of many separate little seed-cases (carpels), but in most flowers there are fewer (commonly 3 or 5) which are joined together. In some flowers, e.g. hyacinths and pelargoniums, the ovary cannot be seen clearly unless some petals and stamens are removed.

● Make large drawings of one or more flowers from the front, and from the side with two or three petals and stamens removed. Use label-lines, as in Fig. 4.8, to show the names of the different parts. Looking carefully as you draw helps you to identify each part of the flower.

4.3: Plant growth and response

Plant growth has already been discussed in a general way, in connection with investigations into plants as living things (Activities 2.2.2, 4.1.1). In this section, some aspects of plant growth will be examined in more detail. A useful approach is to compare and contrast the growth of plants with that of animals such as humans. The main differences between plant and animal growth are, first, that plants grow in particular parts of their bodies, usually at the tips of shoots and roots, whereas the bodies of animals such as humans appear to grow all over. Secondly, the growth of most though not all animals is much more definite and predictable than that of plants. Most animals have fixed numbers of body-parts such as legs and eyes, and a well-defined range of size when adult. In contrast to this, most kinds of plant can vary widely both in size and the number of shoots, leaves and roots they have, depending on the conditions in which they live and grow.

Activity 4.3.1

Patterns of plant growth
The most generally-useful plants for investigating growth-patterns are house-plants (such as pelargoniums and tradescantias, see introduction to this chapter), because children can easily observe them over a period of several weeks or months.

Localized growth in shoots
Marking leaves and measuring the growth of house-plants (Activity 4.1.1) not only provides evidence that they are alive: it also shows in a very direct way that once a particular leaf and section of stem are fully-grown they do not grow any more. However, it is also obvious that at the same time the shoot is continuing to grow by producing more stem, leaves and buds at its tip. Children can readily contrast this localized growth with the 'all-over' growth of their own bodies.

Growth-patterns in shoots
Successful cultivation of plants often involves more than simply providing them with the conditions they need for healthy growth (Activity 4.3.4). In particular, it may be desirable or necessary to control shoot growth. Children can experiment by pruning actively-growing pelargoniums and tradescantias. Remove the end-parts of some shoots (the terminal bud, together with two or three leaves and stem below it), by cutting through each stem just above a leaf with a sharp knife. The parts removed can then be rooted as cuttings (see Activity 4.5.1). After removal of the shoot-tip, one or more axillary buds below the cut will be activated, growing into side-shoots. The pattern of growth in the pruned shoots should be contrasted with that in other, unpruned shoots. Because removal of one shoot-tip usually results in the growth of at least two side-shoots, pruning in this way is likely to make the plant more compact and bushy.

Localized growth in roots
Observing tip-growth in roots has to be rather less direct and involves the use of a little imagination and logic. The best roots to work with are those of vigorously-growing seedlings of white mustard (see introduction to this chapter), about 4–5 weeks old, grown in small plastic pots. Perennial house-plants which are growing actively and are not pot-bound are also likely to have easily-visible young (white) roots.

Equipment: Actively-growing plants in pots; magnifying glass.

- Gently turn a plant out of its pot. Look for young, white roots which were growing down the inside of the pot, on the outside of the root-ball.
- Look for the tips of these young roots: they are smooth, taper to a rounded point

and are often slightly yellowish. Using a magnifying-glass, look carefully behind the root-tip to see where the root-hairs develop (see Activity 4.2.2).

? Do root-hairs grow at the root-tip? (No: they start to grow some way behind it.)
? Imagine the root growing longer by pushing its way through the soil. If root-hairs grew out into the soil while the root was still growing, what would happen? (They would be broken off as the root pushed through the soil.)
? What does this tell you about the way the root grows? (The root grows only at its tip, as the shoot does. Only when the part behind the tip has stopped growing in length can the root-hairs grow out into the soil.)

Activity 4.3.2

Observing germination
Germination is the phase of growth which starts the life-cycle of seed-plants (Fig. 4.13). It begins when seeds start to become active and ends when the young plant is fully independent of the food-store laid up in the seed (see Activity 4.5.4).

Selecting plants to study germination
Children should if possible plant and observe a range of seeds in germination and subsequent growth. These should include both small and large seeds. Small seeds which germinate quickly are particularly useful for investigating the conditions needed for germination, because results can be obtained in a short time. Large seeds, which usually grow more slowly, make it easier to follow the sequence of changes during germination and growth.

For a small, quickly-germinating seed, white mustard (see introduction to this chapter) is ideal because it will germinate and grow well at any time of the year. Readily-available larger seeds in temperate and sub-tropical climates include peas and beans of various kinds, sunflowers and castor-oil. A rather different growth-pattern is shown by grasses and of these, germinating cereals such as wheat and maize (indian corn) provide a useful contrast.

Observing germination in larger seeds
To follow the sequence of changes in the germination of larger seeds it is worth making two kinds of simple growth-chamber, as in Fig. 4.9a,b, both of which are useful. Roots naturally grow in darkness and there is a lot of uncertainty as to what effect, if any, light has on them. Any possible problem can be avoided by putting a sleeve of opaque paper round each growth-chamber, removing it only to observe and record root-growth. Ideally, children should be able to observe germination of a variety of seeds in both kinds of growth-chamber. It is interesting to plant seeds in different orientations (i.e. some upside-down), to observe the responses of emerging shoots and roots to gravity (see also Activities 4.3.7, 4.3.8).

Stages in germination and patterns of development can be recorded in dated drawings. As germination begins these need to be done daily, but in the later stages less frequent drawing will give a clearer record of change.

Patterns of growth in germination
Most seeds which children are likely to observe undergo broadly similar sequences of change as they germinate, though differences will be seen as their shoots emerge.

b: Place a smaller bottle inside a cut-down larger one. Fill the space between with seedling compost

a: Line cut-down bottle with absorbent paper; fill with sand to level of dotted line. Place soaked seeds between paper and plastic; add water until the sand and paper are damp.

Cut drainage holes in the outer bottle. Sow soaked seeds in compost; keep moist.

Figure 4.9

To avoid going into unnecessary detail it is useful to identify three stages.

First stage: The visible changes are that the seed takes in water and swells, usually splitting the seed-coat. What cannot be seen is the activation of the undeveloped plant within the seed (embyro). As the seed absorbs water the embryo begins to digest its food store and use this for growth.

Second stage: The root (radicle) emerges, turns downwards and grows into the soil. Shortly afterwards it begins to develop root-hairs (Activity 4.2.2) which enable the growing embryo to absorb water and chemicals (nutrients) from the soil.

Third stage: The shoot emerges and grows upwards. Leaves expand when it is above ground level. A variety of growth-patterns is shown here. In all the species mentioned except the cereals, the shoot is bent over as it is pushed upwards through the soil, to protect the terminal bud at its tip. In some plants (e.g. mustard, sunflower, french beans and castor-oil) the first leaves to emerge are 'seed leaves' (cotyledons) which were part of the embryo in the seed. In other plants (e.g. peas, runner beans and broad beans) the large seed-leaves stay below ground as the shoot above them grows up. Maize and other cereals grow in quite a different way. They send up an upright, spear-shaped sheath (coleoptile) from which the first leaves and then the shoot emerge.

Activity 4.3.3

Investigating conditions needed for germination

Children can easily investigate three basic environmental conditions to find out what effect they have on germination: water, temperature and light. The other obvious environmental condition, the availability of oxygen, cannot usefully be investigated at primary level, not only because seeds vary very much in their oxygen requirements, but also because the amount of oxygen available can neither be measured nor controlled.

A suggested experimental design is set out below; but older and more able pupils can usefully develop this for themselves, as an exercise in fair-testing and the control of variables.

Equipment and materials: Small seeds (e.g. white mustard); absorbent paper (e.g. paper towels); four dishes; pipette; water; four small clear plastic bags; drawer or box with closely-fitting lid which can hold one dish; adhesive paper labels.

- For each of the four trials, fold a piece of absorbent paper to make a pad, put it on a dish and place 6–10 seeds on it. Have a small clear plastic bag ready to cover the dish. Label and treat the dishes as follows:

- *normal*: Drop water on to the paper and seeds until they are soaked. Cover the dish with the plastic bag so that the seeds are in contact with air but will not dry out. Keep the dish at normal room temperature in full light, e.g. on a window-sill.
- *no light*: Wet and cover the seeds and paper; place the covered dish in a closed drawer or box in the same room as the first trial.
- *cold*: Wet and cover the seeds and paper; place the covered dish in a refrigerator at 0° to +4°C (i.e. do not let the water freeze); keep the light on if possible.
- *no water*: Leave the paper and seeds dry, but cover them; place the covered dish alongside that of the first trial, i.e. in light and at room temperature.

- Each day, uncover the dishes and look for any changes in the seeds. Make a note of changes and differences between the trials, with the dates on which they were observed.

The main changes which will be observed are (in order): splitting of the seed-coat and emergence of the root; emergence of the shoot and growth of root-hairs. The seeds germinated in darkness begin growth normally, but elongate much more rapidly than those under 'normal' conditions. They also fail to produce chlorophyll in their seed-leaves, so that they are pale, spindly and with yellow leaves. Pupils may therefore have grounds to question the commonly-stated view that 'light is not needed for germination', because without it the seedlings cannot grow normally (see also Activity 4.3.4).

? In which trials did the seeds not even begin to germinate? (In the third and fourth trials.)
? What does this tell you about the conditions needed for these seeds to germinate? (They need water and conditions which are not too cold.)
? What additional test do you need to carry out on the seeds in the third and fourth trials to show that this conclusion is correct? (Put both sets of seeds in warm, wet conditions to see if they grow. This is a control procedure: if it is not done, it could be argued that the seeds failed to germinate because they were dead.)

Activity 4.3.4

The effects of environmental conditions on plant growth

The easiest and most effective way of investigating the environmental conditions plants need for normal growth is to grow fast-germinating seeds in sand-culture for 6–8 weeks. The starting-point is the scientific view that plant growth is affected by temperature and by the availability of water, nutrients and light. Plant nutrients are not 'food' in the generally-accepted sense of the term (i.e. complex, high-energy chemicals such as sugar or starch): they are simple chemicals, naturally found in solution in the soil, which are absorbed by the root system (see Activity 4.3.5). Nutrients can be added to the soil artificially in the form of chemical fertilizers which, confusingly, are often referred to as 'plant food'! In order to find out what effect nutrients have on growth it is necessary to grow plants in a medium which contains none, and then supply them in a controlled way. The most commonly-available suitable medium is washed silver-sand.

Equipment and materials: For each set of trials: five small plastic plant pots; damp silver-sand; small seeds (e.g. white mustard); rain or distilled water; plant nutrients in powder or liquid form (e.g. proprietary fertilizer for house or garden plants); two washed plastic bottles; drawer or box with closely-fitting lid; adhesive labels.

- For each set of trials, fill five pots with damp silver-sand. If the pots have fairly large holes, put a piece of wet absorbent paper over the bottom of each to prevent sand escaping. Sow five seeds in each pot and put them on a tray.
- Make up a solution of plant nutrients according to the manufacturer's instructions and keep it in a labelled bottle, but *use only half the recommended amount*: it is very easy to overload small pots with nutrients. Throughout the investigation the trial pots need to be inspected every day. Set up the pots and label them as follows:

- *normal*: Water the seeds with nutrient solution so that the surface of the sand is thoroughly wetted. Keep the pot in full light, but not in direct sunlight, and at room temperature; keep the surface of the sand moist but not wet.
- *dark*: Treat the pot exactly as in the first trial, except that it should be kept in a closed box or drawer which is opened only for inspection and watering.
- *drought*: At the start of the trial, treat this pot as in the first trial; but after that, water very sparingly: the seedlings should be given a little only when they show the *first signs* of wilting. Place the pot alongside that of the first trial.
- *no nutrients*: Water the pot with distilled water or rain water only; keep the surface of the sand moist but not wet. Place the pot alongside those of the first and third trials.
- *cold*: Treat this pot exactly as in the first trial, but keep it in a cool place, for example outdoors in autumn or spring in temperate climates. In temperate summers, warm climates or very cold winters it may not be possible to carry out this trial satisfactorily.

- As the seedlings develop, thin them out so that there are only one or two plants (the most vigorous) in each pot. Every week, record the height, number of leaves and appearance of the plants in each trial. If the plants are growing on a window-sill, turn them every few days so that they keep growing upright.

The effects of different conditions are only partly predictable because conditions will vary and different kinds of plant respond in different ways. As an example, plants of white mustard grown under 'normal', i.e. favourable, conditions have unbranched but very leafy shoots of a clear, slightly yellow green.

The most predictable effect is that of darkness : the young plants will elongate and fail to develop chlorophyll, so they will be tall, weak, spindly and pale. They can make no food by photosynthesis (*4.4) and so have no food available to them apart from the small store in the seed itself. As a result of their uncontrolled length growth and inability to make food they soon fall over and die.

Normal growth in plants involves taking in a lot of water. Plants in drought conditions grow more slowly than normal: they are likely to have fewer and smaller leaves which may be of an abnormally dark green. They may also have more pigments (e.g. purple) in their stems than normal plants.

In the absence of nutrients from the soil, the growing plant is unable to make a wide range of chemicals needed for normal growth, in particular, proteins. The result is that at best growth is poor and the plants are stunted, often of abnormal colours (reds and yellows are common) and they may not survive for more than a few weeks.

As long as temperatures are not low enough to be lethal or prevent germination altogether, plants in the cold are usually quite healthy, but grow more slowly than those in warmer conditions. This is because all the chemical changes involved in growth proceed more slowly at lower temperatures.

Activity 4.3.5

Plants and water

In Activity 4.3.3, it is found that if plants are given a very scanty water supply, they grow far less than those under 'normal' or favourable conditions. If a plant is deprived of water altogether it will sooner or later collapse; a process known as wilting. Children may already be familiar with wilting from seeing changes in plants transplanted in gardens. If a plant begins to wilt but is then watered it will usually recover with no permanent damage. If white mustard plants in the classroom are not watered for a few days they will begin to show the drooping of leaves characteristic of wilting. When children have seen them in this state, water them by putting the pots into a bowl of water to ensure thorough wetting of the soil. Their recovery should also be watched and will usually be complete in an hour or two.

Water taken in by the root system is moved up the stem and into the leaves, carrying with it nutrients the plant needs for normal growth (see Activity 4.3.4). It is important to emphasize that the uptake of water is in itself one of the plant's main transport systems. With care and pre-planning, children can see this for themselves by making plants take up a solution of dye. The most effective way to do this is to use weeds or young mustard plants, dug up carefully and with their root-systems washed off in water. Whatever plants are to be used, it is essential to make sure in advance that they will take up the available dye and that this will be visible in their leaves when they do.

The most effective dye to use is eosin, the main colorant in red writing ink (i.e. not waterproof drawing ink). If red ink is not available, remove the two ends from a scarlet-red felt-tip pen, take out the porous ink cartridge, cut it into pieces and soak these in a small volume of water. Some food-colourings both red and blue have been used with success, but their dye content varies greatly and many are not suitable.

Equipment and materials: Weeds or other small plants with their roots washed off and kept in water; solution of dye; small jars; magnifying glass.

- Look carefully at the leaves with a magnifying-glass, holding them up to the light. Notice the system of veins: in grasses these are more or less parallel but in other weeds they are branched like a net. Usually they are green, but paler than the rest of the leaf.
- Place some plants in jars of dye so that the roots are completely covered by the solution. Place others in water as a control and leave them all in cool, light conditions, *not* in direct sunlight.

- Look at the plants at intervals during the day, comparing the two batches, using a magnifying glass and looking in particular for any change in the colour of the leaf-veins. If no change can be seen at the end of the day, leave the plants overnight and compare them again in the morning.

Once the dye has reached the leaves, it is usually possible to see the network of leaf veins very clearly with a hand-lens, especially if they are held up to the light. The important point to emphasize in discussing their observations with children is that water uptake and movement, as shown by the dye, is a transport system which the plant has to maintain in order to grow and stay alive.

Plant growth and response

Living things characteristically respond to conditions both within themselves and in their surroundings, so that their chances of survival are increased. To do this they have to be able to detect changes (stimuli) and change their behaviour as a result (response). In most plants it is the parts which are actively-growing which detect change, but there are no specialized sensory organs such as eyes or ears. Actively-growing shoots and roots are usually very sensitive to changes in their environment and respond by changing their direction or pattern of growth. Young plants need to become established in their environment, so their responses to the conditions they are growing in are among the most rapid and easily-detected.

Children can investigate three kinds of response in seedlings: the response of shoots to gravity and light, and the response of roots to gravity. For all three investigations, seedlings of white mustard are suitable.

When investigating the response of shoots and roots to gravity it is very useful to have, in addition to the test-plants, larger germinated seeds such as beans planted in humid air growth chambers (Fig. 4.9a); some upside-down and others the right way up. These will show responses to gravity as shoots and roots emerge and are especially helpful in discussing why plants need their shoots and roots to behave as they do.

Activity 4.3.6

Response of shoots to light

Equipment and materials: Seedlings (e.g. white mustard) grown in small plastic pots; box as in Fig. 4.10a; clear plastic set-square.

- For a day or two before the experiment, keep the seedlings in full light and turn the pots twice a day to keep them growing straight up.
- For each trial, use two pots and mark the rim of each. Place one pot in the box as in Fig. 4.10a.
- Place the second (control) pot beside the box with its mark facing the window. Turn this pot through 180° (i.e. half a turn) every hour.
- ? Why is the control pot turned every hour? (To make sure that light falling on the seedlings is not from one side only.)
- Every hour during the day, take the seedlings from the box and look at them from the side. Put a set-square on the table to help you see how much they have changed (Fig. 4.10b). Draw some of the seedlings, showing the angles of stems and leaves accurately.
- Replace the seedlings in the box, making sure the mark on the pot faces the hole. At the same time, turn the control pot.

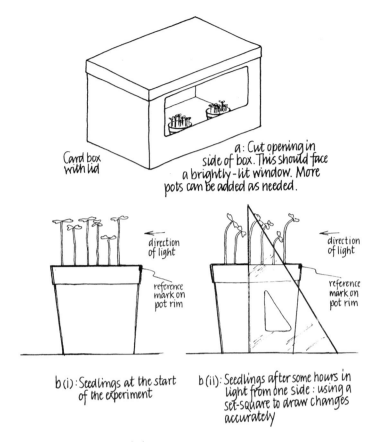

a: Cut opening in side of box. This should face a brightly-lit window. More pots can be added as needed.

Card box with lid

direction of light

reference mark on pot rim

direction of light

reference mark on pot rim

b (i): Seedlings at the start of the experiment

b (ii): Seedlings after some hours in light from one side: using a set-square to draw changes accurately

Figure 4.10 Response of shoots to light

? What does the plants' response tell you about their ability to detect change in their environment? (They can detect a change in the direction of the light falling on them.)

In this case the stimulus is a difference in the amount of light falling on the plant from 'in front' and 'behind'. Their response is positive: they bend *towards* the stimulus, i.e. the high light intensity.

● Leave the seedlings overnight. Next day, turn the pot through 180° so that the mark on the pot rim faces away from the light.

? If the seedlings are left in this position all day, what do you predict will happen? (They will bend back, towards the light.)

? How do the seedlings bend? How is their movement different from the bending of your arm or leg? (The seedlings bend by *changing the direction in which the shoot is growing*. This means that they move slowly and cannot bend to and fro as our bodies can.)

? Why do plants need to respond in this way? (Young seedlings in darkness cannot grow normally and they soon die [Activity 4.3.4]. The ability to sense the direction of light and grow towards it gives them a better chance of survival.)

Activity 4.3.7

Response of shoots to gravity

Equipment and materials: Two batches of seedlings (e.g. white mustard) grown in small plastic pots; box with a lid; modelling clay.

- For a day or two before making an observation, keep the plants to be used in full light and turn the pots through 180° twice a day to make sure they are growing upright at the start of the experiment.
- Place one pot of seedlings on its side in the box as in Fig. 4.11. Mark the uppermost point of the pot rim. Place the second pot upright beside the first; put the lid on the box.

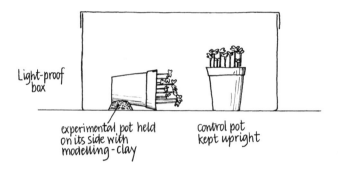

Figure 4.11   Response of shoots to gravity

- Every hour during the day, take the pots out of the box to see how the seedlings have changed. Draw them to show any changes, then replace both pots in the box as before.
- ? What does the plants' behaviour tell you about their ability to detect change in their environment? (The shoots are sensitive to their direction in relation to gravity and the Earth.)

In this case the stimulus is gravity acting on the shoot. The response of the shoots is negative: they bend upwards, *away from* the downward force of their own weight.

- ? What was the purpose of the pot of upright seedlings? (They acted as a control, to show that the test seedlings bent because their position had been changed and not just because they were in the box.)
- ? Why were the plants placed in the box for this experiment? (If they had been in light, their bending might have been caused by more light coming from one side, so the experiment had to be done in the dark.)
- ? Why do plants need their shoots to grow upwards? (When seeds germinate the emerging shoot is usually in darkness. The response of bending and growing upwards gives it the best chance of reaching the surface of the soil and the light and air it needs to survive.)

This last point is shown particularly clearly by comparing large seeds germinated upside-down with those grown the right way up. Older plants also need to respond by growing upwards if their shoots are bent down or flattened by animals or severe weather, so their leaves can still reach the light and their flowers have the best chance of pollination. Weeds and plants of waste ground (mustard is one of these) respond particularly rapidly.

Activity 4.3.8

The response of roots to gravity

To see the response of roots to gravity it is necessary to grow them in humid air. An effective way to do this is to make a small version of the humid-air growth chamber shown in Fig. 4.9a. Small seeds, e.g. mustard, should be planted all round the chamber and allowed to germinate in the dark until their roots emerge and start to grow down-wards. Press the sand down firmly to ensure that the absorbent paper is in contact with the bottle or jar.

Beans or other large seeds, some grown the right way up and some upside-down, are very useful for comparison, especially in the discussion of experimental results.

- Place the growth-chamber on its side, so that the roots are horizontal. Mark the upper side of the chamber and put it back in darkness.
- Look at the roots to see how they change, at least two or three times during the day. Draw the roots to record changes in their direction of growth. Make sure you include the root-hairs in your drawing and be careful to show which part of the root is bending.
? Did all the roots behave in the same way? (No: those at the top and sides of the chamber bend downwards, but those at the bottom keep growing more or less straight.)
? Why did some roots stay straight while most bent downwards? (Those which could bend and grow downwards, did so. The ones which carried on growing straight were prevented from growing down by the wall of the chamber.)
? What does the response of the roots tell you about their ability to detect changes in their surroundings? (They are sensitive to their direction in relation to the Earth and gravity.)

If it can grow downwards, the root responds to gravity and its response is positive, *towards* the stimulus, in the same direction as its own weight. The direct contrast between shoot and root behaviour should be emphasized here.

? Which part of the root bends, i.e. changes the direction of its growth? (The part behind the tip which has not yet developed root-hairs. As Activity 4.3.1 shows, it is only this part of the root which is growing longer.)
? Why do plants need their roots to grow downwards? (Water moves down through the soil, so deeper layers of soil are usually moister than shallow ones. By growing down-wards, roots have the best chance of reaching the water and nutrients the plant needs.)

Roots usually respond most rapidly and positively to gravity just after they have emerged from the seed. As a branched root-system develops (which children should be able to see when germinating larger seeds) the side-roots behave differently from the first or tap-root, growing out from it at an angle to gravity, to exploit fresh volumes of soil. This growth-pattern is very like that of branching shoot-systems in trees: both allow plants to exploit their environment very efficiently.

4.4: Photosynthesis

Photosynthesis is the complex chemical process carried out by green plants to make their own high-energy foods (*4.4). The energy source for photosynthesis is light, and in most plants by far the greatest part of this food-making process is carried on in the leaves. Characteristically leaves are flat and thin, so that they can exchange gases with the atmosphere efficiently, and grow so that they intercept the greatest possible amount of light.

Investigation of photosynthesis as a process requires fairly complex chemical testing and so is not possible at primary level; but children can gain a useful insight into its importance by sampling and investigating some of its products. The knowledge gained is in turn a significant element in developing the concept of plants as the producers of food in almost all ecosystems (*5.7).

Activity 4.4.1

Plants as food-makers

Equipment and materials: Dishes, spoons, knives and cutting-boards used for food preparation only; disposable cups; any edible, uncooked plant material. This could include: roots, e.g. carrot, parsnip; stem tubers, e.g. potato; leaves, e.g. lettuce, cabbage, celery; fruits, e.g. tomato, grape, apple, cucumber, sweetcorn; seeds, e.g. sunflower, peas, nuts; edible processed plant products, e.g. rolled or flaked cereals, sugar, dried fruits.

Safety notes

1) Children **must be asked about any food allergies** they may have before being allowed to sample materials. Allergies to nuts are especially dangerous and should be mentioned explicitly. It is advisable to send a note to parents with a consent-slip before undertaking this activity.
2) All fresh plant materials should be washed and if necessary scrubbed or peeled before use. All materials should be set out (and if necessary cut up) under hygienic conditions with kitchen equipment and utensils which are used **only** for the preparation of food.

- Set out the various plant materials and products in dishes, cut up where necessary. Label each dish with a number or letter. Each dish should have a spoon to dispense its contents; each person should have a plastic cup into which to put a sample before eating it.
- Using a spoon, put a sample of food from a dish into your plastic cup. Before eating it, try to identify it. These questions may help you:
? What plant does this food come from? Which *part* of the plant does the food come from? Do you usually eat this food raw, cooked, both, or not at all?
- Sample at least six plant products. Try to include some you don't know as well as ones which are easy to identify.
? We eat plants for food. Do plants eat anything? (Plants do not eat other living things as we and other animals do.)

At this point some children are likely to observe that a few plants do 'eat' animals, usually insects. This is true; but the insects are not used for food as we eat other animals, rather as a source of nutrients (see Activity 4.3.4).

? If plants do not eat other living things, how do they obtain their food? (They make it for themselves by the process of photosynthesis. Light is the energy source for this process and without light, plants cannot live long, see Activity 4.3.4.)

This is a point at which, if it is appropriate, the link can be made between photosynthesis as a food-making process and the role of plants as the producers in ecosystems (*5.7). Although most humans eat food other than plant material, we are still completely dependent on plants for food, as almost all other animals are, because no animals can make food for themselves.

Activity 4.4.2

Plant products as energy stores

The materials we use for food contain large amounts of energy (chemical-potential energy, *12.2) which we transfer in respiration (*3.6) and use as the energy source for activities such as movement and growth. If it is true that plants make their own food and use food (as we do) for growth, to build up their bodies, then their bodies should have a lot of high-energy chemicals in them. Children's own experience and news items seen on TV show clearly that this is so, because many plant materials burn (see also Activity 9.4.1).

Children can find direct evidence that plants make high-energy food-chemicals, by identifying one kind of plant product (oil) and burning it on a small scale in a controlled way. At the same time they will experience for themselves the transfer of chemical-potential energy as thermal and light energy, and can then consider the implications of this.

Equipment and materials: Metal tray or large, shallow tin, with a layer of sand in the bottom; tin-lid diameter 10–12cm; 15cm thin wire; nuts. e.g. brazil-nuts, walnuts, peanuts (ground-nuts); matches; thin white paper.

Safety note: This activity must be closely supervised. Long hair should be tied back and loose clothing secured. Children with nut allergies should not handle nuts.

- Cut or break a nut in half. Rub the cut surface on to thin, white paper, then hold the paper up to the light.
? What change do you see in the paper? (It becomes much more translucent, letting more light through.)

The paper becomes more translucent because the nut contains oil, which is absorbed by the paper. The oil fills up some of the air-spaces in the paper so light passes through more easily. The nut is a seed and the oil is its main energy source.

- Put the tin-lid on the sand in the middle of the tray. Make a small heap of sand on the tin-lid.
- Bend the wire to make a loop and spike as shown in Fig. 4.12a.
- Place a piece of nut on the wire spike, as shown in Fig. 4.12b, with the wire loop buried in sand to make it more stable.
- Use a match to start the nut burning.
? How does burning transfer energy to the environment? (Energy is transferred as light and by heating the air around the flame which then rises, carrying smoke with it.)

? What is the fuel being burnt? (Oil in the nut.)
? Where did the oil in the nut come from? (It was made by the parent plant, by photosynthesis.)
? Where did the energy in the oil come from? (From the Sun: the plant absorbs part of the light falling on it and transfers this, through chemical changes, to the food materials it makes.)

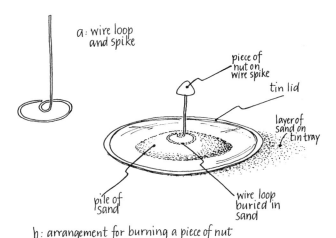

Figure 4.12   Burning a piece of nut

4.5: Plant reproduction

Humans, like nearly all the animals children can observe, make more of their own kind in only one way: by sexual reproduction. Plants also reproduce sexually, but in addition many have asexual ways of increasing their population, which are more directly related to the ways in which they grow.

The life-cycle of plants
The life-cycle of any living thing can be seen as a sequence of events or stages, centred on its reproduction. The life-cycle of plants, including both sexual and asexual reproduction (*2.3), is summarized in Fig. 4.13. Of these stages, germination (which is usually thought of as beginning the life-cycle) is investigated and discussed in Activities 4.3.2 and 4.3.3; growth in activities 4.3.1 and 4.3.4. Of the remaining stages, asexual reproduction is examined in Activity 4.5.1 and sexual reproduction in Activities 4.5.2–4.5.5.

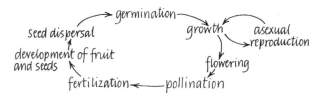

Figure 4.13   Life-cycle of plants

Activity 4.5.1

Asexual reproduction
Children are likely to be familiar with several different kinds of asexual reproduction in plants, though they may not immediately recognize them as such. It is helpful to distinguish between natural asexual reproduction and the artificial propagation (cloning) of plants by cuttings and other means.

Observing natural asexual reproduction
Any plant which 'spreads', such as daisies in a lawn or creeping weeds, is making more plants simply by growing. Outgrowths of the main plant become established as independent plants so that if the main plant is destroyed, they live on. It is worth looking among cultivated plants and weeds to find examples of natural asexual reproduction which are common (and perhaps troublesome) enough to be brought into the classroom. Examples likely to be available for much of the year include most irises, many grasses such as twitch (couch-grass) and willowherbs, all of which spread underground; and strawberries, creeping buttercup and brambles, whose long aerial shoots take root where they touch the ground.

Artificial asexual reproduction: rooting shoot-cuttings
In addition to looking at natural examples, children can experiment with artificial asexual reproduction or cloning of house-plants by using cuttings to propagate them. A cutting is simply a part of a parent plant which is removed and induced to grow independently by developing roots or, more rarely, both roots and shoots. The easiest kind of cutting to work with is a shoot-tip. Because removing shoot-tips changes the pattern of growth in the shoot which remains, this activity can be usefully be combined with Activity 4.3.1.

Tradescantias (see introduction to this chapter) can be readily propagated by shoot-cuttings at almost any time of the year, and pelargoniums during their growing-season. Both usually root well in a mixture of half-and-half soil-less compost and coarse, gritty sand; tradescantias will also root well in water.

Equipment and materials: Plants, (e.g. pelargoniums, tradescantias) with actively-growing shoot-tips which can be removed for cuttings; craft knife; small pots with compost; small jar.

- Using a sharp knife, remove the end of a non-flowering shoot with three or four well-grown leaves in addition to the terminal bud and young leaves round it.
- With the knife, cut off the stem of the cutting just below the oldest (lowest) leaf. Cut (pelargonium) or pull (tradescantia) the oldest one or two leaves from the cutting, so that it is left with two well-grown leaves below the terminal cluster.
- To root cuttings in moist compost, make a hole with a pencil and put the cutting into it so that the lowest leaf is just above soil level. Firm the compost round the cutting.
- Place the pot in a light, warm place but not in direct sunlight. Do not put a plastic bag over the pot, but let air circulate round the cuttings. Keep the compost moist by watering from below.
- To root cuttings in water, put several cuttings into a jar so that the leaves rest on the rim and the bottoms of the stems are in water. Leave the jar in a light, warm

place but not in direct sunlight. Unlike many plants, tradescantias rooted in water usually develop root-hairs.

Activity 4.5.2

Sexual reproduction in plants: gaining an overview

Sexual reproduction in plants is a complex process. A good way of beginning to understand it is to see it as a sequence of events; the central part of the plant's life-cycle (Fig. 4.13). An overview of the process can be gained by observing the obvious changes which flowers undergo, from the growth of the flower-bud to the ripening of the fruit. Children should be acquainted with flower structure and its vocabulary (Activity 4.2.3) before undertaking this activity.

Selecting plants to give an overview of sexual reproduction

There are common plants which, at the right point in their development, show the whole sequence of their sexual reproduction very clearly. In an unbranched flower-spike, flower-buds are produced in sequence so that the oldest flowers have developed into fruits and are shedding seeds while the youngest are still in bud. Looking at these enables children to observe the more obvious events in sexual reproduction in their natural sequence. The examples given are European, but similar flowers are found or cultivated in most north-temperate regions.

Plants of the cabbage-cress family, including weeds and cultivated wallflowers, bloom throughout the spring, when wild and garden hyacinths (English and Spanish 'bluebells') may also be available. Through the summer and into early autumn, foxgloves and a variety of willowherbs are useful wild-flowers, the willowherbs with the ovary *below* the rest of the flower. Among summer-flowering garden plants, hollyhocks show the sequence well, as do lupins and antirrhinums ('snapdragons') though their flower-structure is more difficult to understand.

All flowers which the children are likely to encounter show the same basic sequence of changes, which in the examples suggested can be seen very easily by looking at successive flowers from the top of the spike downwards:

  i) formation and growth of the flower-bud;
 ii) the flower opens;
iii) the flower withers and the petals usually drop off;
 iv) as the flower withers, the fruit begins to grow in the middle of it;
  v) the fruit grows in size and becomes juicy, or dries and splits open, releasing the seeds inside it.

Once these obvious changes and their natural sequence have been identified and observed, the sequence can be used as a framework within which to look in more detail at the stages of sexual reproduction.

Activity 4.5.3

Pollination

Pollination is the process by which pollen is transferred from the anthers where it is made, to the stigma where it develops, which leads eventually to fertilization. With-

out pollination most plants cannot develop seeds. Some flowers can pollinate themselves, but most need some outside agent to move the pollen. The two commonest
pollinators are insects and wind, though birds and bats are also important in some
parts of the world. Wind-pollinated flowers, though common, are mostly very in-
conspicuous and all the flowers children are likely to observe are insect-pollinated.

Natural pollination by insects
A wide variety of insects (not only bees) are attracted to flowers by some combination of colour, scent and food, the commonest food being a sugary liquid (nectar).
Although other parts of the flower may make a contribution, in most flowers it is the
petals which attract insects, this being their main role in the reproductive process.
Children may be able to observe natural pollination in the school grounds, but can
learn more about the process and its results by pollinating flowers artificially.

Selecting plants for artificial pollination
The plants most likely to be useful for artificial pollination are daffodils, lilies and
pelargoniums grown in pots. Of these, daffodils are the most strictly seasonal and
their flower-structure can be confusing. The 'trumpet' (corona) is not the petals, but
a specialized outgrowth from their bases which in natural pollination guides insects
into the centre of the flower. Modern hybrid lilies are easy to cultivate in pots for
summer flowering or can be bought in bud for much of the year and treated as
house-plants. In either case, follow the supplier's instructions for cultivation.

    Pelargoniums have a very long flowering season and can be successfuly pollinated
from May to November in the northern hemisphere. Easiest of all to pollinate are the
'regal' types (see Fig. 4.1c). Of the round-leaved 'zonal' types (Figs. 4.1a and c) those
with wide, overlapping petals are much easier to pollinate than the narrow-petalled
varieties (Fig. 4.8).

Artificial pollination
The plants recommended can all be pollinated by collecting pollen with a small, soft
paint-brush of fine hair and depositing it on a stigma. All three have anthers which split
open at the sides to release their pollen, which is rather like sticky, coloured dust.

    For artificial pollination to be successful, pollen has to be put on to a ripe stigma. In
daffodils the stigma is a slightly feathery cup which opens when ripe. In lilies it is a
three-lobed club which when ripe becomes shiny and covered with a sticky fluid. The
stigma of a pelargonium has five arms. While the anthers are shedding pollen these stay
together; when the stigma is ripe, they open into a star-shaped structure (see Fig. 4.8).

    To pollinate successfully, the children should look for younger flowers which are
shedding pollen and older ones with ripe stigmas. A hand-lens can be used to look at
grains of pollen on the brush and the stigma. The flowers pollinated should be
marked by tying a piece of coloured yarn loosely round the flower-stalk so that
subsequent development can be observed.

Activity 4.5.4

Development of fruits and seeds
This activity is an obvious extension of any investigation into pollination (Activity
4.5.3). Any flower which has been artificially pollinated should be observed closely
over the following days and weeks to see what changes this brings about. These

observations can usefully be supported by any of the plants used to gain an overview of sexual reproduction (Activity 4.5.2).

Biologically the most important event following pollination is fertilization, which in plants as in animals is the central event in sexual reproduction (*4.5). Children cannot observe this process (which takes place at a microscopic scale and is very difficult to observe at all), but they can easily see most of its important consequences, as the ovary develops into the fruit and the seeds develop within it.

The sequence of changes in the development of seed and fruit

The first visible consequence of fertilization is often that the petals and stamens either wither or drop off. At the same time the ovary will begin to develop into the fruit. For example, in pelargoniums the first sign of fruit development is a thickening and lengthening of the 'beak' on top of the ovary, so that it protrudes from the sepals.

It is helpful for children to cut growing fruits open to see the seeds early in their development, using a magnifying-glass or hand-lens, and compare these with ripe fruits, either at the same time or later. All the plants recommended in Activity 4.5.2 are good for this. In most plants the ovary (wall of the developing fruit) is green and juicy, while the immature seeds are soft and white.

As they ripen, seeds undergo many changes. One change which cannot be seen is that they take on a store of food, which is needed for growth and energy during germination (Activity 4.3.2). The main change which can be seen is that their protective seed-coat becomes thicker, tougher and often much darker in colour. Most seeds, though not all, dry out before they are shed, becoming dormant until they germinate (see Activity 2.2.3).

Activity 4.5.5

Seed dispersal

For most plants it is an advantage if their seeds are scattered widely, rather than all falling in the same small area. The means which plants develop and exploit to disperse their seeds are very varied and a major adaptation to their environment (see Activity 5.6.2).

While there are many different means of seed dispersal, children can usefully distinguish three main groups, depending on whether the plant projects its own seeds ('self-dispersal') or they are carried by wind or animals. Usually the most difficult to find are examples of plants which disperse their own seeds, and these may not be available. Much easier to find are examples of wind-dispersed seeds and hooked fruits which can be collected and dried for use at any time of the year. Familiar cultivated or wild fruits can be used as examples of fleshy fruits: modern storage and transport technology means that many are available at all times of the year.

Self-dispersal

In these plants the fruit itself projects the seeds. Most self-dispersing fruits are dry, though children may find the green 'exploding' pods of wild balsams (*Impatiens*, touch-me-not). Apart from these, the two most easily-found groups of self-dispersed seeds among European wild-flowers are the long, narrow capsules of some of the cress-cabbage family (e.g. bitter-cress, lady's smock) and pods of some of the pea family (e.g. gorse and some vetches).

Wind dispersal

Children are likely to encounter or know about three main groups of wind-dispersed seeds. An investigation of 'parachute' and winged seeds and fruits is included as a case-study of adaptation (Activity 5.6.2).

The first and least specialized is the 'pepper-pot' type, in which the dry capsule opens at the top and the small, round seeds are shaken out and scattered like coarse dust as the fruiting shoot is blown about by the wind. Examples include foxgloves, poppies and antirrhinums. More specialized are the 'parachute' fruits and seeds, all of which develop, in a variety of ways, a structure of long, silky hairs which slow the fall of the fruit or seed, allowing air-currents to carry it further from the parent plant.

The other more specialized wind-dispersed fruits are those with wings. Examples likely to be familiar to children in the northern hemisphere include trees such as sycamore and other maples, ash and most species of pine. When released into the air they start to spin as they fall, so that the wing creates lift, slowing the rate of descent and allowing the fruit or seed to travel further.

Animal dispersal

The ways in which animals can act as the conveyors and distributors of seeds are many and varied, but children are likely to be acquainted with or find examples of two: hooked fruits and fleshy fruits.

Hooked fruits are simply that: dry fruits which develop hooks or barbs. As mammals brush by them, these become tangled with furry skin (or hairy clothing) and carried away from the parent plant. Sooner or later they are removed or drop off, so the seeds are distributed. Familiar European examples include goosegrass, burdock and many grasses with a barbed or bristly spike at the end of each fruit.

Fleshy fruits are very varied in structure, but all have in common that they develop a sweet, juicy outer layer which is sought after and eaten by animals and birds. Many wild fleshy fruits are highly poisonous to humans and such fruits should never be eaten unless one is quite sure that they have been correctly identified and are harmless. The seeds of fleshy fruits are often hard and always highly resistant to digestion, so they pass through the animal's gut unharmed and are dropped with its faeces. By that time the animal is likely to have moved away from the parent plant, so the seeds are dispersed.

5

Variety, Adaptation and Interdependence

5.1: Observing a variety of animals

Although most work on animals at primary level is likely to be concentrated on humans (see Chapter 3), children will encounter a variety of other animals, both wild and domesticated, and need to begin observing and learning about them. Children's experience of animals as part of the school curriculum can usefully be considered under four main headings: observing locally-occurring wild animals; visits to outside venues; the long-term care of animals in school and the short-term care of animals in school. If children are to come into close contact with animals, whether in school or elsewhere, it is advisable to consult parents beforehand so that risks from known allergies can be avoided. Any child handling animals at any time must wash their hands thoroughly *both before and after* contact.

Observing locally-occurring wild animals
Wherever possible, children should be encouraged to observe and identify locally-occurring wild animals in their habitats, whether natural or partly man-made. Opportunities to do this are obviously very varied in different localities, but even if children have no access to natural habitats such as ponds or woodland, they can often observe, identify and learn about the behaviour of birds by feeding them, using tables and specialized feeders which are visible from inside the school but inaccessible to cats and squirrels. Such observations can be used as the basis for identifying animals using keys (see Section 5.4) and, if enough information is available, for studying adaptation (see Sections 5.5, 5.6).

Using visits to study a variety of animals
At least some, and perhaps most, of the children's learning about a variety of animals is likely to take place outside school; but to be effective, visits to farms, zoos, wildlife parks, field centres must be supported by preparatory and follow-up work. A preliminary visit by teachers and other responsible adults is highly desirable, to assess not only the centre's resources and its educational potential, but also to make sure that the standard of animal care and welfare is acceptable.

Although the main focus of a visit may be the study of adaptation (*5.5), encountering a variety of animals in a short time is also useful for developing the idea that different animals are related and can be grouped into a fairly small number of large 'families' such as mammals, birds, reptiles and fish, on the basis of criteria which children can learn and apply through the use of keys (see section 5.4).

Depending on the age and ability of the children and the resources of the centre it may be appropriate to construct one or more identification keys (Section 5.4) for use during the visit. These can not only help children to learn criteria used in classification but also focus attention on the animals and encourage purposeful observation of them. For example, at a zoo it reduces the question-load on teachers if pupils can find out for themselves to which broad group animals belong, and their main characteristics. At a farm centre, on the other hand, the range of larger animals is likely to be limited to mammals and birds. In this situation it is useful to construct a key so that children can identify the common domesticated mammals: cattle, sheep, goats, pigs, rabbits, dogs and cats.

Long-term care of animals in school

There should always be well-understood educational reasons for keeping animals in school. Ultimate responsibility for the animals' welfare must rest with *knowledgeable and experienced* adults who are also able to provide or arrange backup care during school holidays, at weekends or if the usual carers are unavailable. Detailed research should be undertaken on the practicalities of keeping the animals under consideration, including equipment, selection, feeding and welfare, both physical and mental. Decisions must also be made at the outset as to whether or not the animals will be allowed to breed, and if they are, how all the offspring and parents are to be cared for.

Short-term care of animals in school

Keeping animals in school for short periods poses far fewer logistical and ethical problems than long-term care, but the same criteria should be applied when assessing its educational value. In particular, can the animals' welfare be guaranteed, and will their presence make it possible to fulfil educational objectives which cannot be met in any other way? If the answer to both questions is positive, there are several possibilities which can be considered if animals are available. The first two discussed below are particularly useful as a preliminary to investigating adaptations to a habitat and feeding relationships within an ecosystem (Sections 5.6, 5.7).

A short-term terrarium

One possibility is the setting-up of a short-term 'terrarium': a tank, preferably of lightweight moulded plastic, with a layer of damp garden soil in the bottom, covered with decaying leaves. When covered with a plastic sheet secured by elastic bands, this provides a humid atmosphere in which a range of common invertebrates, found in most gardens, can be kept for one or two days before being returned to their natural habitat. A terrarium should be kept in fairly dim light and in as cool a place as possible.

Common garden snails, slugs and woodlice can all be kept in a terrarium for a short time without harm, but earthworms cannot, and other animals, e.g. snails, should not be disturbed when dormant. Numbers of slugs and snails should be kept low (two or three of each) or the terrarium will very quickly become foul with their droppings. The animals should be fed on sliced vegetables and fruit such as carrot, lettuce and apple. It is possible to observe and compare their feeding behaviour and preferences, movement and response to their environment. When the animals have been returned to their own habitat, the tank should be emptied completely and thoroughly washed.

A one-day pond

The problem with keeping fresh-water invertebrates in school, even for a few days, is that the water warms up so that its dissolved oxygen content (Activity 6.5.3) is reduced and many animals cannot survive. If a well-stocked pond is available locally (including the school's own grounds), an effective way to use it is to set up one or more 'mini-ponds' in transparent plastic tanks for a day so that children can observe them. 'Mini-ponds', when carefully used, can maximize children's interaction with a variety of animals while minimizing disturbance of the habitat.

This activity requires careful planning, since the animals should be netted on the morning they are required and returned to their own pond on the same day. Inexperienced teachers are strongly advised to seek help from advisers and local wildlife groups in locating suitable available habitats and identifying the commoner animals.

Visiting pets in school

Children and adults may wish to bring pets into school. This can be valuable educationally, especially for children who have little or no contact with animals at home, but a range of precautions must be observed. It is necessary to ensure that animals are brought in only by a well-understood arrangement which must include provision for their welfare while they are in school. Children must be well-prepared for the visit and aware of the need not to subject the animals to stress, for example by noise, crowding or handling. Animals should be handled by people other than their owners only if they welcome this. Strict hygiene must be observed: as always, children must wash their hands both before and after handling animals. Cats and dogs, in particular, should be brought to school only if they have been regularly treated by a vet to eliminate parasites, both external and internal, and the usual precautions with regard to children's allergies and informing parents have been observed.

5.2: Observing a variety of plants

Suggestions for growing a small range of flowering-plants in the classroom and for bringing others in for use in particular activities are given in Chapter 4. Children should also have the opportunity of observing non-flowering plants in natural and artificial habitats.

Growing a wider range of flowering-plants

If the school has a garden children can not only grow a range of flowers and vegetables, but also observe the growth and adaptations of weeds (*5.6). Sowing seeds and observing their development puts learning about germination (Activity 4.3.2) in a practical context. Ornamental annuals which are particularly rewarding include antirrhinums ('snapdragons') pollinated by large bees and ornamental maize (indian corn) pollinated by wind.

Among vegetables, small salads such as radish, lettuce and lambs' lettuce are the most quickly and easily grown. Beans of any kind show the main sequence of events in the plant's sexual reproduction and life-cycle very well (Fig. 4.13; Activity 4.5.2), since some pods can be left to ripen and seed can be collected to be sown the following year. Salads, beans and other crops are likely to attract plant-eating animals such as slugs and snails, so that feeding relationships in the garden ecosystem (*5.7) can be seen in action and the ethics of exterminating pests (*5.9) can be discussed in a real context.

In trying to grow a wider range of flowering-plants in the classroom, the main obstacles are fluctuating temperature, very dry air, and dust. There are many plants which will survive in a classroom, but few which will flourish. The solution is to restrict long-term classroom plants to those which do well and to have others, like pets, on 'visits' for a few days or weeks. From a scientific point of view it is always useful to choose plants which will show structure of shoots and flowers, growth or sexual reproduction clearly, and about which a lot is known. Small-flowered fuchsias, for example, show all of these features, can be pollinated by hand (see Activity 4.5.3) and are unusual in that their sepals are like petals and most of them in the wild (South America) are pollinated by birds.

Observing and growing non-flowering plants
Apart from conifers and their relatives, the three groups of smaller non-flowering plants which children are most likely to encounter are ferns, mosses and liverworts (*5.2). Although some mosses and a few ferns grow in very dry, exposed habitats where there is very little soil, plants of all three groups are found most frequently in habitats which are shady and humid, where there is not enough light or soil for flowering-plants to succeed. In urban environments they can often be found near the ground on shady, north-facing walls, particularly where water seeps into cracks and bricks or stones are permanently damp.

Few non-flowering plants can flourish unprotected in the hot, dry, dusty environment of the classroom. They can be kept for short periods successfully in a cool, humid terrarium (see Section 5.1) with a bottom layer of garden soil covered with damp, decaying leaves. A terrarium of this kind is also useful as a model of the water-cycle (Activity 11.5.2).

Plants of all three groups can be grown in the terrarium, but can flourish only if they are kept cool and shaded. Mosses on small pieces of stone, brick or dead wood can be collected in plastic boxes and brought in undisturbed. Small ferns, which should be obtained from gardens or garden-centres and *not* taken from the wild, can be planted in the soil. The most suitable liverworts are those found under staging in shady, damp greenhouses. They have no leaves and look like a flat or rather curly green ribbon. They should be lifted with a layer of soil and planted on bare soil with as little disturbance as possible. Mosses growing on bare soil can be introduced in a similar way.

5.3: Observing a variety of other living things

Apart from plants and animals, the two groups of living things which affect children's lives most are fungi and bacteria. Often we are unaware of these organisms, or hear about them only when they cause disease and damage, but they affect our lives and the lives of all living things profoundly because they also act as decomposers, breaking down and recycling material in the ecosystem (Section 5.8).

Observing fungi

It is important to emphasize to children that fungi are not plants. They are a group of organisms as distinct from plants and animals as plants and animals are from each other. No fungus can make its own food by photosynthesis and most of them live by digesting dead organic material such as leaves, wood and animal dung. It is this digestion which causes the breakdown we call decay.

Leaf- or wood-decaying fungi may appear in a terrarium being used to cultivate non-flowering plants (see Section 5.2). If they do there is no need to remove them, but the cover of the terrarium should remain in place to avoid any danger of children inhaling fungal spores. The spores of fungi can cause asthma-like symptoms if they are inhaled in very large numbers by susceptible people. Small wood-decaying fungi can be collected, together with the wood they are growing on, and brought to school safely in clear, screw-top jars, but the jar lids should not be removed. The fungi should be returned to their habitat when children have seen them.

Activity 5.3.1

Observing food-decaying microbes

Our food is very easy to digest in comparison with most other dead materials such as wood or straw (see Activity 3.3.1). As a result, microbes can feed and grow on it very easily; a process involving chemical changes (see Section 9.2) which leads to the spoilage of food commonly referred to as 'going sour' or 'going bad'.

Most of the microbes which decay food are bacteria and fungi. The process of decay can easily and safely be observed by children but strict safety precautions have to be in place. Disposable plastic petri-dishes are the best containers to use because the decaying food can be seen more easily, but small, clear, screw-top plastic drink bottles are a safe and practical alternative.

Equipment and materials: Disposable plastic petri-dishes or small screw-top plastic bottles; small samples of food e.g. bread, biscuits, fruit fresh and dried, cheese, breakfast cereal (meat is not recommended); water; dropper; adhesive tape; adhesive labels.

Safety note: Cultures must remain sealed at all times when children are present.

- Choose a selection of food items, e.g. bread, biscuit, cheese, fruit, cereals. Put a sample of each food into each dish or bottle. If the food is dry (e.g. biscuit, cereal, dried fruit) moisten it with a few drops of water.
- Put the lids on the dishes or screw the tops down on the bottles. Seal the lids or tops *all the way round* with adhesive tape so that they cannot be accidentally removed. Put a label on each dish or bottle showing the kind of food and the date.
- Put the containers in a warm place and away from direct sunlight. They do not need to be in the dark.
- Look at the containers every few days and record what changes you see, using a magnifying-glass or hand-lens. Do not shake or disturb the food samples; handle the containers carefully and keep them the right way up.

Detailed identification of the microbes decaying food samples is not possible, but some major groups can usually be distinguished. Blue-green crusts with a white edge and white furry growths looking rather like root-hairs are both fungi (blue moulds and pin-moulds). Dead leaves are also decayed by fungi (Activity 5.8.1).

Slimy or crusty colonies are likely to be seen on the food, starting as spots and then spreading into discs. They may be almost any colour, though most are white, yellow to orange, or brown. Most of these are colonies of bacteria. The majority of bacteria are decay organisms; only a minority attack other living things and cause diseases. Other bacteria children will encounter include those which form a film on teeth (plaque, Activity 3.2.1) as they feed on the remains of food, and which can cause gum disease and tooth decay.

• All decayed food samples must be carefully disposed of. Dishes and bottles can be put into plastic bags *without* being opened and disposed of as household waste after the bags have been tied securely.

5.4: Classification using keys

Keys are devices used to classify or identify unknown members of a population. They are a method of sorting and setting, based on a sequence of questions and decisions. The use of keys for classification reinforces children's knowledge of the criteria used to distinguish the major groups of animals and plants, while at the same time focusing attention and improving the quality of observation. Their use for identification gives children access to stored information about particular organisms in resources such as books and CD-ROMs.

Two types of key
At primary level we need to be concerned with two types of key: decision-trees and statement-keys, each of which has advantages and limitations. Their basic characteristics can most easily be shown by way of examples. Fig. 5.1 shows a very simple decision-tree to classify an animal into one of five groups of common soil-dwelling animals.

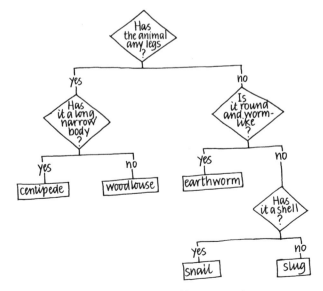

Figure 5.1   Decision-tree to identify five soil-dwelling invertebrates

The same key, in statement-form, could have this layout:

Key to five groups of soil-dwelling animals

1 Has legs 2
  Has no legs 3
2 Body more or less oval, 'feelers' short .... woodlouse
  Body long and narrow; 'feelers' long .... centipede
3 Moves on a flat, muscular 'foot'; eyes on stalks 4
  Body worm-like; does not move on a flat under-surface .... earthworm
4 Has a spiral shell into which the animal can retreat .... snail
  Has no shell, or only a tiny one .... slug

Both keys could be illustrated with simple line-drawings beside each name to give users more confidence that their classification is correct.

From these examples it will be seen that the decision-tree is easier to use, but more limited because it has to be framed as a sequence of simple, short questions with a yes-or-no answer. Statement-keys require greater reading ability and concentration but are much less limited because the user can be given more guidance at each stage.

Constructing and using keys

An effective way for children to learn how keys work is to devise their own, to identify the particular animals or plants which they have in the classroom at the time. The number of items should be small (five or even less for very young children) and it is also helpful if the items are familiar and easy to distinguish.

If asked to construct a key in the form of a decision-tree, inexperienced children (and adults) will usually proceed by separating one member of the population from the remainder at each operation, as shown in Fig. 5.2. In comparison with Fig. 5.1

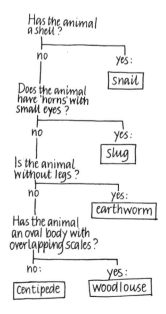

Figure 5.2   A badly-designed 'decision-tree' using only distinctive characteristics

this 'decision-tree' is badly drawn-up, because this linear, one-at-a-time method becomes very cumbersome when the number of items is large. It may also be un-necessarily difficult, because it depends upon finding, for each item, a characteristic which no other member of the population has.

For example, Fig. 5.3 shows a decision-tree to identify five evergreen plants in winter. It would be difficult to identify the five plants on a one-at-a-time basis, as in Fig. 5.2, because three have needle-like leaves and the tips of pine needles feel quite like spines! It is only *after* they have been divided into two sets that the individuals are easy to sub-set and distinguish.

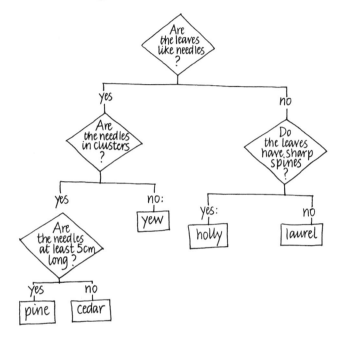

Figure 5.3 Decision-tree to identify five evergreens in winter

As a statement-key, Fig. 5.3 could have this form:

Key to identify five evergreens in winter

1 Leaves narrow and needle-like 2
  Leaves wide; may be spiny 4
2 Needles single on stem, 2mm wide . . . . yew
  Needles 1mm wide or less, in bunches or pairs 3
3 Needles in pairs, at least 5cm long . . . . scots pine
  Needles in bunches (short shoots) 2cm long . . . . atlantic cedar
4 Leaves with a spiny, wavy edge . . . . holly
  Leaves with small teeth at edge, not spiny, more or less flat . . . . cherry-laurel

The final important point to notice is that keys of the kind given as examples here are very specific in their application: they work only for the particular plants or animals which they have been devised to identify. Children need to be aware of the difference between these and more general keys which are much more difficult to construct, but whose use is likely to be essential if animals and plants in local habitats are to be identified successfully.

Developing the use of keys
As with many other activities, learning to use keys can be seen as proceeding in two phases. In the first phase, organisms which may already be familiar are classified or identified in order to learn the skill of using keys. Older children should progress to the use of statement keys in order to classify or identify a wider range of organisms, for example those in local or visited habitats, some of which may up to that point have been completely unknown to them.

The examples given above are of keys to use in the first phase of learning and for children to construct for themselves, dealing with particular, selected groups of animals and plants. In the second phase of learning, the commonest use of keys at primary level is to classify or identify animals and plants found in a particular habitat such as a garden, woodland or pond. This means that the key has to take account of a semi-natural or natural population rather than an artificially-selected one, so it is likely to be significantly more complex. Keys of this kind are available both in books and on CD-ROM.

Wild life parks and nature reserves often include identification-keys in their support material for use by teachers and children. These are very useful in the particular locality for which they were devised, but care needs to be exercised in using them elsewhere, unless it is known that the range of organisms is very similar in both habitats.

5.5: Adaptation

Adaptation is the scientific term for any feature of the body or behaviour of a living thing which fits it for its way of life in its environment and helps it to survive. For example, the feathers of birds are an adaptation of structure, which helps them to conserve thermal energy and so to live in an an environment which is colder than their body temperature; but the fluffing out of feathers in cold weather is an adapatation of behaviour which increases the effectiveness of the feathers as thermal insulation (Activity 12.3.6).

Two approaches to studying adaptation

If children are to develop more than a superficial understanding of the relationship between living things and their environment, the concept of adaptation needs to be firmly established. The most effective way to achieve this is to investigate adaptations in two rather different but related ways, which may to a degree overlap. The first is by way of one or more case studies; the second is by observation of animals and plants interacting with their habitat. The case-study approach emphasizes what could be called the logic of adaptation, seeking to identify features of structure or behaviour which are a positive aid to survival (have adaptive value). The environmental approach seeks to apply this logic to animals and plants in their habitats, whether natural or influenced by human activity.

5.6: Studying adaptation

How children learn about adaptation will usually depend very much on the resources available. Two case-studies are outlined here as examples of this approach, using specimens and organisms for which equivalents can be found in most parts of the world.

Activity 5.6.1

Adaptations of the skulls of mammals

The skull of a mammal gives far more information about its life-style than any other part of its skeleton. This is because the major part of its feeding mechanism (jaws and teeth) are in its head, together with the major sensory organs. In most cases it is productive to concentrate attention on the jaws and teeth, and the position of the eyes as shown by the eye sockets. Suitable skulls may usually be borrowed from museum loans services and the most useful fall into two groups:

1. *hunting predators*: e.g. dog, cat, fox
2. *plant-eaters*: e.g. cow, sheep, deer, horse, rabbit, squirrel, rat.

It is by no means necessary to have a wide range of specimens to make this study worthwhile: only two skulls of contrasting types, such as a cat's (Fig. 5.4) and a

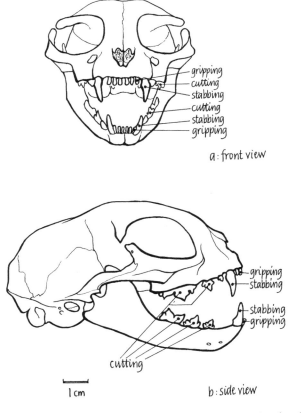

a: front view

b: side view

Figure 5.4 Sketches of the skull of a carnivore (domestic cat) – notice that larger carnivores such as dogs also have large crushing teeth behind the cutting teeth

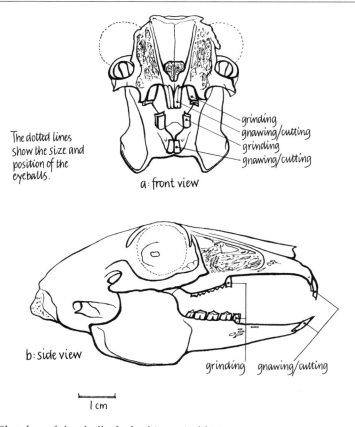

The dotted lines show the size and position of the eyeballs.

a: front view

grinding
gnawing/cutting
grinding
gnawing/cutting

b: side view

grinding   gnawing/cutting

1 cm

Figure 5.5   Sketches of the skull of a herbivore (rabbit)

rabbit's (Fig. 5.5) are needed to observe the main adaptations. Other skulls can then be observed, compared and contrasted as opportunities arise.

Hunting predators
Nearly all mammals (and birds) which actively hunt their prey have both eyes facing forward, which enables them to use binocular vision to judge their distance from their prey very accurately (see Activity 3.10.3). The cat (Fig. 5.4) shows this very clearly because it has an almost complete ring of bone round each eye-socket.

The jaws and teeth of predators have many adaptations. The joint of the jaw is hinge-like, allowing little side-to-side movement and the lower jaw is narrower than the upper one. The result is that the lower teeth pass inside the upper ones as the jaw is closed, so that they can stab and slice. The teeth are specialized so that (from front to back) they can meet and grip; pass and stab; pass and cut; and meet and crush.

The teeth of all predatory mammals are adapted for holding and killing prey, tearing it apart and cutting pieces off before swallowing them. The food is not usually chewed much, but this does not impair digestion because protein and fat are fairly easy to break down in the gut.

Plant eaters

Plant-eaters (herbivores) have skulls which are more varied in structure than those of hunters, but all have adapatations in common (Fig. 5.5). The eyes are at either side, usually high up and protruding which gives all-round vision and therefore a better chance of seeing a predator or other danger.

The jaws of plant-eaters are more loosely hinged than those of predators, so they can be rotated as well as moved up and down, giving a grinding action. They have biting or gnawing teeth in front (sometimes only in the lower jaw), and broad grinding teeth at the back which have sharp ridges to grind plant fibre to a pulp. There is a gap between the two sets of teeth so that the animal can feed continuously, chewing with the back teeth while biting off more with the front ones.

Activity 5.6.2

Adaptations of fruits and seeds to wind dispersal

The specialized development of fruits and seeds for wind dispersal is among the most obvious and easily-investigated plant adapatations. The advantages to the plants of effective seed-dispersal are discussed as part of Activity 4.5.5, and the present activity can be linked to work on parachutes and gliders (Activities 14.3.4, 14.5.4).

Effective wind-dispersal of fruits and seeds depends on slowing their rate of fall, so that when released they will be blown away by the wind and may even gain height in an updraught and be carried still further. There are two main ways of slowing the fall of an object: by creating drag, as a parachute does; and creating lift, as the wings of an aeroplane or the rotors of a helicopter do.

Fruits and seeds with parachutes

Some familiar examples of *fruits* with drag-creating parachutes are members of the dandelion-daisy family, including dandelion, groundsel, and thistles. In all of these plants each 'flower' is a compact head of very small flowers, each of which produces a one-seeded fruit, with a tuft of hairs or a stalked parachute on top.

The commonest plants with parachute-borne *seeds* are the willowherbs, in which the ovary is beneath the flower and develops into a capsule, most often long and slender, which dries and splits open when ripe to release a large number of very small, light seeds, each of which has a tuft of long, silky hairs.

The effectiveness of parachutes

To be effective, any parachute has to slow the fall of its load, in this case a fruit or seed. The slower the rate of fall, the more effective the parachute.

Equipment and materials: Seeds and fruits with parachutes; plastic cups or small boxes; tweezers; strip of coloured or black card about 2x10cm; magnifying-glass or hand-lens.

- Put the different kinds of seeds available into labelled plastic cups or small boxes.
- Using tweezers to lift them by a hair, place one or two seeds of each kind on to a strip of black or coloured card. Look at them with a magnifying-glass or hand-lens. Notice any differences in the sizes of the seeds and the form of their parachutes.
? Predict which you think will be the most efficient parachute.

- Test your prediction by having 'races' between seeds of different kinds. Work in pairs in as still air as possible: people moving past will disturb your trials.
- Using tweezers to lift them by a hair, place seeds of two different kinds near the edge of the card, then release them together by tilting the card. Watch the seeds to make sure the 'race' is fair (both should begin to fall at the same time) and to see which lands first. Repeat the 'race' five times.
? Which kind of seed has the more efficient parachute? (The one which takes *longer* to fall.)
- If you have a third kind of seed, test the more efficient of the first two against it. Keep on testing in this way until you find which parachute is the most efficient of all those you have.
- To see how much difference the parachute makes, break the parachute off a seed with tweezers and compare its speed of fall with that of another seed whose parachute is undamaged.

On a day with a gentle breeze, children can see the effect of wind on the movement of parachute fruits and seeds outdoors. The larger fruits such as those of dandelion and thistle are the most suitable for this: smaller ones such as groundsel and willowherb are very difficult to see as they blow away.

Fruits and seeds with wings
Lift is an upward force generated when a wing slices through air (or water in the case of a hydrofoil). Lift, generated in different ways, is the force which enables birds to glide and soar and gliders, aeroplanes and helicopters to fly. Many fruits and seeds have wings which are efficient adaptations for seed dispersal. As these seeds and fruits fall they spin, making their wings slice through the air, generating lift and slowing down the rate at which they fall. The most easily-obtained winged fruits are likely to be those of sycamore (Fig. 5.6a), other maples and various species of ash (Fig. 5.6b), while some species of pine have winged seeds.

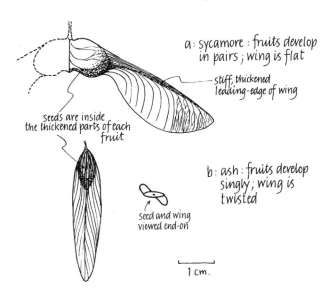

Figure 5.6   Sketches of winged fruits

A first look at winged fruits
It is easy for children to make sycamore fruits 'fly' by throwing them outwards and upwards or simply dropping them. In either case the fruit will spin, but what is noticeable is that it does not begin to spin until it has fallen some distance, i.e. reached a certain speed through the air. Notice also that if the fruit fails to spin, it drops to the ground very quickly.

To make ash fruits 'fly' they have to be thrown and if they are dry, many will not spin, because drying them has distorted their wings. If they are soaked in water for a few minutes, then surface-dried with a paper towel, a much higher proportion will spin successfully.

How do wings slow the fall of fruits?
Characteristically, winged fruits and seeds falling in still air spin rapidly and some clearly fall in a spiral path.

Equipment and materials: Large winged fruits (sycamore are particularly good; ash fruits need to be dry to start with); white correcting fluid or pen.

- With the white correcting-fluid or pen, mark the wings of some fruits, across the width of the wing. Put one stripe on one side; two on the other.
- (If dried ash-fruits are being used, they should be soaked for a few minutes *after* being marked and then surface-dried before use.)
- Work in a place with bright overhead light. Throw the fruits and watch them spin as they fall. You should see either one or two white stripes on the rotating wing. This will enable you to tell which way up the fruit is, and which way it is rotating (clockwise or anti-clockwise).
- ? How does the fruit moves as it spins? (It moves in a downward spiral.)
- ? Try dropping a fruit so that it does *not* spin.
- ? What happens? (It falls much faster than when it spins.)

The upward force slowing the fall of the fruit is not drag, as in the parachute seeds, but lift generated as the spinning wing slices through the air.

- Test a range of fruits of the same kind, and different kinds if you have them.
- ? Do the fruits always spin the same way? Do they always spin with the same side uppermost?

Sycamore fruits can normally spin clockwise with one side up, or anti-clockwise with the other side up. Ash-fruits (almost) always spin anti-clockwise, and there is no obvious reason why they should not spin either way up, but in fact they never do: an interesting research project for an enterprising class, perhaps?

The adaptive value of winged fruits and seeds
Winged fruits and seeds are mostly much bigger and heavier than those carried by parachutes, and they are mostly produced by tall forest trees. This is significant, because a parachute slows the fall of a fruit or seed as soon as it is released whereas, as we have seen, a wing generates lift only when it is spinning, and it starts to spin only when the fruit, seed or model is falling fast enough. Parachutes can help to disperse the seeds and fruits even of very small plants; those with wings are likely to travel far only if they are released high above the ground.

The release of these fruits and seeds is also significant. Whereas those with parachutes can drift away on the slightest breeze, those with wings are most likely to be released in windy conditions, which is exactly the situation in which the spinning winged fruit, with its long, slow fall, is most likely to be carried furthest from the parent tree, ensuring efficient dispersal.

Activity 5.6.3

Adaptation and environment

As already suggested (Section 5.5), developing an understanding of adaptation requires not only investigation of particular examples through case studies (Activities 5.6.1–5.6.2) but also first-hand observation of plants and animals in their habitats. This activity also creates a useful bridge between learning about living things as individual organisms and the broader issues of the ways in which they interact and are interdependent in ecosystems (Sections 5.7–5.9).

Detailed guidance on investigating how plants and animals in different habitats are adapted to their environment is beyond the scope of this book, because the work undertaken by particular schools and classes depends very largely on the particular habitats they can use as resources; but some general points may usefully be made.

Selecting habitats

Whenever possible, children should study adaptation in at least two habitats which are strongly contrasted in character. It is a great advantage if at least one of these habitats also lends itself to aspects of work on interdependence such as feeding relationships, decay, recycling and human influence (see Sections 5.7–5.9) because much of the preparatory work needed will serve all these activities equally well.

When selecting habitats to observe adaptations they should in most ways be contrasted; but there are some practical criteria which they all need to satisfy. These basic practical issues are ease of access from school, availability at different times of the year and the robustness of the habitat: can it withstand invasion and investigation by children? Will children's investigations be in conflict with, or hampered by, the needs and rights of other members of the community? If there is a choice, an apparently rather bleak and uninteresting habitat which is very easily accessible is likely, with good preparatory work, to have far more potential for first-hand investigation by children than a wonderfully rich habitat which they can visit only once or twice a year.

The following lists are suggestive rather than exhaustive; habitats likely to be available only to a small minority of schools are given in brackets.

Land habitats, natural or semi-natural: woodland and scrub; heath and moorland; uncultivated grassland e.g. downland; rural hedgerows; urban wildlife areas; (sand dunes).
Land habitats, made or strongly influenced by humans: farmland, especially field margins; gardens; parkland and playing-fields; walls and buildings.
Aquatic habitats, natural or semi-natural: mature ponds; streams; (rocky sea-shore).
Aquatic habitats, made or strongly influenced by humans: newly-established ponds, e.g. in school grounds.

Two important and interesting types of habitat have been excluded from this list on safety grounds: roadside verges and heavily-polluted areas, whether aquatic or terrestrial.

Many schools have limited potential for creating habitats suitable for investigating adaptation and interdependence, but relatively few have none. Even a small garden or wildlife area can act, and should be managed, as a significant educational resource. In doing this it is important to avoid making gardens too tidy and ornamental by eliminating weeds and over-pruning shrubs, as this removes some of the very resources which make them valuable educationally. If children grow vegetables, pesticides should not be used: the pests and their natural predators should be studied instead.

Preparing to help children investigate adaptation in a habitat
Sound preparatory work is essential. The first step is to find out the range of animals and plants which inhabit or visit the habitat, because this gives access to stored information on animals and plants in books and other resources, which is likely to be essential in understanding how they are adapted to their environment.

The second line of enquiry is into the range of environmental conditions in the habitat. Detailed measurements are not usually needed at primary level, and much of the necessary information comes from everyday experience and common-sense. Factors to consider are: light, temperature, rainfall and humidity of the air; and how they vary, both daily and seasonally. Human influence in the habitat also needs to be assessed, in terms both of structures such as walls or paving, and activities such as cultivation, control of vegetation (including mowing, pruning, and weeding), trampling, control of animal pests and pollution (see Section 5.9).

5.7: Ecosystems: feeding relationships

Both logistically and educationally it is helpful if children's investigations into the interdependence of organisms within a habitat can be linked with their learning about adaptation (see Section 5.6), though the range of habitats in which feeding relationships can be studied successfully is usually much narrower. Learning about identification and adaptation within a suitable habitat is likely to be the best foundation for wider considerations of how organisms are inter-related in terms of feeding, how materials are re-cycled within the habitat (Section 5.8) and what impact human activity has upon it (Section 5.9).

Activity 5.7.1

Developing the concept of a food-chain
Before attempting to find out how animals and plants are inter-related in an ecosystem, it is helpful to develop some basic concepts on feeding relationships in a familiar context. The animal whose feeding relationships we know best is ourselves: the human species. Investigating the sources of some of our foods is a useful way to develop three concepts which are essential to the understanding of any ecosystem: food-chain, producer and consumer. Feeding relationships and the concepts needed to understand them can be investigated and developed effectively by asking the children to focus on the origins of a range of basic foods, some natural (e.g. fruit, eggs, milk, meat and vegetables) and others man-made (e.g. bread, jam, butter,

cheese, chips, margarine, yoghurt). If necessary, lists of ingredients of man-made foods can be obtained from food labels.

A good strategy is to consider natural foods first, to trace the origins of those discussed and to present these graphically. In this way, the origins of natural foods appear as simple food-chains (Fig. 5.7). These serve to show an important feature of all the food-chains children will investigate: every one has plants at its base, because only plants produce food materials (by photosynthesis, Activity 4.4.1) whereas animals consume them.

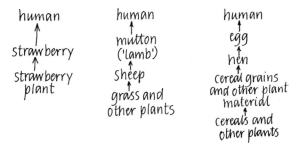

Figure 5.7   Some simple human food-chains

When natural foods have been discussed, some man-made foods such as bread, cheese and butter should be considered. Here the food-chains usually become more complex (Fig. 5.8), either because the food has several ingredients (e.g. bread) or because one animal product is used to make several foods (e.g. cheese and butter). It may be helpful at this stage to introduce the idea of levels in a food-chain, which children will need when investigating food-chains in an ecosystem.

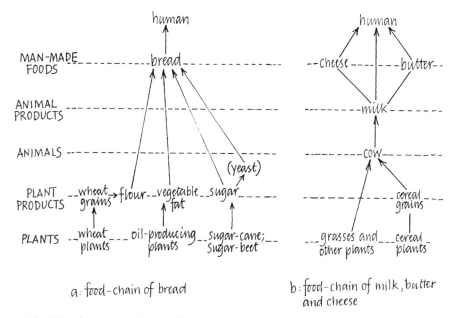

Figure 5.8   Two less simple human food-chains

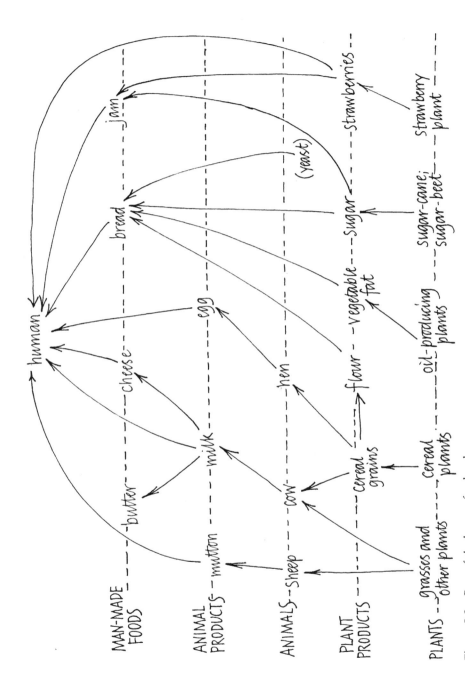

Figure 5.9 Part of the human food-web

Food-chains drawn up in this way can be combined into food-webs, in which all or part of an animal's diet is charted so that the inter-relationships between its parts can be seen. A simple food-web involving some basic items of human diet is shown in Fig. 5.9, which incorporates the food-chains shown in Figs. 5.7 and 5.8. This human food-web once again reinforces the roles of plants as the producers of food at the base of the food-web, and animals as consumers.

Investigating feeding relationships
Having established the basic concepts of food-chains, producers and consumers, these can be applied and used to investigate feeding relationships within a habitat. The most accessible and rewarding habitats for this kind of study are likely to be found in school gardens and grounds, or nearby parkland. More natural habitats such as woodland and ponds, which are very valuable when studying adaptation, are likely to pose formidable problems when feeding relationships are being considered: woodland because the very wide range of organisms is likely to make any investigation very complex; ponds because children will be able to observe very little feeding behaviour for themselves.

A successful investigation of feeding relationships within an ecosystem usually begins with identifying the range of plants and animals which inhabit the area. This is the key which gives access to stored information which children would find it difficult if not impossible to obtain for themselves. The information needed includes, for plants, which animals eat them and, for animals, what they eat and what, if anything, they are eaten by. This information-finding route is essential because children are unlikely to observe more than a small proportion of the feeding behaviour in even the most favourable and accessible habitat. Comprehensive information of this kind can be built up only by long-term, detailed observation, which children cannot usually carry out. What they can do, once an animal or plant has been identified, is use the records of others to fill in the gaps in their own observations.

Activity 5.7.2

Food-chains and food-webs within a habitat
During the course of identifying the plants and animals which live in or visit a chosen habitat, some feeding behaviour is likely to be observed. A good strategy is to concentrate on this and build up information from these initial observations.

For example, observation of blue-tits on an apple tree, pecking at leaves and bark, showed that they were feeding on aphids, which suck plant sap, and caterpillars (larvae, usually of moths) which eat the leaves. This information can be summarized in two simple food-chains (Fig. 5.10a,b). When confirming the presence of caterpillars and aphids, the larvae of ladybirds and lacewings and adult ladybirds were also found and identified. All these animals prey on aphids, so more food-chains could be drawn (Fig. 5.10c,d).

These food-chains, like those of human feeding, can be better understood by charting them using levels, but here the levels are somewhat different. At the bottom, as always, are plants which are the producers of the ecosystem. Above them are their products which are eaten by the first level of consumers, the plant-eaters or herbivores. These animals often fall prey to a second level of consumers, which are animal-eaters or carnivores.

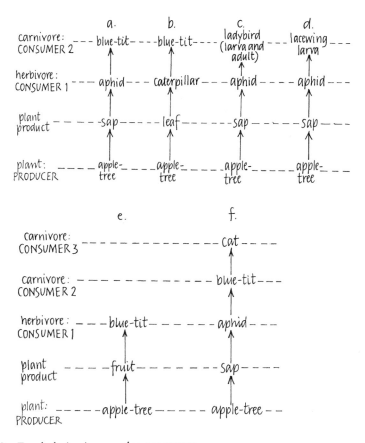

Figure 5.10 Food-chains in a garden ecosystem

Later in the year, more information emerged from ongoing observations. For example, blue-tits were seen pecking fallen fruit, and evidence could be found that a local cat had destroyed a nest of blue-tits and eaten the fledglings. The first observation added a new food-chain to the collection (Fig. 5.10e), while the second added another level, that of a third-level consumer, to food-chains involving blue-tits (Fig. 5.10f).

At this stage the limitations of food-chains again become apparent. Food-webs not only give a better account of inter-relationships than the food-chains on which they are based, insofar as these are known, but also are more compact. For example, all the information included in the six food-chains in Fig. 5.10 can be combined to make one fairly simple food-web (Fig. 5.11). Notice that the cat and the ladybird are at the top of their parts of the food-web. Neither has any natural predators, so they are sometimes called top-carnivores. This food-web is not hypothetical, and most if not all this feeding behaviour can easily be seen in many gardens in most years.

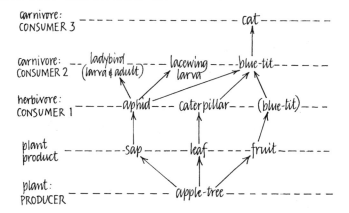

Figure 5.11   Part of the food-web of an apple tree

5.8: Ecosystems: decay and recycling

The feeding relationships of plants and animals make up the more obvious part of the ecosystem. The less obvious part is the decay and recycling of dead material by scavenging animals and microbes. The microbes are mostly fungi and bacteria (see Section 5.3), which collectively are known as decomposers.

Although some materials such as wood and bone decay slowly, most leaves and the soft tissues of animals are broken down quickly and disappear within a year or two. Plant material decaying on the soil surface rarely smells offensive, but decaying bodies of animals do, and should not be touched because they can be potent sources of infection. The most easily-seen sequence of decay in most localities is the breakdown of leaves at the soil surface. Those of deciduous trees (apart from beech, which decay very slowly) are likely to be the best. A range of scavenging animals, as well as microbes, is involved in leaf breakdown and decay. The main leaf-scavengers are earthworms, but a wide range of other invertebrates, including woodlice and springtails, also feed on the leaf-litter and are hunted by their predators.

Activity 5.8.1

Observing the breakdown of leaves

To observe the sequence of leaf breakdown, find a place in a garden or woodland where the soil is never cultivated and there is a layer of dead leaves on the soil which looks undisturbed. To sample it, a spade, a board about 60x60cm and a large plastic bag are needed. Cut out a square about 20x20cm by driving the spade through the dead-leaf layer into the soil beneath. Lift a layer of soil on the spade with the dead leaves on top, disturbing them as little as possible. Slide this on to the board and cover with the plastic bag to conserve moisture. Keeping the sample damp, use tweezers to pick dead leaves from the surface layer one by one and lay them out on a large sheet of paper. The degree to which the leaves are broken down is easily seen (Fig. 5.12).

5 cm

Figure 5.12   Stages in decay of leaves

At this point, one of two rather different situations is likely to become apparent. The first is that as the leaves are removed layer by layer, the amount of breakdown increases fairly steadily. This situation is most common in woodland, where the leaf-litter is not disturbed much. The second situation is that, although different degrees of breakdown can be seen, leaves in different stages of disintegration are mixed up: almost entire leaves may be lying below others which are fragmented and appear to have been decaying for much longer. This happens most often in gardens and appears to be the result of foraging by birds (in Britain, particularly blackbirds) and by hedgehogs, which fling the dead leaves about while hunting for worms and other invertebrates which are feeding on them.

When the decayed leaves have been laid out, it is noticeable that in most cases it is the soft parts of the leaves which are eaten or decayed first so that the leaves become skeletonized before they break up, a process which in a garden takes between one and two years to complete. This rapid decay and recycling can usefully be contrasted with the inability of decomposers to break down many of the man-made materials used for food packaging and which pollute the environment in the form of litter (see Section 5.9).

5.9: Ecosystems: human activity

The environment and ecosystems all over the world have been profoundly affected by human activity, which has left relatively little of the planet unaffected. Children need to learn about the effects of human activity on the environment in at least two ways, both of which have profound social as well as scientific implications.

First, there is a need to find out how and why habitats and ecosystems in the area in which they live have been, and continue to be, affected by human activity; secondly there is a need to understand some of the ways in which human activity has destructive, long-term effects such as pollution. Both these kinds of knowledge are needed if children are to begin developing the foundation for a balanced view of human exploitation and conservation of the environment.

The impact of human activity on ecosystems

In general, ecosystems dominated by human activity are much simpler than natural ones, with short food-chains and much less diversity. One pair of vividly contrasted habitats is likely to be enough to make the main points about the effect of human activity on the ecosystem, but both must be familiar to the children. In Britain, the contrast could be between the natural habitat, broad-leaved forest, and human-dominated habitats such as school playing-fields which have, with reason, been referred to as 'green deserts'. The playing-field is in stark contrast to natural woodland populated by hundreds of plant and animal species, though the situation does have one educational advantage. Because so few groups of animals and plants are present, playing-fields are a habitat where adaptation and feeding behaviour can be much more easily observed by children than they could be in a forest.

Pollution

In contrast to human activity which modifies habitats for human use and which can be reversed (cities can return to forest), pollution is an entirely destructive human activity. Pollution is a major world issue which children should be aware of in both a social and a scientific context. Much of their learning about it is likely to come from resources such as books and TV news items; but there are two aspects of pollution which affect them directly and which they may be able to investigate for themselves: air pollution and litter.

Activity 5.9.1

Observing the effects of air pollution

Air pollution is a significant problem globally, but children can begin to learn about some of its effects through short and simple observations. Two are suggested here: one on solid-particle pollution and the other on acid rain.

Trapping solid pollutants in the air

Solid particles are emitted into the air by many kinds of combustion, particularly when it is incomplete (*9.4), often in the form of smoke or exhaust fumes from motor vehicles. In a city environment, particularly near busy roads where pollution is heavy, pollutants in different places can be compared by trapping particles on sticky tape.

The easiest way to do this is to fasten 5cm lengths of double-sided adhesive tape to white cards. In dry weather, fix the cards with Blu-tack on to horizontal surfaces in a variety of places at least 1.5m above ground level and at varying distances from the main sources of pollution. Remove the protective strip to expose the adhesive and leave the cards for 24 hours. Varying levels of pollution in different places will usually be apparent simply by looking at the cards. If the particles trapped on the adhesive are examined under a microscope it will come as no surprise to learn that they can irritate the lungs and are a major cause of bronchitis and, probably, asthma. Similar particles are produced by incomplete burning in a candle-flame (Activity 9.4.1).

Gas pollution: acid rain

The most serious gas pollutant which children can detect is sulphur dioxide, the main cause of acid rain. This gas is produced both by motor vehicles and power stations. Particularly in cities, sulphur dioxide dissolves in falling rain, making the water acidic. This can be detected by collecting rain-water and testing it immediately using strips of universal indicator paper available from photographic stores and pharmacies. Pure water is not acidic; it has a pH of 7. Rain in most cities is distinctly acidic, shown by the colour it produces when dropped on to the indicator paper. Even in rural areas, rain-water may be detectably acidic, especially downwind of large power-stations.

Activity 5.9.2

Litter

Litter is a problem which affects most children and schools. Most urban litter comes from packaging for food and drink, and a study of it can usefully begin with classification of packaging from foods which the children themselves consume.

Safety note: Litter in the environment should **not** be collected by hand: this is why cleaning operatives use a special tool to pick it up. There is a significant risk of cuts and infection, even if disposable gloves are worn.

The main categories are: paper and card; plastic (bags, bottles, trays and cups); glass (bottles); steel (cans) and aluminium (cans, 'silver paper', food-trays and foil tops). These can be discussed in two contexts: first, the danger each category poses to humans and wildlife; secondly, the degree to which the various materials are bio-degradable. Paper and card will be decayed slowly and steel cans may eventually rust, but the other materials will break down much more slowly, if at all. It is this inability of the environment to break down and recycle many man-made materials which makes them pollutants, and they can usefully be contrasted with natural materials such as leaves which break down rapidly (see Section 5.8 and Fig. 5.12).

6

States of Matter and Physical Change

6.1: Solids, liquids and gases

Most materials and objects which children encounter in everyday life are fairly obviously in one of three states of matter: solid, liquid or gas. Observing materials to find out how they are classified in this way is an essential preliminary to investigating changes between the three states and ways in which they may be brought about. The three states of matter are sometimes written or spoken about as if there were always sharp distinctions between them; but particularly between the solid and liquid states the distinction is not always clear (Activity 6.2.2) and even when it is, it may not appear to be (Activity 6.1.2).

Activity 6.1.1

Distinguishing solids from liquids

Equipment and materials: A range of (unlabelled) solid objects in a variety of materials, e.g. wood, stone, rubber (elastic bands), paper, modelling clay, plastics, metals. A range of liquids in labelled screw-top jars or bottles with tops sealed on, e.g. water, vegetable oil, thick sugar syrup, PVA glue; disposable cup; dropper; plastic or metal tray.

- From all the objects in front of you, pick out the bottles or jars with liquids in them. Put them on one side to look at later.
- Look at the objects which are left. Try to identify the materials of which they are made.
- Try to change the shape of these objects by bending, pulling, squashing and twisting them in your hands. Do not break any of the objects: just find out if you can make them change shape.
- ? Are these objects solid or liquid? (They are solid.) Are they all solid? (Yes.) Are some more solid than others?

Children may mistakenly answer 'Yes' to the last question because they may equate solidity with rigidity or hardness and think that soft, squashy and stretchy materials like modelling clay and elastic bands are less solid than hard materials such as metal or stone.

? What properties do all these objects have which makes us call them 'solid'?

This may need some discussion. The scientific view is that solids maintain their shape without support, although these shapes can be changed by applying forces to them. As children might put it, solids 'have their own shape' and 'stand up on their own'; but there are solid materials which need further investigation to find out how they behave (Activity 6.1.2).

- Now look at the liquids in their containers. (Make sure the lids are on tightly.) Tilt the containers fairly slowly and watch the liquids inside them.
? As the container is tilted, does the liquid stay the same shape, as a solid object such as a brick does when it is tilted? (No; the liquid runs down to the bottom of the container.)
? Do these liquids have a shape of their own? (No: they take their shape from whatever container they are in.)
? Do the *containers* change shape? (No: they are solid and maintain their shape.)
- Tilt the container of water. As its shape changes, look for the direction of something which stays the same.
? When the container is tilted, what direction stays the same? (The surface of the water stays level, i.e. horizontal, Fig. 6.1a.)

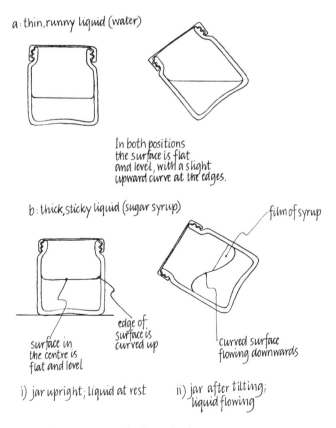

Figure 6.1   Liquid surfaces at rest and when tilted

- Do the same with the other containers.
? Do all the liquids behave in the same way?

The simple answer is, no: but the behaviour of very thick, sticky (viscous) liquids such as sugar syrups or glues needs to be observed more closely. The surfaces of these liquids tilt as the container is tilted, but then flow slowly downwards. While they are flowing the surfaces are curved, not flat (Fig. 6.1b). Eventually these liquids do form a surface which is flat and level, at least in the middle of the container, but this may take some minutes.

- What happens if a liquid does not have a container round it? To find out, stand a plastic or metal tray on a level table-top and pour a little water on it.
? What does the water do? (It spreads out to form a layer which has a flat, level surface, except for its curved edges.)

These simple observations show three properties of liquids which children need to be able to identify. The first property is that liquids have no 'shape of their own': they cannot maintain a shape without support. The second property is that liquids in a container always flow to form a surface which is flat and level in the centre, though it may be curved up or down at its edges. The third property is related to the second: if a liquid is poured on to a level surface it will form a layer which itself has a flat and level surface, apart from its edges.

Activity 6.1.2

Solids which 'flow'
A solid object is one which can maintain its shape without support (Activity 6.1.1). Children may have difficulty in understanding the behaviour of materials which do not seem to have a definite shape and which appear to flow, but which nevertheless feel dry and are said to be solid. Investigating these materials, which are made up of small, solid particles, is a good way to consolidate learning about the differences between solids and liquids.

Equipment and materials: Dry particulate materials in screw-top jars. These could include: wheat or rice grains, coarse gritty sand, fine washed (silver) sand, granulated sugar, salt. Samples of the same materials in shallow boxes or bowls; tray; magnifying-glass or hand-lens (microscope if available).

- Look at each material in the jars. (It is helpful, particularly with younger children, to look at materials with larger grains first.) Feel the same material in a bowl or box.
? Does this material feel like a liquid? (No: it does not wet your hands and it is made of little solid bits.)
- Tilt the jar and watch what happens.
? How does the material in the jar move? (The grains slide and tumble over each other.)
? When the jar is tilted, does the material run down to the bottom of the container, as a liquid does? (No. It does run down and fill the bottom of the container, but its surface is not level as the surface of water is.)
- Pour a small amount of the material you are looking at on to a tray.

? What happens? (The material forms a heap on the tray.)

? Would a liquid do this? (No: a liquid would spread out to form a layer with a flat, level surface.)

? Does the material change shape as a liquid does? (No. The mass of material changes shape, but does not form level surfaces. Also, each individual grain keeps its own shape, which shows that although the material may appear to flow rather as a liquid does, its particles are solid.)

This activity should be repeated with at least one other material whose particles are too small to be distinguished easily with the unaided eye (e.g. very fine sand or salt). A magnifying-glass, hand-lens or microscope can then be used to see that each particle, though small, is still a solid object.

Activity 6.1.3

Gases and their properties

Gases, like liquids, have no shape of their own. Unlike liquids, they do not collect at the bottom of a container but fill it completely. Showing that gases have this property, and even that they are real materials which have substance, needs thought and care because nearly all gases are invisible (i.e. transparent and colourless) and those which are not are highly poisonous.

The gas with which children are likely to experiment most at primary level is air, the gas mixture which makes up our atmosphere. With young children especially, a range of experiences is most likely to develop the concept of air and other gases as materials which are invisible but which are real, can exert forces on other objects and completely fill containers within which they are confined.

Air can exert forces on other objects

A wide variety of simple, short investigations can be used to show that air is a real, though invisible, substance. The scientific view is that moving air-streams exert push-forces on objects in their path. Useful ones to experiment with are: model windmills and turbine wheels made of paper and card, held in wind outdoors or in the air-stream from an electric fan or hair-dryer indoors; objects and materials such as table-tennis balls and liquid paint, moved by blowing on them with a straw; blowing on card sails attached to model boats or lightweight trolleys (see Fig. 14.8a; add dowel for a mast).

It is also helpful for children to experience, in the context of an investigation, the forces generated as they move through still air, for example by running with a paper or card windmill, or while holding a large, lightweight board (at least 1 × 1m) above their heads at different angles.

Air fills whatever is containing it

While it is obvious that a liquid runs to the bottom of a container, it is not so obvious that a gas such as air fills any container completely, because it is invisible. The point can, however, be made by inflating a balloon with air and feeling it. When the balloon is inflated, air is squashed into it. This air pushes out all the time, stretching the rubber. Feeling the balloon shows that the air is pushing out evenly all over its surface: there is not more air in one part of it than another, so the (compressed) gas is filling its container completely. Activity 12.3.1 provides more evidence, based on the way in which air expands and is expelled from one end of a container when the *other* end is heated.

6.2: Changes of state: melting and freezing

There is a variety of ways in which materials can change state between solid and liquid or *vice versa*. In this section we investigate changes of state brought about by transfer of thermal energy to or from the material, i.e. by heating or cooling, which also result in changes of temperature (Section 12.3). These changes are known as melting (solid to liquid) and freezing (liquid to solid). Other changes of state are associated with evaporation (Section 6.3) and dissolving (Section 6.5).

Most simple materials, i.e. those which are not mixtures, exist either as solids, liquids or gases with no intermediate or transitional states between them, though solids may soften as they are heated. Under the same conditions the same material will always melt and freeze at the same temperatures (its melting- and freezing-points) and the change in either direction will be sudden, though it may not always appear to be. Children may associate 'freezing' only with changes which take place at temperatures they experience as 'cold', but scientifically freezing is the reverse of melting, regardless of the temperature at which it takes place.

Activity 6.2.1

Observing melting and freezing

The most useful material for introductory investigations into melting and freezing is candle (paraffin) wax. Ordinary white (i.e. uncoloured) candles should be used, since materials used to colour candles or crayons can interfere with observation of melting and freezing. Any sample of paraffin wax will melt and freeze at a definite temperature, usually between 50°C and 60°C and the change between the two states can easily be seen.

These and other investigations which involve the heating and cooling of small amounts of material (see also Activity 6.2.3) can effectively be carried out using small food trays or containers made of fairly thick aluminium foil, floating on water.

Observing melting and freezing of wax

Equipment and materials: White (i.e. uncoloured) candle; knife; small aluminium foil food containers; plastic bowl; electric kettle or other means of heating water; cold water; thermometer, range −10 to 110°C; a long-handled spoon.

Safety note: Water hot enough to melt wax can cause some discomfort and even scalding of skin. Children should at no time splash or put their fingers into the hot water.

- Heat water until it is nearly boiling; mix with cold water in a bowl until the mixture is at about 70°C.
- Cut a few *small* chips of wax (i.e. not more than a few millimetres across) from a white candle. Put them in a small aluminium container and, using a long spoon, float this on the water.

? What happens to the wax? (It quickly melts.)

? How does its appearance change? (The wax chips lose their shape as they melt and turn from white solid to colourless liquid with shiny surfaces.)

● Using the spoon, remove the tray from the hot water. Watch the drops of liquid wax as you put the tray down on the table.

? What happens? (The wax becomes solid again, i.e. it freezes.)

? What is causing these changes?

The answer to this question needs to be expressed with some care. The causes of melting and freezing are heating and cooling, i.e. the transfer of thermal energy (see Section 12.3). It is important neither to state nor imply that they are caused by changes in temperature, because melting, freezing and temperature are all effects brought about by heating and cooling.

Softening and melting

When wax is just below its melting-point it is solid, i.e. it keeps its shape without support although it is very soft. Many materials show softening as they are heated and this may cause confusion because children may think of it as a kind of half-melting, although it may take place well below the melting-point of the material.

Equipment and materials: as above.

● Put enough wax into two aluminium foil containers to make a layer 3–4mm deep in the bottom of each. Melt the wax by floating the containers on water in a bowl at about 70°C.

● Remove the containers and allow the wax to cool. As it begins to freeze, touch the surface with a finger. Keep testing by pushing a finger on to the wax every few minutes, until you can no longer dent the surface with your finger-tip.

? What do you notice as the wax freezes? (The surface freezes and forms a solid but soft 'skin' over the wax below it which is still liquid. Later, the surface is firm but can still be dented with a finger-tip because the wax below it is still soft. Later still the whole mass of wax hardens.)

? A very small sample of wax freezes all at once and hardens very quickly. Why does this larger sample take longer to freeze and harden? (Because freezing and hardening depend on cooling, i.e. transfer of thermal energy from the material to its surroundings. The outer layers of wax cool much faster than the middle.)

● When both samples of wax are cold, gently break them from their containers and then put them back. Keep one sample of wax cold, and heat the other on water to a temperature 10°C *below* its melting-point for a few minutes.

● By bending and squashing, compare the properties of the warm and cold wax samples.

? In what ways are their properties different? (The warm wax is much softer and its shape can be changed by bending and squashing, but the cold wax breaks into pieces.)

? Is the warm wax solid? (Yes.) Is it as solid as the cold wax? (Yes; but its physical properties are different. The warm wax is softer, more flexible and plastic; the cold wax is harder, less flexible and more brittle. These observations should be linked to those on the physical properties of materials, see Chapter 7.)

Activity 6.2.2

Solid or liquid?

Children are likely to be familiar with materials which can exist in a state intermediate between solid and liquid, and which may show a gradual transformation between one state and the other. All of these materials are mixtures and many of them are foods. Examples include chocolate, ice-cream, cornflour custard, blancmange and other quick-setting desserts, but the most easily-investigated is jelly, made from gelatine.

A good standard mixture can be made by dissolving 10g of gelatine powder or granules in 60ml of hot water, always adding the gelatine to the water and stirring until it is dissolved. This will set into a very stiff jelly which can then be cut into pieces and used as the basic material for children's investigations.

Equipment and materials: Stiff gelatine jelly (see above); five small plastic bowls or aluminium foil food containers; medium-sized plastic bowl; 15ml measuring spoon; electric kettle or other means to heat water; lolly-stick; refrigerator.

Safety note: Children need to measure hot water with a 15ml measuring spoon (a 'standard tablespoon'). This activity should be supervised to prevent danger of scalding.

- Cut the stiff jelly made from 10g gelatine into six equal parts. Keep one part as a reference sample; put each of the other five into small basins or food-containers.
- Heat water until it is nearly boiling; pour into a plastic basin.
- Using a spoon, carefully measure 15ml hot water and pour on to one piece of jelly. Allow it to dissolve, stirring gently if necessary with a stick.
- Dissolve the other samples, using increasing amounts of water for each: 30, 45, 60 and 75ml. Allow the mixtures to cool overnight at room temperature; do not put them into a refrigerator.
- Test the cooled mixtures to see if they are solid, liquid or somewhere between the two. Useful ways to test them are to:
   i)   Tilt the container slowly. (Does the mixture keep its shape or start to flow?)
   ii) Touch the mixture with a finger.(Does the mixture wet your finger? Does the finger leave a mark?)
   iii) Try to turn the mixture out of its container into another one. (Will the mixture keep its shape when unsupported?)

These tests should show that some of the gelatine-water mixtures are liquid, some solid and some have intermediate properties.

- Replace the samples in their containers and put them in a refrigerator for at least two hours.
- Re-test the cold mixtures as before.
- ? What change has cooling made? (The mixtures are more solid than when they are at room temperature.)

As well as showing states intermediate between solid and liquid, jelly and other mixtures like it also change gradually between the two states if they are heated and cooled slowly. These properties can be contrasted with the melting and freezing of both wax and water, in which the change of state is sudden.

Activity 6.2.3

Freezing and melting of water

Although water is the material which children are likely to see freezing and melting most often, it has some very unusual properties and is best investigated when the basic concepts of freezing, melting and freezing-point have been established using materials such as wax (Activity 6.2.1). Most of the simpler aspects of the freezing and melting of water can be investigated using small aluminium foil food containers, transparent plastic containers such as drink bottles with their tops cut off and plastic ice-cube trays, in the freezing compartment of a domestic refrigerator.

Observing freezing and melting of water

Equipment and materials: Small aluminium foil food containers or trays; cold water; dropper; freezing compartment of refrigerator; thermometer which can measure down to −10°C; magnifying-glass or hand-lens.

- Put two or three drops of water into each of six foil containers; place these in the freezing compartment of a refrigerator with a thermometer; leave for five minutes.
- Open the freezer; find the temperature inside. (It is usually about −8°C but varies according to the setting of the thermostat.)
- Take out one foil container and look at the water in it.
- ? How has the water changed? (It has frozen into ice. The ice will usually appear white.)
- Watch the ice carefully for a few seconds.
- ? What happens? (The ice melts, turning to transparent colourless liquid again.)
- Have a magnifying-glass or hand-lens ready. Replace the first container in the freezer and take out another (frozen) one. Without any delay, look at the ice with the magnifying-glass and put a finger-tip on the metal under the ice-drop. Watch carefully to see how the ice melts.
- ? Does the ice melt quickly or gradually? (Very quickly.)

With the magnifying-glass it can be seen that the heating effect of a finger-tip on the metal container and the ice is almost instant. This sudden melting can usefully be compared with the melting of wax (see Activity 6.2.1).

- Replace the container in the freezer and take out another (frozen) one. Look at the ice with a magnifying glass or hand-lens.
- ? Can you see why the ice is white rather than transparent?

This may be difficult to see, but most of the ice-drop is full of tiny air-bubbles. Air is normally dissolved in water (this is the air that fish and other aquatic animals breathe, Activity 6.5.3) and when the water is frozen the air comes out of solution and appears as bubbles of gas. The ice-cubes made in a refrigerator usually have much bigger air-bubbles which can easily be seen when the cubes are floating in cold water.

Freezing and melting a larger quantity of water

Equipment and materials: 1 litre colourless transparent drink bottles; cold water; freezing compartment of refrigerator; thermometer.

- Cut the bottom 5cm from two 1 or 2 litre plastic drink bottles. Colourless transparent bottles are best. Fill these containers two-thirds full of cold water and put them into the freezing compartment of a refrigerator, with a thermometer which can measure down to −10°C, until ice starts to form.

Ice begins to form both on the liquid surface and as plate-like crystals growing inwards from the wall of the container. Both can be seen more clearly if the container is held beside a table-lamp and tilted.

? What is the temperature inside the freezing compartment? (This will be variable according to the thermostat setting, but will be well below 0°C.)
? What is the temperature of the water? (If ice is forming, it will be 0°C.)
? Why does ice form on the surface and inside the container, rather than in the middle of the liquid? (Because the water surface and container are in contact with the air in the freezer which is much colder than they are, so that thermal energy can be transferred from those parts of the water most rapidly.)

- When ice formation is more advanced (usually after about an hour), squeeze the container to free the ice and pick out pieces. Test the hardness and flexibility of the ice with your fingers by trying to dent thicker pieces and bend thin pieces.
? Can you dent or bend the ice? (No: the thick pieces are too hard to dent with a finger-nail and the thin pieces break if bending forces are applied to them.)
- When the water in it has frozen completely, take out the second container which has not been disturbed, squeeze it and turn the ice out of it. Feel and try to grip the ice as it starts to melt.
? What does the ice feel like? Can you grip it? (It is cold, hard and solid but very slippery so it is difficult to grasp it firmly.)
? Why is the ice slippery? (Because it is starting to melt and is covered with a thin layer of liquid water. This acts as a lubricant, so the friction forces (*14.3) between your hand and the ice are very low and you cannot easily grip it.)
? When it is just below its melting point, wax becomes very soft. From your observations, do you think ice does this? (No: ice seems to stay quite hard right up to the point at which it melts.)

The expansion of ice

Most materials become smaller as they are cooled. One of the most unusual properties of water is that it expands as it freezes, and continues to expand as it is cooled and its temperature falls further and further below its freezing-point. One result of this is that a kilogram of ice has a volume larger than a kilogram of water (i.e. 1 litre), so that solid water (ice) will float on liquid water. Children can see this effect very simply by floating ice on water.

The expansion of ice can have very destructive effects. If a *thin* glass jar is filled about two-thirds full with water, put into a plastic bag and then into a freezer, the ice will usually crack the glass as it expands on freezing. If the jar is strong enough to withstand the force from the ice, take it from the freezer, wipe it dry and immediately put an adhesive paper label on it to show the level of the ice. When the ice has melted, it can be seen that the water level is below the label, showing how much greater the volume of the ice was.

The expansion of ice is a major cause of the weathering of rocks in the colder parts of the world (*11.8) where it may also cause damage to buildings. Children may observe flaking and crumbling of porous brick or stone, where water has seeped in, frozen and forced the material apart.

6.3: Changes of state: boiling, condensation and evaporation

Changes of state between liquid and gas always involve the transfer of thermal energy (*12.2). Liquid may be changed into gas in two ways. Boiling is caused by heating and takes place only at or above a characteristic temperature (the boiling-point). For example, water boils at 100°C and produces water in gas form, known as steam, which can continue to exist as a gas only at or above that temperature. The other mode of change takes place when a liquid surface is exposed at or near the temperature of its surroundings, which may be far below the liquid's boiling-point. This kind of change is called evaporation and produces a cool gas phase called a vapour. For example, when wet objects dry in air, water is evaporating from them and the water vapour produced is passing into and mixing with the air above or around them.

The change of any gas into liquid is called condensation. The liquid children are most likely to see boiling, condensing and evaporating is water, so attention is focused on it in the following activities.

Activity 6.3.1

Boiling of water
The boiling of water can most easily be observed in a glass vessel, but this must be safe and capable of withstanding direct heating. A large (2 litre) chemical beaker is ideal, but if a glass vessel is not available, an ordinary large saucepan can be used. If there is a choice, a thin-based pan is easier to use and control than a thick-based one.

Equipment and materials: Pan or beaker to hold hot water; means to heat it safely; cold tap-water; thermometer range −10 to 110°C.

Safety note: Water must be heated and boiled in such a way that children can look at it without risk either of spillage or scalding by steam. Boiling water must always be viewed by looking from well to one side of the vessel. In particular, no one should ever look directly downward on a pan or kettle of boiling water: the risk of scalding from steam or small, hot droplets is very high.

- Half-fill the pan with cold tap-water. Do not re-use water which has recently been heated or boiled.
- Place the pan on the heating equipment; heat it as rapidly as possible, measuring the water temperature with a thermometer, but not stirring the water with it.

As the water temperature reaches 20°C or 30°C, small bubbles are likely to appear on the bottom of the vessel. These grow in size as the temperature rises and some come to the surface and burst. The appearance of these bubbles is not caused by boiling but by air coming out of solution (see also Activity 6.5.3).

As the temperature of the water reaches 100°C the rate of bubble formation suddenly increases and the whole liquid starts to boil. If a glass vessel is being used it should be possible to see that bubbles are being formed in the middle of the liquid, not only at the bottom.

? What is the temperature of the water when it boils? (100°C.)
? What is this temperature called? (The boiling-point of water.)
● Reduce the rate of heating so that the water is boiling fairly slowly, and look at the bubbles being produced.
? What do the bubbles in the water look like? (They are colourless and transparent.)
? Are they filled with solid, liquid or gas? (Like all bubbles, these are filled with gas).
? What gas is it?

Some children may think that the bubbles are filled with air; but where could the air be coming from? In fact they are filled with water in the hot gas phase, commonly known as steam, and a simple observation shows that in some conditions they have a very unusual property.

● Switch off the heating equipment and allow the water to cool to about 80°C; then re-heat it slowly and watch the bubbles which form very carefully, especially when they leave the bottom of the vessel and move upwards.
? What happens to the bubbles? (They disappear and do not reach the surface.)

These are not air-bubbles: the water at the bottom is boiling, because it is being heated more rapidly than the rest of the water in the vessel, which is still below boiling-point. As a steam-bubble starts to rise, it moves through water which is below 100°C, so the steam condenses almost instantly into liquid water again and the bubble disappears.

What is produced when water boils?

If children are asked this question their verbal reply will probably be correct: steam is produced. If, however, they are asked what steam looks like, they will probably reply, incorrectly, that it looks like clouds. The situation is less simple, and more interesting.

Equipment and materials: Kettle, preferably with a spout, not an automatic jug-type; means to boil water in it safely; water; thermometer; oven gloves; 30cm thin cotton thread.

Safety note: Steam from a kettle-spout must never be directed towards people since it can scald skin almost instantly. Apart from the person taking the temperature of the steam, who should wear oven-gloves, no one should be nearer than 1m to a boiling kettle.

● Fill the kettle one-third full of water. Replace the lid and heat the water until it boils. Reduce the rate of heating but keep the water boiling and look carefully at the spout.
? What do you see? (A short distance above or out from the spout a stream of cloud starts to form, which moves upwards and outwards; but just above and inside the spout there is nothing to see.)
● While the kettle continues to boil, and keeping your hand well clear of the hot cloud-stream, hold a piece of thin thread so that the end hangs over the end of the spout.
? What happens to the thread? (It is blown upwards and outwards.)

? What does this show? (That there is a stream of gas coming from the kettle-spout.)

- Wearing oven-gloves, take the temperature in the kettle-spout, just outside it and in the cloud-stream. The thermometer should be held in one place until the temperature shown is constant.

The temperature inside and just outside the kettle-spout, where the gas-stream is invisible, is 100°C. The invisible gas is steam, i.e. water in the hot gas phase. The temperature of the cloud further away from the spout is always *below* 100°C, so it cannot be steam, although this is what it is commonly called. It is in fact exactly what it looks like: a cloud, but a hot cloud of tiny water droplets suspended in the air. Steam coming from the spout at 100°C has been cooled and changed back to liquid water. This is an example of condensation (see Activity 6.3.2), which is also responsible for the drops of liquid water which form on the thermometer.

Activity 6.3.2

Condensation

Any change from gas to liquid is called condensation. The condensation of water in the gas phase (from steam or water vapour, see Activity 6.3.3) is not only easy to investigate in the classroom but is also likely to be a common occurrence in the lives of children, both in the home and in their wider environment, since it is involved in many kinds of weather such as rain, fog and dew (see Sections 11.4, 11.5).

Condensation of steam

Equipment and materials: Kettle, preferably with a spout, not an automatic jug-type; means to boil water in it safely; oven gloves; cold water; crushed ice; clear plastic drink bottle with screw-top; clear plastic cup or other receptacle (e.g. cut-down drink bottle).

Safety note: Steam from a kettle-spout should never be directed towards people since it can scald skin almost instantly. Apart from the person collecting condensed liquid, who should wear an oven-glove, no one should be nearer than 1m to a boiling kettle.

- Wearing an oven-glove, hold a bottle half-full of ice-water in the cloud-stream from a boiling kettle.

Drops of water form on the bottle and can be collected as they drip from it. The change from gas (steam) to liquid water is condensation, which is always caused by cooling and reverses the change brought about by boiling. The water which condenses is distilled water and is very pure. A more familiar form of condensation occurs under cool conditions when no water has been boiled, and this needs to be investigated in more detail.

Condensation under cool conditions

Equipment and materials: Clear plastic (not glass) bottle half-filled with ice-water; magnifying-glass or hand-lens; paper towel.

- Stand a clear plastic bottle, half-filled with ice-water, on a table. Wipe it dry with a paper towel, then watch it.
? What happens? (The lower half of the bottle, in contact with the ice-water, mists over.)

- Leave the bottle for a few minutes. Look at the part which has misted over with a magnifying-glass or hand-lens.
? What do you see? (The misted part of the bottle is covered with tiny drops of clear liquid.)

Children are likely to be familiar with this kind of condensation through seeing mist and water-drops obscuring windows in rooms and cars on cold days. That the liquid is water cannot be proven without chemical testing, but the only *commonly-occurring* clear, colourless runny liquid which has no smell is water. Once it is accepted that the droplets are indeed condensed water, the investigation can continue.

? If the liquid droplets are water, where was the water in gas form before it condensed on the cold bottle? (Again the obvious answer is the correct one, i.e. that it was in the air. In this case, however, the bottle itself gives us some evidence to support this hypothesis.)
- Tilt the bottle.
? What is the difference between the lower and upper parts of the bottle? (The lower part has a mist of liquid droplets all over it; the upper part is clear and dry. There is a clear, sharp boundary between the two which corresponds to the level of the ice-water.)
? Why are the two parts different?

The only difference between the two is that the ice-water cools the lower part of the bottle, which in turn cools the air in contact with it. The result is that water already in the air in the form of a gas condenses on the lower part of the bottle. The upper part is not cooled and so is at the same temperature as the air around it. As a result, no water condenses on it. Water in gas form below 100°C is known as water vapour and is normally present in the air around us. How it gets there is investigated as part of Activity 6.3.3.

Activity 6.3.3

Evaporation
This activity follows on from Activity 6.3.2, but starts with a situation very familiar to children: the drying of wet porous material, returning later to further observations on the water which condenses on cold objects.

Drying paper towels

Equipment and materials: Paper towels cut into strips about 5 cm wide; water; dropper; saucer or shallow basin; clear plastic bottle; paper-clips; thread; any of the following: electric fan, room-heater; blow-heater; hair-dryer; refrigerator.

- Dampen each paper strip with the same number of drops.
- Hang strips using paper-clips and thread if necessary in a variety of places, e.g. in still air in the middle of the classroom, over a room heater, in a refrigerator and inside a bottle with the top on; in an air-stream from an electric fan and in a *warm* air-flow from a hair-dryer or blow-heater. Make a note of the time when your observations start.

? How can you tell when a strip is completely dry? (The most reliable difference is that a strip which is even slightly damp feels cooler than one which is completely dry. This is a significant observation which will be referred to again in Activity 6.3.4.)

● Keep checking the strips. As each strip dries completely, write down the time on it, then subtract the starting-time to find out how long it took the strip to dry.

● Make a list of the time it took strips in different conditions to dry, and note the strips which did not seem to dry at all.

? If still air in the classroom is taken as 'normal', which conditions allow the strips to dry more quickly than this? (Warmth and wind, especially if they are together, as in the air-stream from a hair-dryer.)

? Which conditions slow down or prevent drying? (Cold, or being in a small enclosed space such as a bottle.)

? When have you experienced fast and slow drying of liquids or wet materials? (Examples could include: drying of washing in open air and tumble-dryers; drying-up and persistence of puddles on hot and cold days; drying one's body and hair after swimming in different conditions.)

? When a material such as a paper towel dries, where does the water go?

To find the answer to this last question, we have to carry out a second, very simple investigation which can usefully be set up and begun at the same time as the first one and then observed when it is needed.

Finding out where the water goes when a material is dried

Equipment and materials: Completely dry plastic drink bottle, preferably a tall one with a screw-top; strip of paper towel; water; dropper; room heater or other means of gently warming the bottom of the bottle.

● Drop water on to the paper until it is wet but not dripping. Roll the paper longways until you can drop it into the bottom of a dry plastic bottle without it touching the neck or sides. Screw the top on to the bottle.

● Place the bottle where it will be warmed gently, e.g. on or near a room heater but not in sunlight. (The bottle should be left until needed. If it is left for a day or two the effect will be even more obvious.)

? Look carefully at the bottle. Has its appearance changed? (A mist of condensation will have formed inside the bottle, usually near the top. Larger drops may have formed and run down the sides.)

? What are the mist or droplets? (They are water which has condensed from the air on to the cooler parts of the bottle.)

? Where did the water come from? (From the only source of water in the bottle, i.e. the paper towel.)

Taken together, these observations show that when an object 'dries' in air, liquid water is changed into a gas which mixes with the air and can be changed back to liquid water by condensation. This process is called evaporation. Water which has evaporated is in the cool gas phase and is known as water vapour. Water vapour is always present in the atmosphere and if air is cooled enough, water will condense as cloud, rain, hail or snow (*11.5).

Comparing and contrasting evaporation and boiling

This may be an appropriate point at which briefly to compare and contrast evaporation with boiling (see Activity 6.3.1). Boiling can take place only at or above the boiling-point of the liquid, whereas evaporation can take place at much lower temperatures. Boiling of water produces steam, i.e. water in the hot gas phase, which can exist only above 100°C. Evaporation of water produces water vapour, i.e. water in the cool gas phase which, mixed with air, can exist at any temperature down to and even below 0°C. Boiling takes place inside a liquid; for example bubbles of steam can arise anywhere in a pan of boiling water. Evaporation can take place only at the exposed surface of a liquid; in the examples we investigate, the interface between liquids and air. This point is shown very clearly in Activity 6.3.4.

Activity 6.3.4

The cooling effect of evaporation

A useful starting-point for this activity is the observation, made in Activity 6.3.3, that a drying strip of paper towel, even if it is only slightly damp, feels cooler than one which is completely dry. The present activity sets out to observe this effect, to discuss its importance to humans and how it occurs.

Evaporation of water and cooling of the skin

Equipment and materials: Water; dropper.

- Before carrying out this investigation, make sure you are cool, i.e. not hot and perspiring.
- Hold out your hand horizontally, palm downwards. Blow gently on to the back of your hand for about 10s.
? What do you feel? (It feels cooler than normal.)
- Using a dropper, put one drop of water on to the middle of the back of your hand, so that it stays as a drop and does not spread.
- Gently blow on to the back of your hand for 10s as before.
? What do you feel? (Most of the hand feels cool, as before; the water drop may feel slightly cooler still.)
? Did the drop appear to dry up when you blew on it? (No.)
- Now spread the drop of water with a finger-tip so that it forms a thin film all over the back of your hand, and blow on it for 10s as before.
? What do you feel? (The skin feels much cooler than before.)
? Did the water-film dry up as you blew on it? (Yes. If the water is spread very thinly, blowing on it for 10s will often dry the skin.)
? Does the water evaporate faster when it is in a compact drop or spread into a thin film? (When it is in a thin film.)

This simple observation reinforces two important features of evaporation: it can take place at temperatures much lower than the boiling-point of the evaporating liquid, and is a surface phenomenon. When the water is spread out into a thin film over a large area, it dries up much faster than when it is in a compact drop.

The importance of the cooling effect to animals and humans

? In what other situations have you experienced the cooling effect you have just felt? (Examples could include getting out of a bath, shower or swimming pool: even in quite warm conditions one can feel suddenly cool or even cold because evaporation of water is cooling the thin film of water on the skin.)

This investigation, and experiences of suddenly feeling cool when we are wet and exposed to air, model what happens when our bodies become overheated and we sweat (Activity 3.9.3). The cooling effect of evaporation is crucial to the survival of many mammals including humans, because it enables them to avoid overheating while remaining active. In the case of humans this is achieved by sweating (perspiration). In animals which do not perspire, such as dogs, a similar effect is achieved by panting, which forces water to evaporate from the tongue, so the blood flowing through it is cooled.

Evaporating liquids other than water
Children may have experienced the cooling effect of evaporation with liquids other than water. The most likely is the medical use of an alcohol swab to surface-sterilize the skin before an injection or taking of a blood sample. The cooling effect of alcohol (ethanol) can easily be shown by putting a drop of surgical spirit on the skin and blowing air on it, as in the first part of this activity. It spreads more readily than water and evaporates much faster, so the cooling effect is felt immediately. If children blow air on to a single drop of surgical spirit spread into a thin film, it evaporates so fast that the cooling effect may not be felt very distinctly, but blowing air on to three or four drops spread over the hand produces a very marked cooling effect.

Explaining the cooling effect of evaporation
Although evaporation can take place at temperatures much lower than the boiling-point of the evaporating liquid, it still requires the transfer of thermal energy from the liquid to the vapour. One result, as the first part of Activity 6.3.3 showed, is that the warmer conditions are, other things being equal, the higher the rate of evaporation. As thermal energy is transferred to the vapour, which then mixes with the air, the liquid is cooled. If the liquid is in contact with another object (e.g. water in a film on human skin) thermal energy will in turn be transferred from this object to the liquid, so the object will be cooled as well.

The thermal energy transferred to the vapour as a liquid evaporates is known as latent heat of vaporization (*12.2) and is of great importance in understanding weather, particularly the more violent kinds of event such as thunderstorms, hurricanes and typhoons (*11.6).

6.4: Physical changes, mixtures and their separation

Physical change and reversibility
Melting, freezing, boiling, evaporation and condensation are all examples of physical changes. These are changes which alter the physical properties and often the appearance of materials, while the actual substances involved remain the same. However fundamentally a material seems to alter when it undergoes physical changes, the kind of material it is does not change at all. Changes which do involve making new kinds of material are chemical changes (Section 9.1).

It is important to avoid any confusion between the concepts of physical and chemical change on the one hand, and reversible and non-reversible change on the other. These pairs of ideas are quite independent of each other. There are physical changes which are reversible (e.g. melting ice or dissolving sugar in water) and others which are non-reversible (e.g. cracking and beating an egg or grinding grain to flour); and similarly with chemical changes.

Because physical changes are very varied and often encountered in everyday life, it is useful to think of them as falling into broad groups, depending on their causes. Changes of state brought about by the transfer of thermal energy are investigated in Sections 6.2 and 6.3; those caused by applying forces to objects and materials in Chapter 7; while those brought about by mixing and separation are investigated in the remainder of this chapter.

Mixtures

A mixture is made when two or more materials are physically combined or mixed together while remaining chemically distinct. To understand mixtures and their properties it is necessary not only to mix materials and observe the changes this brings about, but also to use and if necessary devise the means of separating them again. Of the nine possible kinds of mixture (all of which exist), children can easily make and investigate four:

1. *solid dispersed in solid*: particulate mixtures (Activities 6.4.1–6.4.3);
2. *solid dispersed in liquid*: solutions and suspensions (Activities 6.5.1, 6.5.2);
3. *gas dispersed in liquid*: solutions (Activity 6.5.3);
4. *liquid dispersed in (porous) solid*: (Activity 6.6.1).

Particulate mixtures

These are made when two or more solids in small particles are mixed. A useful way to investigate and classify such mixtures is to find the means of separating their constituents. It is worth remembering that although the mixtures suggested can all be easily separated, so that in these cases mixing is an easily-reversible change, not all particulate mixtures are of this kind. For example, a mixture of two materials such as finely-ground salt and sugar, both of which are highly soluble in water, is remarkably difficult to separate.

Activity 6.4.1

Separating particulate mixtures by particle size

The two most commonly-used methods of separating materials by particle size are sieving and sedimentation. Sieving is more useful for separating larger particles, sedimentation for smaller ones; and while sieving is a good introduction to this kind of separation, sedimentation is more likely to be useful in conjunction with other methods when investigating complex materials, such as soils (see Activity 11.10.2).

Sieving

Sieving consists of sorting particles by their ability to pass through meshes with apertures of different sizes. Garden sieves can be used to remove large particles (usually between 5 and 10mm) from a mixture. Kitchen sieves are usually available in a range of sizes (larger ones are more useful) and at least two grades of mesh, made either of nylon or plated steel wire. The coarser mesh usually separates particles larger than 1mm; the finer, those larger than 0.5mm.

The most useful materials to introduce sieving are the sand, grit and stone mixtures used for making concrete and available bagged from builders' merchants and hardware stores under such names as 'fine mixed ballast' or 'concreting sand'.

Wholemeal bread flour can also be sieved, a process which models the industrial process of 'bolting' flour to refine it. With the two commonly-available grades of kitchen sieves it can be separated into coarse bran, fine bran and white flour, but is much slower to separate than sand and stones, so smaller samples should be used.

Sieving should be carried using materials *thoroughly* dried on trays in warm air for some hours, so that particles do not adhere. Any sieving activity can be much easier to manage if thoroughly-mixed samples (200g of minerals; 50g of flour) are made up for children to work with.

Equipment and materials: Dry mixtures to be separated; sieves; large sheets of paper; dry containers for separated fractions (the number needed will be the number of sieves plus one).

- Make sure the mixture you are to separate is thoroughly mixed-up. Spread a large sheet of paper on a table or the floor. Place your sieves in order, coarsest (i.e. largest holes) first.
- Put the sieve with the coarsest mesh on the paper; pour some of the mixture into it. Do not fill any sieve more than one-quarter full.
- Shake the sieve from side to side till no more particles fall through.
- Pour the material left in the sieve into a dry container: pour the mixture which passed through the first sieve into the second one for re-sieving.
- Sieve and separate the material fractions as before; repeat this process until all the sieves available have been used. Compare the appearance and texture of the separated fractions. Feel the finer particles with your finger-tips and see if you can tell which fraction you are feeling without looking at it.
- ? How are sieves used in garden and kitchen? (To remove lumps or large particles of material when preparing food or fine soil mixtures.)
- ? In what industries would this process be useful? (Sieving, usually known as 'screening', is an essential part of preparing crushed stone or quarried gravel for use as roadstone or in construction. After milling, flour is passed through a coarse sieve to remove large particles including pieces of grain or chaff and then, if white flour is required, through a finer one to remove bran.)

Activity 6.4.2

Separating mixtures by dissolving and filtering
If two solid materials with particles about the same size are mixed together they cannot be separated by sieving, so other methods have to be used which exploit different properties. If one of the materials is soluble in water (*6.5) it can be dissolved and the insoluble material separated from the mixture by filtration.

Filtration
Filtration is simply a kind of wet sieving, which separates the solid and liquid parts of a suspension (see Activity 6.5.1) and can remove all but the very smallest solid

particles. Children will already be familiar with coarse filtration through making tea and coffee. In chemical analysis special filter-papers are used, but if these are not available a very effective substitute can be made using a double layer of paper towel (see Fig. 6.2).

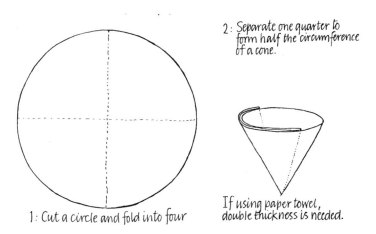

2: Separate one quarter to form half the circumference of a cone.

1: Cut a circle and fold into four

If using paper towel, double thickness is needed.

Figure 6.2 Folding a filter-paper

Suitable mixtures for separating in this way include a soluble and an insoluble ingredient, in equal proportions by volume, for example:

– *soluble ingredients*: salt (sodium chloride), white sugar (sucrose)
– *insoluble ingredients*: sand, powdered chalk (calcium carbonate).

If it is available, children can also refine natural rock-salt by dissolving and filtering, which removes clay and other coloured minerals. This models the process by which much salt is mined and refined commercially.

Although salt and sugar are the most easily-available soluble ingredients for mixtures of this kind, the use of neither is entirely straightforward because they cannot, under most classroom conditions, be recovered from solutions as dry solids without being heated (see Activity 6.5.2). In addition, commercially-available table or culinary salt has magnesium carbonate added to it to prevent caking. This chemical is insoluble in water and so will be filtered out. If a chalk and salt mixture is being separated it will not be distinguishable, but mixed with sand will appear as a white solid in the filter-paper.

Equipment and materials: Dry mixture to be separated; dry spoon; jar with lid for mixing with water; water; spoon for stirring; plastic funnel; filter-paper or substitute; two jars in which funnel will rest upright; shallow dishes (e.g. small foil food containers or trays); means to heat these gently over a period of some days.

- Stir the mixture to be separated with a dry spoon to make sure it is well-mixed.
- Add a flat teaspoonful of dry mixture to 100ml water in a jar; stir to dissolve the soluble part.
- Fold a filter-paper (or double thickness of paper towel) as shown in Fig. 6.2; put into a plastic funnel; rest the funnel upright in a clean, dry jar.

- Stir the liquid mixture and continue stirring as it is poured into the filter-paper. Make sure that the level of liquid stays below the edge of the filter-paper.
- Pour some of the clear, filtered solution into a clean, dry, shallow dish (e.g. a small foil food container). Place this where it will be gently heated for a few days; cover with paper to prevent dust settling on it.
- Pour more water into the mixing-jar; shake to gather up any solid particles and pour into the filter-paper. This will rinse the solid material. Unfold the filter-paper; leave it and the solid material to dry.
- When water has evaporated from the solution and the insoluble material is dry, the two materials which were mixed can be put into separate containers for inspection.

Activity 6.4.3

Separating mixtures using other properties

Older and more able pupils can usefully be encouraged to devise ways of separating mixtures by considering the properties of the materials which make them up. These may include properties not investigated so far. One interesting mixture is a small amount of powdered iron ('iron filings') in fine, dry silver sand. The iron is a relatively 'heavy' (dense) and magnetic material. The dry mixture can be separated by using a magnet (in a plastic bag to make recovery of the iron easier), or it can be 'panned' in a shallow dish, over a bowl, with a slow stream of water. The solids and water are swung gently in the pan, so that the lower-density sand is carried out and the iron particles remain.

6.5: Solutions and suspensions

When a solid is dispersed in a liquid, the mixture produced is either a solution, a suspension, or both, depending on whether or not the solid will dissolve in the liquid. As a solid is dispersing in a liquid it may look as if it is melting, but it is not. It is important to emphasize that the changes of state brought about by making and separating solutions and suspensions are quite different from melting and freezing (Section 6.2), which are caused by transfers of thermal energy.

If the solid (solute) will dissolve in the liquid (solvent) it becomes dispersed as individual chemical particles (molecules) among the molecules of the solvent. This has three consequences, all of which can easily be observed: a solution passes through a filter; it never separates unless changed in some other way; and it appears clear, i.e. not cloudy, when light is passed through it. If the solid will not dissolve, it remains as solid particles. If small enough these stay suspended in the liquid, but scatter light, making the mixture cloudy. In most cases these can be removed by filtering and will eventually settle out at the bottom of the liquid by sedimentation.

Activity 6.5.1

Distinguishing solutions and suspensions

All solutions and suspensions investigated at primary level can use water as their solvent or dispersing liquid and the use of other solvents is best avoided.

Comparing a solution and a suspension

Many solutions children use and drink are colourless, but it is helpful to begin work on solid-in-liquid mixtures by using coloured solids, so that children are in no doubt that there 'really is something in the water'. Two useful solids are red pottery clay (terracotta) and instant coffee. If the clay is hard or dry, break it into small lumps and soak it in water for a day or two, then decant the water and present the clay in the form of a thick paste, which will disperse easily.

All that is required at this stage is to mix a little of each solid with water so that solid particles are dissolved (coffee) or dispersed (clay), compare the appearance of the resulting mixtures and then filter them. For instructions on filtration, see Activity 6.4.2. The clay forms a suspension which is cloudy, with particles which settle out to form a sediment; whereas the instant coffee forms a clear solution which forms no sediment at all. When the two mixtures are filtered the instant coffee solution is unaffected, whereas nearly all the suspended clay particles are separated and appear as a residue in the filter-paper. It may, however, be noticeable that the water passing through the filter is still slightly cloudy. This is because the very finest clay particles, which will never settle out into a sediment, are so small that they can pass through ordinary filter-papers.

Some mixtures are suspensions of solids in a solution. Separation of these is discussed as part of Activity 6.4.2. Two other mixtures of this kind, which children can separate by filtration are: coffee brewed using a nylon mesh 'filter'; and table-salt mixed with water, which contains insoluble magnesium carbonate.

Activity 6.5.2

Solutions and their separation

Once children can distinguish reliably between solutions and suspensions, the concept of a solution needs to be developed and reinforced in two ways. First, children must be convinced that when a solute dissolves it is still present, even though it may seem to have vanished. It is particularly important to make this point in the context of colourless solutions. Finding this out for themselves leads children on to the second important point, that dissolving does not change the nature of a solute, i.e. it is a purely physical process. Both points are emphasized by tasting, and by recovering solutes from solutions by evaporation.

Dissolved solids are still present in the solution

This activity can be linked to the investigation of basic tastes (Activity 3.10.6).

Equipment and materials: Granulated (white) sugar; salt; instant coffee; water; disposable cups; short (3cm) pieces of drinking-straw.

Safety note: Solutions should be freshly made up under hygienic conditions. Sections of drinking-straw should be used once only and then discarded. If a straw which has touched anyone's tongue is dipped into a solution, that solution should be thrown away and a fresh one made up.

- Put a little water into a disposable cup. Wet the end of a piece of drinking-straw, dip it into instant coffee, then taste the coffee. Using a fresh piece of straw each time, taste sugar and salt in the same way.

- Put a little of each solid into a disposable cup and add a little water; shake gently until the solids dissolve.
? Can you see the solids when they have dissolved? (The coffee makes a coloured solution; the salt and sugar disappear.)
? If the salt and sugar are invisible, what has happened to them? (They are dissolved in the water, but some children may still think that they have vanished entirely.)
? How could you tell if the salt, sugar and coffee are still in the solutions? (By tasting them.)
- Taste all three liquids, using pieces of drinking-straw to put them into your mouth.
? Can you taste the dissolved materials? (Yes.)
? Do they taste the same as they did before? (Yes.)
? What does this tell you?

The observations are significant and the question is crucial because taste is the body's way of discriminating between different chemicals in the mouth (Activity 3.10.6). Tasting the solutions shows not only that the substances dissolved are still present in them and have not vanished, but also (because they taste the same) that they are the same kinds of material that they were before. This makes the point very clearly that dissolving is a physical change, not a chemical one. The converse argument, that a change in taste means a change in the nature of the material being tasted, is important when investigating chemical change (Chapter 9).

Separating solutions
The second way of showing that dissolving is a physical change is to recover the solutes by evaporation, which can be related to work on evaporation (Activity 6.3.3) and separating mixtures (Activity 6.4.2). This is not difficult to do, but solutions of salt and sugar usually have to be heated if dry solids are to be recovered. Solutions of table-salt should be filtered before use (see note in Activity 6.4.2).

Equipment and materials: Solutions of sugar, salt and instant coffee; shallow dishes (e.g. used petri-dishes and lids or small foil food containers); means to heat these gently over several days; paper towel; adhesive labels; magnifying-glass or hand-lens.

- Label shallow dishes; pour into each enough solution to cover the bottom. Place the dishes where they will be warmed gently and not disturbed. Lay a piece of paper towel over each dish to keep dust out.
? What happens to the water in the solutions? (It evaporates and mixes with the air as water-vapour.)
- Look at the dishes three or four times a day until the changes in them are complete. A magnifying-glass or hand-lens is useful to see how solids re-form as the water evaporates. Write down what you see each day, with the date and time.
? What differences are there in the way the three solutions change?

The salt and sugar solutions will form crystals (see Section 8.6); the sugar solution will thicken to a syrup before these appear, but the salt solution will not. The instant coffee solution thickens and finally dries to leave a thin, brittle sheet with no structure visible. As long as the making-up of the solutions and the evaporation process have been carried out under hygienic conditions, children can again taste the three solids to show that they are still the same substances they were before being dissolved.

Activity 6.5.3

Solutions of gases

Children are likely to encounter two gases in solution in water. The more significant, but the one they are less likely to be aware of, is air; the other is carbon dioxide.

Air dissolved in water

Tap water always contains some dissolved air; rain, pond and river waters contain even more if they are unpolluted. When substances such as salt and sugar are dissolved in water, more will dissolve in hot water than in cold, but with gases this is reversed: it is cold water which can carry the most dissolved gases, which usually include oxygen. The effects of this can be observed in a variety of ways. One is to watch the breathing action of a fish, which is the apparent 'drinking' of water, co-ordinated with the movement of the gill-covers at the back of the head. As water passes over the gills, dissolved oxygen is taken from it into the blood-stream and waste carbon dioxide is given out into the water, again in solution.

Other observations include freezing tap-water to observe the air-bubbles which form in the ice (Activity 6.2.3); and heating cold tap-water in a pan to observe the formation of bubbles of dissolved air while the water is still only warm (Activity 6.3.1). When water has been freshly-boiled, it contains very little if any dissolved air, so iron and steel will not rust in it as they will in tap and rain-water. This is used as a control test when investigating rusting (see Activity 9.5.1).

Carbon dioxide dissolved in water

Children are likely to be familiar with carbon dioxide in solution mainly in the form of fizzy (effervescent) drinks. By dissolving it under pressure, water can be made to hold far more carbon dioxide than it normally would. When the pressure in a bottle or can is released, the 'extra' dissolved gas comes out of solution as bubbles and the drink fizzes.

6.6: Absorbency, chromatography and waterproofing

Porous materials

The activities in this section are concerned with what happens when a liquid be-comes dispersed in a porous solid. Porosity simply means that the solid material has more or less small holes or cavities throughout its volume, which are filled with air when it is dry, and may fill up with liquid if it is wetted. Although many porous materials will take up a variety of liquids, attention will be focused here in their interaction with water. If a porous material easily takes up water in contact with it, it is said to be absorbent; if all the cavities in a porous material are filled with water, it is said to be waterlogged.

Children will already be familiar with many porous materials, including sponges both natural and man-made, cloth, paper and sand. The porosity of these materials is obvious because of their absorbency, but many other materials which do not appear to be absorbent are porous and may take up water under some circum-stances, for example brick (*10.2), wood and cork (Activity 7.2.1).

Activity 6.6.1

Investigating absorbency

Water moves into the cavities in absorbent materials because it is attracted to the solid surfaces and clings to them. The smaller the cavities, the greater the attraction. Because the forces of attraction between water and the porous materials are greater than the weight of the water, one of their most remarkable properties is that water can flow uphill in them.

Making water flow uphill

Equipment and materials: Plastic or metal tray 30cm or more long; blocks or books to hold one end up; Blu-tack; ruler; dry, fine silver-sand; strips of 2 or more absorbent papers 5cm wide and at least 20cm long; adhesive tape; water; dropper.

● Set up a tray at a slope of about 25°, with a strip of dry sand and strips of paper, as shown in Fig. 6.3.

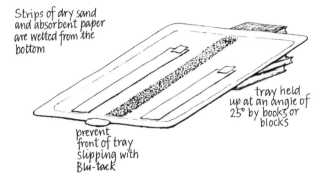

Strips of dry sand and absorbent paper are wetted from the bottom

tray held up at an angle of 25° by books or blocks

prevent front of tray slipping with Blu-tack

Figure 6.3   Absorbency: making water run uphill

● Using a dropper carefully and gently to avoid washing any sand downwards, wet the end of the sand-strip, then wet the bottom of each paper strip. Keep the bottom of each strip in a pool of liquid during the rest of the experiment.
● Watch carefully to see what happens as the bottom of each strip is wetted.
? What do you see? (Water begins to move up the strips.)
● Compare and make a note of how quickly the water begins to move up the different materials.

This may be an appropriate point to introduce the idea that, since water is moving uphill in all the strips there must be a force pulling it up, acting against gravitational force (i.e. the weight of the water). This force is a result of the attraction between the water and the porous materials.

? Has the water risen to the same level in each strip? (Usually not.)
? Compare the speed with which water began to rise up the strips, with the height it reached in the end. What pattern do you notice in the results? (The usual pattern is that the faster the water rises up a material at the start, the shorter distance it rises overall.)

This difference comes about because water can penetrate small cavities only slowly, but is more strongly attracted to them so it rises up further.

Comparing the absorbency of different materials
Comparing different materials is a useful way of developing and reinforcing the concept of absorbency, while demonstrating its relevance to everyday life. It is suggested that absorbent papers should be used and that comparisons should be made on the basis that 'the most absorbent material is the one which can take up the greatest amount of water per unit area before it starts to drip'.

Equipment and materials: Absorbent materials (e.g. paper towels, kitchen rolls and toilet tissues); ruler; plastic bag; soft wooden stick or dowel and the means to fix it horizontally; pins, (preferably map-pins); dropper; water; stop-clock or watch to count seconds.

- Work in pairs. Fix a soft wooden stick or dowel so that it can be reached easily. (It will be necessary to fix pins into this wood.)
- Cut 5 × 5cm squares from each of the absorbent papers to be tested, and from a plastic bag.
- Test the samples one at a time. Pin a sample and plastic square to the stick as shown in Fig. 6.4: the plastic is to prevent the stick absorbing water.

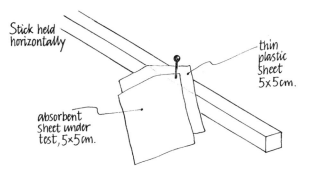

Put one drop of water every ten seconds at the base of the pin until one drip falls from the lower corner of the absorbent sheet. Number of drops gives a comparative measure of absorbency.

Figure 6.4   Comparing absorbency

- Using a dropper, one partner puts one drop of water on the upper corner of the absorbent material, at the base of the pin. Using a watch or stop-clock, add a further drop every 10s. The other partner counts the drops added and watches the spread of the water. When one drop falls from the lower corner of the sample, note how many drops had been added.
- This should be repeated three times for each material, to find out how reliable a test it is.
- Compare the amounts of water added to the samples. The most absorbent is the one which holds the most water without dripping.

Absorbency is not the only property an absorbent paper may need if it is to be effective in use. A useful exercise linking science and technology is to compare kitchen roll with paper towel, which may have about the same absorbency, in mopping up spilt water and drying hands. The main properties to look for are speed of absorption and strength when wet, which can be linked to technological issues, in particular the needs and purposes which the products have been designed to meet.

Activity 6.6.2

Chromatography

Chromatography (literally, 'colour-writing') is a method of separating a mixture of solutes in a solution. It depends on the fact that, as a solution is absorbed by paper, a variety of solutes will be carried up to different levels as the water advances. Chromatography can be a very precise method of chemical analysis, but can also be carried out very simply (and enjoyably) by children, analysing dye mixtures used in the ink of felt- and fibre-tipped pens.

Equipment and materials: White blotting-paper; selection of non-waterproof felt- and fibre-tipped pens (including more than one of each colour if possible); large (2-litre) plastic drink bottle; cane or thin dowel; adhesive tape; plastic bag; scissors; thin elastic band which will fit round the bottle, but not tightly.

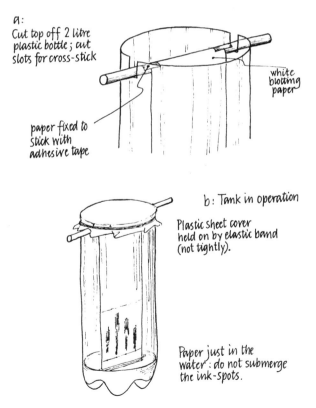

a:
Cut top off 2 litre plastic bottle; cut slots for cross-stick

white blotting paper

paper fixed to stick with adhesive tape

b: Tank in operation

Plastic sheet cover held on by elastic band (not tightly).

Paper just in the water: do not submerge the ink-spots.

Figure 6.5 Making a chromatography tank

- Set up a simple chromatography tank as shown in Fig. 6.5. Each ink-dot near the bottom of the paper should be 'loaded' with ink several times to give a concentrated spot of colour.
- Leave the tank undisturbed until the water has nearly reached the top of the paper, then lift out the paper, detach it from the dowel and dry it.

Using this method it can be shown that inks which appear be the same colour are in fact made of different dye mixtures. Black inks are particularly interesting. When a selection is analysed a wide variety of colourful dye mixtures is likely to be found. Forged signatures have been detected when chromatography has demonstrated that the forger used a different kind of ink from that in the remainder of the document.

Activity 6.6.3

Waterproofing

A good way of showing how absorption takes place is to attempt to prevent it, by waterproofing an absorbent material. Suitable materials for a simple, introductory investigation of waterproofing are paper towel and white (uncoloured) candle-wax.

Equipment and materials: Paper towel; wax (candle or crayon); scissors; electric iron; water; dropper.

- Cut three 10 × 10cm squares of paper towel. Leave one untreated; in the centre of the other two cover a circular area about 5cm diameter with wax without crumpling the paper.
- Heat an electric iron to a 'cool' setting and iron the wax into one of the pieces of waxed paper. Leave the other unchanged. Make sure that the iron is hot enough to melt the wax, which should penetrate so that it can be seen on the underside of the paper.
- Place all three pieces of paper side by side. Using a dropper, place (i.e. do not drop) three separate drops of water near the centre of each, then watch carefully so see what happens.
? What happens to the water on the three pieces of paper?

The water quickly spreads and is absorbed by the untreated paper. On the paper with a layer of wax on its surface, the water lies as globules for a short time but is then absorbed into the paper underneath. On the paper with the wax ironed-in, the water lies as rounded globules indefinitely and is not absorbed.

- Very carefully, put as small a drop of water as you can on to the paper with the wax ironed into it.
? What shape is the water-drop? (If it is very small, it is almost spherical; larger drops are partly flattened by their own weight.)

This shows that the wax is water-repellent: the water cannot wet the wax, so it contracts into a nearly-spherical drop. This can be confirmed by holding the paper with ironed-in wax at about 45° to the horizontal and dropping water on to the waxed area: the drops run off without wetting the surface.

? Why does the water stay on the surface of the paper with ironed-in wax? (Because the spaces between the paper fibres have been filled with a material which repels water, so the water cannot get into them.)

? Why does the paper with only a surface layer of wax absorb water after a little delay? (Because the paper underneath the wax layer is still absorbent, so if there is the tiniest crack or hole in the surface coat, water will get through it and be absorbed.)

Natural waterproofing is much more effective than any man-made material. Leaves of land plants have waxy coatings and some, e.g. those of most cabbages and 'nasturtiums' (*Tropaeolum*), are completely unwettable unless damaged by being rubbed. Children can also experiment with feathers of aquatic birds, such as the small breast-feathers of ducks, which are virtually unwettable, so that it is very difficult to make even a small drop of water stay on the convex outer surface. Waterproofing of this kind is an adaptation (see Section 5.5), essential to the survival of most aquatic birds since without the layer of air trapped by their unwettable feathers, their thermal insulation is completely inadequate and they die of 'cold' (hypothermia).

7

Mechanical Properties of Materials and Objects

The mechanical properties of an object or material relate to the way in which it responds when the forces acting on it are increased, decreased or exerted in a different direction.

7.1: Forces, materials and objects

When unbalanced forces (*14.1) act on an object, they can bring about change in two ways: change in the object's movement (Chapter 14) or its shape. Changes in shape, which are investigated in this chapter, include denting or scratching the surface, deformation and fracture.

Throughout this work it is very important that children learn to distinguish clearly between properties of materials and those of objects. A material property is one which does not depend on the size or shape the material happens to be in. Material properties include compressibility, hardness, elasticity, plasticity, brittleness and toughness. Object properties, on the other hand, are dependent partly on the size and shape of the particular object being used or tested, and partly on the material of which it is made. Two object properties are investigated: stiffness (which includes flexibility) and strength. The difference between object and material properties can be understood most easily by testing pairs of objects made of the same material, but which differ in size or shape. For example, thin steel wire and a thick steel nail differ in stiffness (object-property) but have the same hardness (material property).

When investigating compressibility (Section 7.2) we are concerned mainly with gases, but also with liquids and solids. Gases are also perfectly elastic (Section 7.6), but all the other properties investigated in this chapter are shown only by solids and the relationships between them are summarized in Table 7.1.

7.2: Compressibility

If an object or material can be squashed into a smaller volume when forces are applied to it, it is said to be compressible. The scientific view is that gases are compressible, whereas liquids and solids are not, but children may be puzzled by solids which appear to be compressible.

Table 7.1 Summary of mechanical properties of materials and objects

Type of shape change	Material property	Object property
Dent/scratch surface	**Hardness:** measure of how easy/difficult it is to dent or scratch.	

Deformation	When force is no longer applied to deformed material, it:
	    returns to original shape: **elastic;**
	    retains new shape: **plastic.**
		Object cannot be deformed: it is **rigid.**
		Object can be deformed: it is **flexible.**
		Measure of resistance to deformation is **stiffness** (specify whether in compression, tension or bending).

Fracture	How (in what manner) does fracture occur?
	    suddenly (cracks spread easily): **brittle;**
	    slowly: **tough.**
		Size of force required to cause fracture is measure of **strength** (specify whether in compression, tension or bending).

The compressibility of air and water can be investigated in a number of ways. One of the simplest and most convincing is to use fairly large disposable plastic syringes, but in a social context where these may be associated with drug abuse, experimenting with them may be unacceptable. Substitutes, which can be used in much the same way, are bicycle pumps and plastic drink bottles.

Activity 7.2.1

Investigating compressibility

Equipment: Bicycle pump (the simplest form is the most useful); large plastic drink bottle with gas-tight screw-top; balloon; bucket; water.

- Take a bicycle pump to pieces to see how the piston moves in the barrel, then put it back together again.
- Pull the pump-handle out, put the forefinger of the other hand over the hole on the other end of the pump so no air can escape, and push the handle in again.
- ? What happens? (It gets harder and harder to push the handle in until it cannot be pushed in any more.)
- ? When you cannot push the pump-handle in any more, what do you know about the forces acting on the handle? (They must be balanced. There must be a force pushing out equal to the force you are exerting by pushing in.)
- ? What could be exerting this outward push force? (The air in the pump pushing on the piston and the handle.)
- ? How has the air been changed so that it pushes in this way? (It has been squashed [compressed] into a smaller space by the piston.)
- Let the handle go.
- ? What happens? (The outward push force from the compressed gas makes the handle spring out again.)

It is useful to repeat this investigation using a large plastic drink bottle with the top screwed on tightly. As the sides of the bottle are squeezed inwards, the compressed air inside pushes outwards harder and harder until the hands cannot compress it any more. When the bottle is released, the air pushes the sides out until the original shape is regained. If a bottle without its top on is squeezed and then released, it usually stays partly collapsed because there is no force acting outwards to push the sides out again.

● Now repeat both investigations with the pump and bottle filled with water, making sure that all the air has been expelled from the pump and the bottle is filled completely by immersing it in a bucket.
? What happens when you try to push the piston in or squash the bottle? (The piston cannot be pushed in and the bottle cannot be squashed smaller.)
? What property of water does this show? (That it cannot be squashed: it is incompressible.)
● When you have finished, dismantle the pump and dry it carefully.

These simple investigations show first, that air can be squashed (compressed) into a smaller space than it normally occupies whereas water cannot. Secondly, they show that when air is compressed it pushes outwards with a force equal to that applied to it. Another way of showing this is to inflate a balloon: as air is compressed into the balloon it pushes outwards, stretching the rubber (see also Activity 14.1.4).

Solids which appear to be compressible
Children may be puzzled by porous materials such as sponge or cork which appear to be both solid and compressible. When they are squashed, the solid material is not compressed but distorted, so that the spaces within the object become smaller and the air or liquid filling them is forced out. Soft, non-porous solids such as modelling clay and Blu-tack, on the other hand, do *not* become smaller when squashed: they simply change shape.

7.3: Hardness

Hardness is a material property (see Section 7.1), which is estimated by finding out how difficult it is to scratch or dent the surface of the material.

Activity 7.3.1

Comparing and estimating hardness
Objects for comparing hardness should have a point or edge with which to scratch or dent other objects, and a surface which can be scratched by them. Suitable materials and objects, roughly in a descending order of hardness, include:

– *hard steel*: an old file or hacksaw blade;
– *hard rocks*: granite, quartz or hard sandstone;
– *mild steel*: a large nail or screw; a piece cut from a thick tin lid (smooth edges to avoid risk of cutting hands);
– *brass*: large screw or mirror-plate (test with magnet; should be non-magnetic);
– *copper alloy*: 'copper' coin;
– *aluminium*: bottom cut from drink can (smooth edges; test with magnet as some cans are steel);
– *finger-nail*: your own; use with care!

– *plastics*: a wide variety is possible here; drink bottles and their tops provide two useful examples;
– *slate*;
– *chalk*;
– *woods*: in variety, which may have a wide range of hardness;
– *candle wax* (cold);
– *modelling clay*.

Harder materials are usually easier to test by scratching, but care may be needed when testing hard rocks with metals. The metal may leave a silvery streak on the rock and appear to have scratched it, but some metal may simply have been rubbed off by the rock. Wetting the streak and rubbing it off with a rag will show whether the rock has actually been scratched or not. Softer materials are usually easier to test by denting: for example, a harder wood will dent a softer one but may not scratch it.

When comparing the hardness of materials, begin with a few which are clearly different, (e.g. mild steel, aluminium, finger-nail, chalk and modelling-clay).Place these in order as 'bench-marks', then introduce other materials which can be compared with them and placed in the series. The simplest scientific scale of hardness, which relates to rocks and minerals (Moh's scale) ranges from 1 (softest: talc) to 12 (hardest: diamond). The importance of children's testing for hardness lies in their ability to compare and order materials. Reference to an absolute scale is not necessary, but if children are interested, some typical values on Moh's scale of materials they might test are: hard steel file 6–7; steel knife-blade 5.5; 'copper' coin 3; finger-nail 2–2.5.

Variable hardness
Although it is usually possible to determine the hardness of materials fairly accurately by comparison, the hardness of some materials can vary markedly. Heating causes many materials to soften, and the softening of wax is investigated in Activity 6.2.1, in the context of melting and freezing. The working of many metals throughout history has depended on changing and controlling their hardness by heating and cooling in different ways, e.g. the tempering of steel.

7.4: Compression, tension and bending

When investigating the simpler mechanical properties of materials children are likely to learn most effectively through experience of handling a wide range of materials and subjecting them to forces in a variety of ways.

Activity 7.4.1

Applying forces in different ways
In order to learn, understand and predict how materials behave under stress, children need to be aware of and identify the ways in which forces can be applied to them. An effective way to begin this process is for each child to have a piece of plastic foam about 2 × 8cm and at least 1cm thick, preferably thicker. Ordinary sponge-like foam is adequate, but the more resilient 'closed-cell' foam is better. Polystyrene foam is not suitable. There are five main ways of applying forces, illustrated in Fig. 7.1, which children need to distinguish. Children can apply forces to plastic foam in all five ways and immediately see and feel the results.

If forces in the same straight line are acting towards each other, the material is squashed: this is compression (Fig. 7.1a). If they are acting away from each other the material is pulled and in some cases stretched: this is tension (Fig. 7.1b). Bending occurs either when an object is held at one end and a force is applied at the other (cantilever, Fig. 7.1c), or when it is held at both ends and a force is applied in the middle (beam, Fig. 7.1d).

If the object is held at one end and the other end is turned, the object is twisted: this is known as torque (Fig. 7.1e). A spanner tightening a nut (Fig. 14.11) is an example of torque in action. If an object is cut with a pair of scissors, the blades move past each other very close together. The forces act towards each other as in compression, but not in the same straight line. This way of applying forces is known as shear (Fig. 7.1f). Children can hold their plastic foam samples in scissors to see how the forces are applied, but actual cutting is better done using box-card (Fig. 14.12), as the foam samples are likely to be used later.

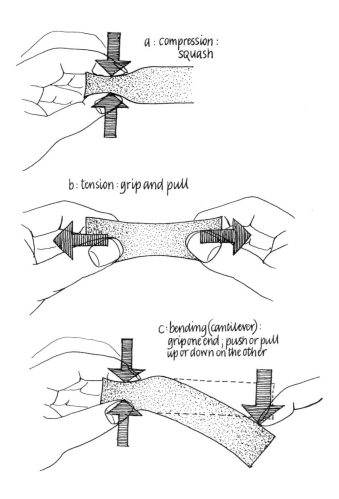

a : compression : squash

b : tension : grip and pull

c : bending (cantilever) : grip one end ; push or pull up or down on the other

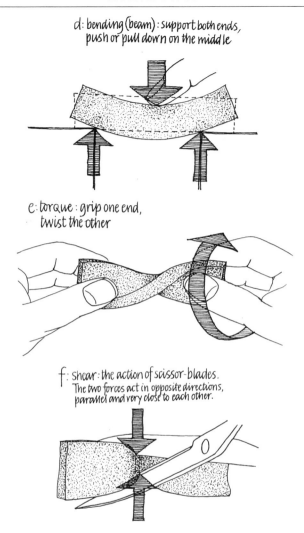

d: bending (beam): support both ends,
push or pull down on the middle

e: torque: grip one end,
twist the other

f: shear: the action of scissor-blades.
The two forces act in opposite directions,
parallel and very close to each other.

Figure 7.1   Applying forces in different ways to a strip of plastic foam

As they continue to investigate and manipulate materials in a variety of ways it is useful for children to have their samples of plastic foam available for re-testing and to act as a reminder when they are trying to decide exactly how forces are being applied and materials are responding.

Deciding how to test a material or object
Plastic foam is unusual in that it responds in an easily visible and understandable way when forces are applied to it in all five ways. Most materials are not like this and children need to be able to decide in a logical way how any particular material is to be tested, which is usually related to the way in which it is used. For example, when string is used it is pulled and bent, so we would test it to see how it responds to tension and bending, but would not usually need to find out how it responds to

compression. Throughout their investigations of mechanical properties children should be encouraged to relate the properties of the materials and objects they test to their uses. Using this kind of information and knowledge is the focus of Section 7.9.

7.5: Stiffness and flexibility

Stiffness is a measure of an object's resistance to changing shape when unbalanced forces are applied to it. Flexibility is a descriptive term and is the counterpart of stiffness: the less stiffness an object has, in compression, tension or bending, the more flexible it is. Children are also likely to meet the term 'rigidity'. When an object is described as being rigid, what is meant is that it has a very high degree of stiffness and does not appear to change shape under the forces being applied to it at the time. For example, as far as children bending objects with their hands are concerned a six-inch nail is rigid; but if it were held in a vice and hit sideways with a hammer, it would be found that it is not.

Activity 7.5.1

Experiencing stiffness and flexibility
A productive way to investigate stiffness and flexibility is to compare and contrast samples of familiar materials in ways related to the ways in which they are used.

Materials: (Bending): thick and thin samples of, e.g., wooden dowels, plastic covered garden wire, thin paper and stiff card, string and rope; (Tension): string and elastic bands, strips of paper, thin polythene and rubber sheet e.g. cut from kitchen gloves; (Compression): brick, plastic foam block, cork, plastic erasers, warm and cold modelling clay.

Stiffness in bending

- Hold up an object to see if it will bend under its own weight.
- If it will not, test the object by bending it in your hands (Fig. 7.2) but do not break it. Test each object with your hands different distances apart. Find out how the force needed to bend the object changes as you move your hands.

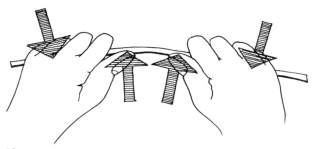

If an object bends easily when held at its ends, bend it again with your thumbs close together.

Figure 7.2   Comparing stiffness in bending

- Carry out the same tests with thin and thick objects made of the same material.
- What difference does the thickness of the object make? (Thicker objects require greater forces to bend them, i.e. they are stiffer and less flexible.)
- What effect does changing the position of your hands have? (The nearer the hands are together, the greater the force needed to bend the object.)

These simple tests emphasize that stiffness and flexibility are object-properties: the size and shape of the object and the way in which forces are applied to it all affect how large a force is required to bend it.

Stiffness in tension
An object which is rigid in tension will not extend when pulled. The most instructive objects to test are those which are very flexible in bending but which behave under tension in different ways. Simply pulling on string, elastic bands and strips of paper, polythene and rubber sheet will enable children to experience a range of materials with different stiffnesses in tension which can be related to the ways in which they are used.

Three points need to be made here. First, low stiffness in tension is not shown only by elastic materials (see Activity 7.6.1): polythene is also extensible. Secondly, rubber and polythene can be extended only to a limited degreee: if they are pulled enough, they will reach a point at which they cannot be extended any more (see also Activity 8.5.1). Thirdly, as in bending, stiffness in tension is affected by the thickness of the object. If a material can be extended at all, a greater force is required to extend a thick object made of it than a thin one. This is important when elastic bands are used in work on forces (see Activities 14.1.3, 14.2.1).

Stiffness in compression
Many materials such as brick and stone are useful because they are rigid or very stiff in compression and do not change shape when squashed. Others are useful because they can be squashed easily, for example plastic foam used in upholstery and packing. Children should attempt to squash both kinds of material with their their hands, and others which are of intermediate stiffness, such as corks and plastic erasers. It is also useful to compare cold modelling clay (kept in a refrigerator) with a similar, warmed sample, which can be squashed much more easily.

Activity 7.5.2

Stiffness and shape
Stiffness and flexibility depend on the size and shape of the object as well as the material of which it is made, so they are object properties (see Section 7.1). Children can investigate this by making a range of structures which have properties different from those of the material from which they were made; an activity which can be closely linked to the design and building of structures in technology.

Equipment and materials: A4 photocopier paper; glue; bamboo cane or dowel 30cm long; scissors.

- Roll a sheet of A4 paper lengthways to make a cylinder about 2cm in diameter. Glue down the outside edge, using a cane or dowel *inside* the cylinder so that you can press the edge down from the outside. Allow the glue to dry thoroughly.

- Hold a flat sheet of A4 paper by one short edge. Try to hold it horizontally.
? What happens? How stiff or flexible is the paper? (The paper is bent down by its own weight. It has very low stiffness in bending.)
- Hold up the cylinder you have made by one end.
? How is its stiffness in bending different from that of the flat sheet? (The cylinder is very much stiffer and does not bend at all under its own weight.)
- Assess the stiffness of your cylinder by bending it as shown in Fig. 7.2 until it collapses in the middle. This confirms that it is much stiffer than the sheet.
- After assessing stiffness in bending, use the same cylinder for another test. Mark and cut 3 or 4 cylinders each 2cm long from one end of your paper cylinder (they should be undamaged by the bending test).
- Put a 2cm cylinder upright on a table. Place the palm of your hand on top of the cylinder and push down, slowly increasing the force until it collapses.
? How is force being applied to the cylinder? What does this test estimate? (The cylinder is being compressed. The test estimates the stiffness of the cylinder in compression.)

These simple tests show how change in shape can bring about very significant changes in the stiffness of an object. They emphasize that stiffness is an object property and could be used as the starting-point for children's own inventions and tests.

7.6: Elasticity and plasticity

If an object distorted by forces returns to its original shape when released from those forces, it is said to be elastic. Gases are perfectly elastic; a property observed when investigating their compressibility (Activity 7.2.1). If an object retains its new form and does not move back at all when released, it is said to be plastic. The two properties are counterparts, elasticity being the positive property and plasticity the lack or absence of it. Unlike stiffness, elasticity is a material property and not dependent upon the size or shape of the object being observed (see Section 7.1).

Many common materials show a combination of both properties, but these can be investigated more effectively after children have observed the behaviour of materials which are almost perfectly elastic and plastic.

Activity 7.6.1

Observing elasticity and plasticity

Equipment and materials: Modelling-clay; selection of elastic bands, including some long, thick ones.

- By squashing, pulling, bending and twisting the warm clay and the elastic bands, find out what happens when you make them change shape and then let them go again.
? When the clay and bands are released, what happens? (The clay keeps its new shape and does not change at all; the bands always spring back into the same shape that they had before.)
- Repeat the observations with thinner and thicker bands, and with clay pieces of different shapes and sizes.

? Do size and shape make any difference to the way in which the materials behave when they are released? (No.)
? What does this tell you? (That elasticity and plasticity are material properties.)

These observations show first, that the bands are, as their name implies, almost perfectly elastic, while the clay shows no elasticity, i.e. it is an almost perfectly plastic material. Secondly, children should also notice that (unless the elastic bands are pulled so hard that they break) both materials show their characteristic properties no matter how forces are applied to them. This is significant because not all materials behave like this. In particular, there are many materials in common use which show elasticity up to a certain point but which, if distorted beyond that point, cannot regain their original shape.

Materials with limited elasticity

Materials: Strips about 2 × 15cm cut from a plastic drink bottle.

● Bend and twist a strip 2 × 15cm cut from a plastic drink bottle, to see how you can make it change shape, and what happens when you let it go. Start with small changes of shape: do not do anything extreme yet.
? What property does the material have when bent or twisted a little? (It is elastic.)
● Now try changing the shape of strips more drastically by folding, rolling or twisting them as much as you can.
? What happens when the plastic strip is released from this more extreme distortion? (It springs back a little, but partly keeps its new shape. If it is pulled gently out of this new shape and then released, it will spring back into it again. This is a good example of an irreversible physical change following a reversible one.)

The behaviour of the bottle-plastic can be related to a wide range of familiar sheet materials with similar properties which are very important technologically. Observations can usefully be made on paper, card and sheet metal (e.g. aluminium foil from food containers) when they are bent, rolled, creased and folded. Many activities and industrial processes, from paper sculpture to pressing sheet metal for vehicle bodies, depend on this combination of properties.

7.7: Strength

Strength is an object property (Section 7.1). The strength of an object is measured by finding the force which it can withstand before it breaks (fractures). Care must be taken to distinguish between the ability to resist deformation or distortion (stiffness) and the ability to withstand fracture (strength). If an object will not break under forces applied in a certain way, its strength cannot be tested in that way. For example, a piece of thin, flexible wire might be thought of as being weak (i.e. having low strength) in bending; but this is both incorrect and misleading. It certainly has low *stiffness* in bending, but unless it breaks when it is bent, we do not know anything about its bending-strength. Similarly, in Activity 7.5.4, short paper cylinders are compressed until they collapse; but although this distorts them they are not fractured, so it is their stiffness which is being tested, not their strength.

In addition to simple investigations into tensile, bending and compression-strength, an investigation into the tearing-strength of paper is suggested, which gives excellent opportunities for fair-testing and measurement.

Activity 7.7.1

Measuring and comparing strength

Approaches to investigating the strength of materials need to be varied depending on the kind of test being carried out. The tensile strength of threads and the bending strength of rods can be measured and compared fairly accurately, but compression strengths can be compared only in a very approximate way.

Tensile strength

Equipment and materials: Selection of threads and yarns, e.g. sewing threads, thin fishing-line, thin knitting yarns; thick dowel or cane; two desks or tables; 100g 'weights' (masses) with a hanger; pad of newspaper.

Safety note: In this and the next activity, no one should at any time put their hands under suspended 'weights' (masses), since if these fall unexpectedly they could cause pain or injury. Masses must be added to the load from the side, not from below, and should not exceed 10kg.

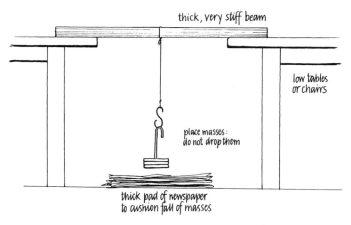

When measuring tensile strength of elastic materials, allow for extension when deciding where to place the beam.

Figure 7.3   Measuring the tensile strength of thread

- Tie a loop in either end of the thread to be tested. Hang the thread from the dowel as shown in Fig. 7.3.
- Add 'weights' (masses) 100g at a time until the thread breaks; record its breaking-strength in newtons (N): 100g has a weight of approximately 1N.
- Each mass must be added by placing it carefully on the hook or loop used for suspension, so that it does not fall off and shock-load the test-piece, or the test will not be fair and accurate. It is prudent to put a thick pad of newspaper under the test area to prevent falling masses denting the floor.

Notice that the tensile strength ('breaking-strain') of the thread is not related to the amount by which it extends before it breaks. Children often believe, intuitively and incorrectly, that inextensible threads are stronger than those which stretch under load.

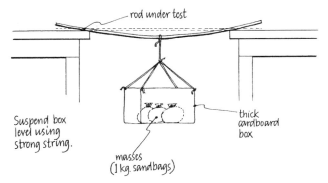

The span between the tables must be kept constant for all tests

Figure 7.4   Testing bending strength

Bending strength
The easiest way to carry out this kind of test is to use the test-rod as a beam, with masses ('weights') hung in a cardboard box from the centre of the span (Fig. 7.4). For this test to be a fair comparison of different objects, the same span has to be used throughout, so it is necessary to pre-test objects to find a span at which they can all be broken under a load which children can apply. It is suggested that loads of over 10kg (100N) should not be used.

Suitable materials for testing include thin wooden dowels, thin ,bamboo canes or split lengths of thicker ones. Plastic materials should not be used, since plastics which will fracture in this kind of test are likely to be brittle and sharp splinters may fly out at high speed when they break.

Equipment and materials: Rods to be tested (see note above); two tables of the same height; 10 × 1kg masses ('weights'), e.g. sand in plastic bags; thick cardboard box; string.

- Set up the rod to be tested as in Fig. 7.3, making sure that the string loop is exactly in the centre of the span and the box is hanging level.
- Add 1kg load so that the box stays level. Carry on loading the box, keeping it level, until the rod breaks. As it bends and fractures, notice *how* it breaks: this observation will be useful later.
- To find the bending-strength of the rod at the span used, mutiply the load in kg needed to fracture it by 10, to give its weight in newtons (N).

If rods of the same material but of different thicknesses can be tested, this will emphasize that strength, like stiffness, is an object property: the thicker the object, the greater the force needed to break it.

Compression strength
Testing materials for strength in compression is difficult because the materials in which this is an important property are so strong that any forces children can exert unaided will not crush them. Compression forces cannot be measured without specialized equipment, but children can learn a lot by using simple machines to squash weaker objects until they fracture.

The most effective and easily-controlled machines for this are a carpenter's G-cramp or a nut-cracker which compresses using a screw-thread in the same way. Either can be used to compress and fracture a range of objects, and children can at the same time observe the way in which the objects break to see how tough or brittle they are (see introduction to Section 7.8). Suitable materials include short pieces of chalk and wax crayon (which crumble); nuts (most of whose shells are fairly brittle and fracture cleanly); and short pieces (1–2cm long) of bamboo and softwoods. So that children can appreciate how strong these materials are in compression, and how large a force they can exert with the aid of a machine, they should attempt to crush a piece of wax crayon without using it. It can be done under a hard shoe-heel, but not with the hands, yet the cramp or nut-cracker crush it very easily.

Bamboo and wood are particularly interesting in tests of this kind. When compressing them along the grain (i.e. force exerted on the end-grain), their strength is so great that even with a G-cramp children may not be able to break a sample as small as a 1cm cube, whereas when compressed across the grain dry bamboo will usually shatter and softwoods will fail by being crushed.

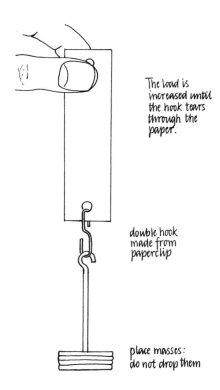

The load is increased until the hook tears through the paper.

double hook made from paperclip

place masses: do not drop them

Figure 7.5   Testing the tearing-strength of paper

Activity 7.7.2

The tearing-strength of paper
One very important property of paper is its tearing-strength; that is, its resistance to being torn apart. Older and very able pupils could be asked to devise and evaluate a test for this property; the procedure suggested here is one of many possibilities.

Equipment and materials: Strips 10 × 2.5cm of a variety of papers (e.g. paper towel, photocopier paper, cartridge paper, sugar paper, brown wrapping-paper); hole-puncher; plain wire paper-clip; 100g 'weights' (masses) with a hanger.

- Using a hole-puncher, make holes near either end of a paper strip. Make sure that the holes are in the middle of the strip and the same distance from either end.
- ? Why is it important that the holes are all the same distance from the sides and ends of the strip? (Because if they were not, this could affect the force needed to tear the paper, so the test would not be fair.)
- Unfold a plain wire paper-clip to form an 's'-shaped double hook. Hold the paper up and use the hook to hang a 100g mass from it, as shown in Fig. 7.5.
- Continue adding 100g masses by placing, not dropping them, until the hook tears through the paper and the masses fall. Write on the end of the paper the load (in grams) needed to tear it.
- ? Why is it important to place each mass on to the hanger and hook, and not drop it? (Dropping the mass would shock-load the paper in an uncontrollable way. This could cause the paper to tear under quite a small load.)
- Test the other end of the same piece of paper in the same way. Record the result on the paper.
- Test the other papers in the same way. When you have finished, convert your results to newtons: 100g weighs (exerts a downward force of) 1N.
- ? How reliable do you think this test is? (Each sample has been tested twice: if differences between the results from the same sample are only small, this indicates that the test is reliable. A more thorough evaluation would be to test five samples, giving ten readings, and again see by how much they varied.)
- ? How could this test be extended?

One simple way is by measuring wet-strength. When most papers are soaked in water their tearing-strength is reduced, and an important test in paper technology is to measure this reduction. This could be done in the present context by punching holes in sample strips, soaking them for an hour, then testing them as before and comparing the results.

7.8: Brittleness and toughness

Brittleness and toughness are properties which relate to the way in which objects fracture, so they are quite distinct from strength, which measures the force needed to cause fracture. They are material properties, which depend on the way in which cracks and fractures spread through materials. If a small fracture forms and spreads through a material very easily, the object will break apart completely with very little extra force being applied. Often this will happen suddenly, with no warning and characteristically the fractured faces will be 'clean' and sharp-edged. Glass and ceramics are examples of hard materials which break in this all-or-nothing kind of way, and which are said to have the property of brittleness.

The counterpart of brittleness is toughness. In a tough material, cracks spread slowly and even then only when additional force is applied. If a tough material begins to fracture and the force on it is released, it does not break any further. Cardboard, good quality paper, polythene, many fabrics and some woods are examples of tough materials in which fractures tend to be irregular, with rough edges.

Attention is focused here on very simple testing of materials in bending and tension. Suggestions for observing the fracture of materials under compression are found as part of Activity 7.7.1.

Activity 7.8.1

Observing brittleness and toughness

Children can observe brittleness and toughness in bending and tension by bending and pulling carefully selected materials until they fracture. In all cases the force applied should be increased slowly, with attention being concentrated on the way the fracture occurs and the appearance of the fracture-faces. Good materials to use are:

- *brittle in bending*: dry pasta of any shape; thin, transparent plastic cups;
- *tough in bending*: thin sticks or canes (split bamboo smoothed to remove splinters is especially good);
- *brittle in tension*: 'cellophane' sheet or 'sellotape';
- *tough in tension*: paper, card and polythene.

When testing the sheet materials in tension, cut them into strips, make a tiny cut in one long edge and pull this edge apart. In all cases, children should observe:

- whether the material fractures suddenly or gradually;
- if, once the fracture has begun, a large or small force is needed to make it continue;
- whether the edges and faces of the fracture are ragged or 'clean' and smooth.

7.9: Linking properties of materials to their uses

Investigating the properties of materials shows one of the important two-way relationships between science and technology. In many enterprises, scientific investigation provides the knowledge and understanding necessary for effective design and use of materials; while knowledge gained from practical experience feeds back to increase scientific insight. These issues are taken up again in the context of the ways in which we obtain and make materials (Section 10.1) and how some of these are used in specific activities (Section 10.2).

As with much scientific knowledge, an effective way to consolidate and reinforce learning about materials and their properties is to use it in practical problem-solving. In order to be effective this must involve materials with which children are familiar and whose properties they can assess, used in the context of a problem they can readily understand. An interesting (and even entertaining) group of problems centres around the protection of a fragile object from mechanical shock and breakage. Some of the background to this in terms of forces is discussed in Activity 14.2.3. Depending on the age and ability of the children, problems can be presented in a more directed or a more open-ended way.

An example of a more directed approach would be to ask children to select materials for packing and sending a fragile, valuable object by parcel-post. The actual objects used could be old pottery mugs which will be no loss if they do not survive! The children have to discuss what tests their parcels will have to undergo, e.g. being dropped from a height of 2m, rolled downstairs, thrown into a corner and left out in the rain. Working in teams, they have to test and select packing materials, pack the fragile object (which will be safer in a polythene bag if it does break), make up the parcel, test it and evaluate the results.

An example of a more open-ended approach, which could be worked on within a strict time-limit, would be to ask the children to devise and make some means of dropping an egg from 1m on to the floor without breaking it, and then to discuss the results in terms of the properties of the materials they have used.

8

Explaining Physical Changes

In order to explain why many materials behave in the ways they do it is necessary to understand something of atomic theory, at least in a very simple form (*8.1). Simple investigations can help in the development of such an understanding and are likely to be particularly useful for older and more able pupils. Those suggested here are of two kinds: making models of materials, and observing more closely some materials and changes which may already be familiar. The aim in both is similar: to show how the properties of materials and the changes they undergo depend on the behaviour of atoms and molecules.

8.2–8.4: Explaining the properties of solids, liquids and gases

Models can be effective in helping to explain and understand the basic properties of the three states of matter: solids, liquids and gases, even though modelling a gas is too complex to undertake at primary level.

Using sand to model molecules

A useful material to model molecules in solids and liquids is fine, washed silver-sand. As in all such exercises it is important to appreciate the scale of the model. In modelling the Solar System, for example (Activity 18.1.1), we use objects which are five thousand million times smaller than the real Sun and planets. In using sand-grains as models of molecules, we go to the other extreme and use objects (small sand-grains) each of which is between 100 000 and 200 000 times *bigger* than an actual molecule.

In Activity 6.1.2, materials such as sand, which are made up of small solid particles, are investigated. These materials can be poured rather as a liquid can (though they are quite different in other ways) because their grains can slide or roll past one another. This gives us a starting-point for a model of a solid. The scientific view is that solids behave as they do because the atoms or molecules which make them up cannot move past each other: they are bonded together. If we use sand-grains as models of molecules, and can make the individual grains bond together, it should be possible to make sand behave much more like a solid mass.

Activity 8.2.1

Modelling a solid

Equipment and materials: Dry, fine silver-sand; teaspoon; water; plastic tray or shallow container; sheet of paper.

- Measure six level teaspoonfuls of dry sand on to a tray or shallow container. Tilt the container gently and watch the sand move. Notice how it can 'flow' because the grains can move over each other.
- Add one spoonful of water, mix the sand to a paste and tilt the tray again.
- ? How has the behaviour of the sand changed? (It no longer 'flows' and the grains cannot move past one another.)

What has happened is that the water is acting like a weak glue, bonding the sand-grains together; an effect which is also seen in soils (Activity 11.10.1). In a solid material the atoms and molecules are bonded together, not by glue or water, but by forces of attraction acting between them. In the model, the water is acting like these forces.

- Mould the sand paste between your fingers to make as tall and pointed a cone as you can.
- Pour some dry sand on to a piece of paper. Try to mould it into a cone.
- ? Why can you not mould dry sand into a tall cone? (Because the grains will not bond together.)
- ? Which behaves more like a solid in keeping its shape: dry sand or sand-paste, and why? (Sand-paste behaves more like a solid, because its particles are bonded together.)

This simple model makes the point that solids can 'keep their shape' only because their molecules are bonded together.

- Tilt the tray with the sand-cone on it. Pour some water into it, then tilt the tray back and forth so that the water washes round the base of the cone.
- ? What happens? (The cone softens, appears to melt, and collapses.)
- ? Why does this happen? (Because the extra water makes it possible for the sand-grains to move apart.)

This models what happens when a solid softens and melts (Activities 6.2.1 and 6.2.2), but it is important to emphasize that this is a model: making a solution or suspension does not involve melting, and neither does the collapse of the sand-cone. In the model, the 'glue' effect of a thin layer of water round each sand-grain is lost as the extra water is added, so the bonding between the sand-grains is weakened. As a solid material is heated, thermal energy (*12.2) makes the atoms and molecules move more and more violently so that the bonds between them may be weakened (so that the solid softens) and are finally broken, so that it melts.

Activity 8.2.2

Modelling a liquid

Equipment and materials: As above, but add some clear plastic jars (e.g. cut-down drink bottles).

- Put some of the wet sand-paste into a plastic jar. Add water until, when the jar is still, there is a layer of water on top of the sand.

- Tilt the jar and watch the mixture.
? Does this mixture behave like a liquid? (No: the sand layer at the bottom is a solid sediment.)

To make this mixture into a model of a liquid we have to input some energy, to agitate the sand-grains which are our model molecules. In a melting solid the energy is thermal energy (*12.2), which makes the molecules move so violently that they cease to be bonded together and become a liquid. We can make the sand-water mixture 'melt' by shaking or vibrating it, supplying kinetic energy to keep the sand-grains suspended and moving independently of one another.

- Shake and swirl the sand-water mixture round the jar, tilting it at the same time and watching the behaviour of the mixture.
? While it is being shaken, does the mixture behave as a solid or as a liquid? (It behaves as a liquid.)
? What happens when you stop shaking the mixture? (The sand settles out and behaves as a solid again.)

The model is unlike a liquid in that we have to keep up a continuous input of energy in order to prevent the sand-grains settling out. In contrast, as long as a liquid does not cool down by transferring thermal energy to its environment, it will stay liquid for ever.

Children may be interested to know that solid-liquid models of this kind are of great importance in research into some kinds of earthquake damage. The vibration from an earthquake can liquefy wet sediments just as shaking liquefies the sand-water mixture in the jar, so that roads and buildings collapse and sink into the ground.

Using the models to think about gases
Although we cannot make a model of a gas, our experience of modelling solids and liquids can help us to imagine what it would be like. If a liquid is heated until it boils, its atoms or molecules move so fast that they break away from each other entirely and become a gas.

If we could use sand-grains as models of molecules, a model of a gas would be rather like a violent sand-storm, with the grains suspended in air, moving very fast and colliding violently with each other. This would model what we cannot model: the space between the molecules of gases, which explains their unique property of compressibility (see Section 7.2). Because the molecules or atoms making up solids and liquids are in contact with one another, no force that we can exert can compress them into a smaller space, but because the molecules of a gas have space between them, they can be squashed into a smaller volume.

Although we cannot see the molecules of a gas moving, nor even make a good model of them, we can see their effects. When a balloon is inflated, the force which stretches it is exerted by the molecules of the air squashed inside, bombarding the rubber. As well as seeing what air molecules do, we can even hear them. If we sit in what seems to be total silence, there is always a faint, high-pitched hiss in our ears. This is the sound of air molecules bombarding the ear-drums. If a large sea-shell is held up to the ear in very quiet conditions, the sound like the breaking of distant waves is the same sound, amplified by the shell.

8.5: Explaining the properties of some flexible materials

When unbalanced forces are applied to flexible materials they change shape and show a range of properties such as stiffness, elasticity and strength (see Chapter 7). These mechanical properties can be understood much more clearly when a little is known of the molecular structure of the materials in relation to the forces being applied to them. The next activity assumes that children are already familiar with investigations of the stiffness, flexibility, elasticity and strength of materials (Activities 7.5.1, 7.6.1, 7.7.1).

Activity 8.5.1

A closer look at materials in tension and bending
The materials whose behaviour children can most readily interpret in terms of molecular structure are those with long-chain molecules (polymers, *8.5) when they are under tension. Examples include elastic bands, cotton string and very thin pieces of wood, all of which behave differently in ways which reflect, and can be explained in terms of, their molecular structure.

Materials: Elastic bands, cotton string and thin slivers cut from a bamboo cane, all about the same thickness. Smooth the cane slivers with fine sandpaper to remove sharp edges.

When pulled, cotton string and thin pieces of cane behave in similar ways. Neither can be made longer by pulling it, but if either is pulled hard enough it will simply break. This is because both are fibrous materials, made up mostly of cellulose, whose long, straight-chain molecules run more or less along the length of the fibre. Because they are straight these molecular chains cannot stretch, and large forces are needed to break them, so both materials are inextensible with high tensile strength.

    In bending, however, they behave differently. The cotton string is very flexible, whereas the cane is stiffer and springy (elastic). This is because the cellulose molecules of the cotton fibres are only weakly bound (cross-bonded) to those around them, so that each fibre and the whole mass can be bent by a very small force. In bamboo the cellulose molecules and fibres are strongly cross-bonded, by materials which give the cane and other woods their brown colour (pure cellulose is white). The result is that these materials are both stiffer and elastic: much larger forces are needed to bend them and they spring back when released.

    Elastic bands, like string, have low stiffness in bending (are very flexible) because their long-chain molecules are only weakly bonded to each other. In tension, however, they behave quite differently because their molecular chains are not straight, but tangled up. When pulled, they start to straighten out, so the rubber becomes longer when only a small force is applied to it, and its length increases as a greater pulling force is exerted. If this force is released the molecules and the band return to their original shape: the material is elastic.

    If an elastic band is pulled hard enough, a point is reached at which it will not stretch any more (its elastic limit). At this point, all the long-chain molecules are stretched out straight, with the result that the rubber now behaves much more like string. It will not extend any more, but if pulled hard enough it will break as the forces holding the molecular chains together are overcome and they snap.

8.6: Crystals

The structure of solid materials is governed by the ways in which they bond together, which on an atomic scale is often very orderly. We become aware of this order when a solid object big enough for us to see has an orderly arrangement of atoms or molecules throughout its volume: we call such objects crystals. Crystals are formed by many materials, including water, all metals and most minerals; either when molten material cools and freezes, as in the formation of ice (Activity 6.2.1) and rocks such as granite, or when solutes come out of solution as the solvent evaporates (see Activity 6.5.2).

Children can observe crystals with a hand-lens in a solution of salt as water evaporates from it; but if a microscope is available they can see the process in a much more dynamic way. Suitable materials include salt (sodium chloride), copper (II) sulphate and alum (potassium aluminium sulphate). It is worth making special solutions, dissolving as much solid as possible in a small volume of hot water, filtering the solutions (essential if table-salt is used) and storing them in small bottles.

To observe crystals forming, put one drop of solution on to a glass micro-slide, spread it into a thin layer and watch it under about x40 magnification. Crystals usually begin to form at the edges and spread inwards, often at high speed. What is remarkable is to observe the high degree of order in the crystals as they form. This comes about because individual molecules can bond on to the growing solid structure only in particular ways and directions, so once it has begun to form, the structure at the molecular level is perfectly repetitive, the structure of the individual crystal is perfectly ordered and we see a beautiful geometric solid with flat faces, straight edges and sharp corners.

9

Chemical Changes

9.1: The nature of chemical change

Chemical changes result in the formation of kinds of material which were not present before the changes occurred. This is in contrast to physical changes which, however much they may transform the appearance of a substance, do not change what kind of substance it is (see Chapter 6 and, especially, Activity 6.5.2).

There is no simple, straightforward way by which chemical and physical changes can be distinguished. In particular it is important to avoid any suggestion that chemical changes are irreversible, while physical changes are reversible. The kind of change which is occurring has no connection at all with whether it is reversible: all that teachers (at any level) can do is to find out whether particular changes do or do not involve the formation of different kinds of material and introduce them to children accordingly.

The chemical changes which affect children's lives most profoundly are those upon which all life depends: the processes of respiration (*3.6) and photosynthesis (*4.4). These are much too complex to be studied in detail at primary level, but other kinds of chemical change, which also have a direct relevance to children's lives, can be investigated very productively. It is suggested here that attention should be focused on two groups of chemical change: one associated with some simple forms of cooking; the other with chemical reactions involving oxygen. Before looking at either in any detail, however, it is necessary first to introduce and begin development of the concept of chemical change in contrast to physical change.

Activity 9.1.1

Introducing the idea of chemical change
An effective way to introduce the idea of chemical change is to carry out a modified version of Activity 10.1.2, which is concerned with the sources of materials. In the present context, attention needs to be focused on the kinds of change which are undergone by raw materials in the production of familiar refined materials and artefacts. To start with, a selection should be made in which only one refined material or artefact is made by a process involving chemical change: all the others should be made by way of physical changes only. Other artefacts produced by

chemical change can be introduced later. An introductory selection which has proved successful is:

– a split log of wood and a carved or turned artefact;
– raw fleece or cotton and an (undyed) knitted garment;
– lump of granite and crushed, sieved roadstone;
– grain and (wholemeal) flour milled from it;
– rock-salt and refined salt;
– red clay and (unglazed) pot, pipe or brick.

The critical question here is, which of the raw materials was changed into a different substance in the making of the product? Children usually guess correctly that it is the clay which, when fired into pottery, becomes a kind of material which was not there before. Firing of clay is therefore a chemical change. Making all the other products involves only physical changes (see Activity 10.1.1).

One other product of chemical change which could usefully be introduced at this point is cheese, made from milk. Our sense of taste is one way we have of detecting chemicals in our environment, and we can distinguish between a very large number of them, especially when they have to do with food. Both cheese and milk should be tasted if possible, since their different flavours show that they contain different chemicals, so the nature of the raw material has been changed in making the end-product (contrast Activity 6.5.2). This example can also be used to introduce the other examples of chemical changes related to food investigated in Section 9.2.

9.2: Chemical changes in cooking and food

The aim of food preparation is to make food more palatable and attractive, more digestible, or both. Most societies and cultures have since prehistoric times eaten food which is cooked; a process which relies at least in part on changing raw materials by heating them. Not all food chemicals are changed by heating. Fats and carbohydrates are often either unchanged or changed only in a physical way, for example the swelling and softening of starch in rice and pasta as it is cooked in boiling water. Most of the interesting chemical changes in cooking come about because proteins are changed chemically (and irreversibly) by heating. Children can see this happening by cooking egg-white (Activity 9.2.1) and can investigate more complex examples by baking cakes and bread (Activities 9.2.2 and 9.2.3). They can also observe some of the many chemical changes brought about in food by microbes (Activity 9.2.4).

Activity 9.2.1

Cooking egg-white
When heated, the proteins in raw food materials become changed chemically and irreversibly by a process known as coagulation. Egg-white is a solution of protein in water. When cooked, the large complex protein molecules collapse, contract and solidify, clinging together in a mass. The change in this case is very easy to detect because, as the protein coagulates, the transparent pale yellow solution becomes an opaque white solid. This change will occur only above a critical temperature.

Equipment and materials: Egg; small and large plastic bowls; teaspoon and long-handled cooking spoon; water and the means to heat it safely (preferably a saucepan and hot-plate with heating control); thermometer; aluminium cooking-foil; oven glove; felt-tip pen about 2cm in diameter; scissors; teaspoon.

Safety note: This activity should be closely supervised and water should be heated only in appliances which cannot be upset accidentally. To avoid risk of scalding, children should put samples into hot water and retrieve them only using a long-handled spoon and wearing an oven-glove.

- Cut 4cm squares of cooking-foil. Fold these around the end of a thick felt-tip pen and cut their edges level, to make small cylindrical containers (at least 6 will be needed).
- Break an egg into a small plastic bowl; be careful not to break the yolk.
- Heat water on a hot-plate until it is at 80°C; or boil water in a kettle and mix in a bowl with cold water to the same temperature.
- Using a teaspoon, put a little egg-white into a foil container. Place this on a long spoon and, wearing an oven-glove, float it carefully on the hot water. Observe any changes.
- ? How does the appearance of the egg-white change? (It becomes white and opaque.)

Egg-white is protein, a kind of food chemical, dissolved in water. The change when it cooks is called coagulation of the protein. It is a chemical change brought about by heating and is irreversible.

- Put a larger quantity of egg-white into another container, float it as before, keep the water at 80°C and watch how the change progresses.
- ? How does the change progress through the liquid egg-white? (It starts on the outside and moves inwards.)
- ? Why does this happen? (The change is brought about by heating: the egg-white which changes first is nearest the metal foil and so is heated most strongly.)
- Stop heating the water and allow it to cool down, mixing in cold water if necessary. At each 5°C step, test a small sample of egg-white to see if it still cooks. This should enable you to find out the lowest temperature at which this chemical change will occur.

The lowest temperature at which egg-white will coagulate is between 55°C and 60°C. This is significant, because when hot water or fat falls on the skin, it injures us by 'cooking' the proteins of the skin-cells, so injuring or killing them. This observation shows that water far below its boiling-point can cause changes of this kind and can therefore cause scalding to tender skin.

- Cook two similar samples of egg-white at 80°C, one for one minute and the other for six minutes. When they have cooled, undo the foil containers and compare their textures.
- ? What difference do you notice? (The timing may need to be varied, depending on the freshness of the egg, but the objective is to have one sample cooked until it is firm, while the other is still semi-liquid.)
- ? What does this difference show? (That this chemical change is progessive: the longer a protein is cooked the firmer it will become, until it is fully coagulated. An egg boiled until its protein is fully coagulated is said to be 'hard-boiled'.)

Sponge cakes and bread

Sponge cakes and bread both have a distinctive porous, springy texture. Before cooking both are doughs: mixtures in the form of a semi-liquid paste. During cooking, two processes of chemical change occur at the same time: thousands of bubbles of carbon dioxide gas are formed, inflating the cooking mixture, whose proteins are being coagulated into the elastic 'skeleton' which gives well-baked bread and sponge-cakes their springy properties. These bubbles are enlarged by steam from water in the mixture. From the point of view of children's investigations of chemical change, the twofold focus of interest in both kinds of baking is the source of the protein and the way the carbon dioxide is produced.

Activity 9.2.2

Investigating sponge-cakes

Equipment and materials: Instructions, ingredients and equipment for mixing and baking plain Victoria sponge-cakes (usually using self-raising flour); plain flour; baking powder; two small plastic bowls; teaspoon; water and the means to heat it safely; dropper; sharp kitchen-knife.

Safety note: Since children are to eat the cakes they bake, this investigation should be carried out under hygienic conditions with equipment and utensils which are used **only** for the preparation of food. Because the recipe contains eggs, children should not taste the uncooked dough.

- Put a teaspoonful of plain flour into a small plastic bowl. Adding water a few drops at a time, mix the flour into a small ball of dough; leave this to stand for a few minutes.
- Squeeze and roll the dough into a long, thin cylinder, Gently pull or twist the dough a few times, watching what happens when you release it.
- ? What property does the dough have? (When pulled or twisted a little and released, the dough springs back, showing that it is slightly elastic.)

The elasticity of the dough is caused by the proteins (gluten) in the flour taking up water: this is a physical change.

- Heat some water until it boils, then allow it to cool slightly. Put a teaspoonful of baking-powder into another small plastic basin and pour some very hot water on to it.
- ? What happens? (The mixture fizzes and produces a lot of bubbles of colourless gas.)

The gas is carbon dioxide. There was no gas in the powder or the hot water, so it is a different material produced by a chemical change when they are mixed. During baking, the baking-powder mixed with flour and other ingredients releases bubbles of carbon-dioxide into the cooking mixture (dough).

- Mix and bake your Victoria sponge mixture in the form of small cakes. (Recipes usually call for self-raising flour, which is flour which has baking-powder mixed with it ready for use.)
- When the cakes are cool, cut one open with a sharp knife. Notice its porous, spongy texture. Squeeze the cake gently and let it go: notice that it is elastic.

? What are the main changes in the dough as it cooks? (It turns from a semi-liquid paste to a spongy, porous solid.)

The change from semi-liquid to solid is largely the result of chemical changes as the proteins from the flour and eggs are heated and coagulated. The bubbles are carbon dioxide produced by the baking-powder: they inflate the cooking mixture.

? When the baking-powder was put into hot water, the bubbles of carbon dioxide produced rose to the surface and escaped. Why do the bubbles stay in the cooking dough? (They are trapped by the mixture, which is thick, sticky and elastic because it contains proteins which are being made solid by coagulation.)

Activity 9.2.3

Investigating bread
If possible, children should make and bake their own bread. Even if this is not possible, a good deal can be learned from cutting open a ready-made loaf. Bread from a craft bakery or made in a home bread-making machine will be more informative than that made by mass-produced steam-baking. When making bread it is important to use 'strong' bread flour and to make sure that the dough is prepared and baked in a way appropriate for the kind of yeast being used. Three kinds are commonly available: fresh, dried and 'instant' or 'easy-blend'; all of which require different treatments.

Equipment and materials: Instructions, ingredients and equipment for mixing and baking a loaf of bread; 'strong' bread flour; small plastic bowl; teaspoon; water; dropper; bread-knife and board.

Safety note: Please see the previous activity. Children can taste bread dough because it contains no eggs.

• Put a teaspoonful of 'strong' bread flour into a small plastic basin. Adding water a few drops at a time, mix it to a soft dough; leave this to stand for a few minutes.
• Squeeze and roll the dough in your fingers to form a long, thin cylinder. Squash, twist and pull the dough a little, watching what happens when you release it.
? What property does the dough have? (It is elastic.)

If plain flour is available, make a dough sample in the same way for comparison. The 'strong' flour dough is more elastic than that made with plain flour, because it has a higher protein (gluten) content.

• Make and bake a loaf of bread. Before it is baked, take a small piece of dough, put it into a plastic basin and keep it in a refrigerator.
• When the baked bread has cooled, cut it open and look at its texture: it is spongy and, if you pull and release it, elastic.

Like the Victoria sponge-cakes (Activity 9.2.2), the bread is a moderately elastic porous solid because the cooking dough has been inflated by bubbles of carbon dioxide and proteins in the wheat flour have been coagulated. Both of these are the result of chemical changes.

? Taste the bread and the dough kept in the refrigerator. Does they taste the same as, or different from, each other? What does this tell you? (They taste very

different. This shows that they contains different chemicals, i.e. different kinds of material, which in turn shows that baking must bring about chemical changes; see also Activity 3.3.1.)
? No baking-powder is used in making this bread. Where does the carbon dioxide gas come from? (It is made by the yeast.)

Yeast is a living organism (a microscopic fungus) which in the dried forms is dormant (see Activity 2.2.3). It feeds on sugar and starch, producing carbon dioxide as a waste product of its respiration (*3.6). The structure of the bread shows how the yeast is affected by the cooking process.

● Look at the sizes of the gas-bubbles in different parts of the cut surface of the bread.
? Where are the gas-bubbles largest, and where smallest? (They are largest in the middle of the loaf; smallest in the crust.)
? Why are the bubbles so small in the crust? (Because that part of the dough was heated most strongly early in the baking, so the yeast in it was killed off before it could make a lot of gas.)
? Where in the loaf did the yeast carry on producing carbon dioxide longest, and why? (In the middle, because the dough there was insulated [*12.3] by the bread around it and so was heated up more slowly.)

As a loaf of bread is baked, the inside keeps growing in size, stretching the outer layer which has already begun to form a crust. One result is that the loaf rises up in its tin as it is baked (don't fill tins with dough!); another is that the top crust is often split by the force from inside it, rather as the bark of a tree is.

Activity 9.2.4

Food and microbes
Micro-organisms (*5.3) affect the production, storage and consumption of food by humans in a very wide variety of ways (*9.2), some of which are helpful and others destructive.

Yogurt
If they have made bread, children have already used one helpful micro-organism: yeast. A group of useful bacteria whose action can easily be investigated are those which coagulate milk-protein to make yogurt. They change the protein chemically and irreversibly, not by heating it but by producing acids. Coagulation of milk protein by acid can be seen very easily by adding a few drops of lemon-juice to a little milk in a glass: the protein and fats separate as they curdle and solidify. Again this is an irreversible chemical change.

Yogurt can be made in school using home yogurt-makers which are supplied with recipes and instructions. Yogurt-making bacteria coagulate milk proteins more gently than lemon-juice, so that the mixture thickens but does not separate. These bacteria flourish in rather unusual conditions: much warmer (41°C) and more acidic than most bacteria will tolerate. Children can test the acidity of milk and yogurt, using universal indicator test-papers available from pharmacies and photographic dealers. There will be fall from pH7 (neutral) to about pH5 (distinctly acidic) during the process, which is also detectable in the sharp, slightly sour taste of the yogurt. This is another example of our sense of taste being able to detect the results of chemical change.

Food spoilage
The staling and spoilage of food by bacteria and other microbes is an aspect, particularly important to human commerce and health, of the much wider processes of decay and recycling in the ecosystem (see Section 5.8). Activity 5.3.1 includes the safe observation in the classroom of food decay by microbes.

9.3: Reactions with oxygen

One of the most fundamental ways in which living things depend on each other for survival is the balance between the consumption of oxygen during respiration and its production by plants during photosynthesis (*5.8). The oxygen in the Earth's atmosphere is involved in a very wide variety of chemical changes, some natural and others brought about by human activity. Many of these affect children's lives directly and so have immediate relevance to them. It is suggested that two of these can usefully be investigated in some detail: burning and rusting.

9.4: Burning

Burning is the general term for a very large variety of chemical changes, all of which are irreversible and result in transfer of chemical-potential energy to the environment as thermal and light energy (*12.2; see also Activity 4.4.2). All burning requires three factors in order to occur and continue: fuel, oxygen from the atmosphere and a high temperature: the so-called 'triangle of fire'. If any of these is absent, burning cannot be started and will stop if it is in progress.

Activity 9.4.1

Observing the burning of a candle
The safest, most convenient and informative example of burning for children to study is an ordinary candle, whose fuel is wax.

Equipment and materials: Candle, preferably one which has been lit before and has burned down a little; matches; shallow metal container (e.g. biscuit tin or foil food-tray); dry silver-sand; strip of thick aluminium foil at least 8cm long; a piece of thin aluminium cooking-foil 15 × 7cm.

Safety note: This activity must be closely supervised. Long hair should be tied back and loose clothing secured.

- Put a layer of dry sand 2cm deep into a shallow metal container; place a candle upright in the sand with its base resting on the metal.
- Light the candle with a match. Watch the flame and the base of the wick carefully during the two or three minutes after lighting it.
- ? How does the size of the flame change? (It usually starts quite large, becomes smaller and then larger again.)
- ? What happens at the base of the wick? (Wax melts and forms a pool of liquid.)

When the candle is lit, the match flame heats and vaporizes solid wax in the wick, then ignites it. The flame then becomes smaller as the fuel in the wick is burnt, but at the same time it heats the wax at the base of the wick and melts it. Liquid wax moves up the porous wick (see Activity 6.6.1), is heated by the flame, vaporized and finally burnt. As this sequence is established the flame becomes bigger again.

Putting a candle out safely
Lighting a candle shows that all three factors in the 'triangle of fire' are needed for the wax to be ignited. Once burning has begun it usually continues until all the fuel has been consumed, but it can be stopped. Many people stop candles burning by blowing the flame out, but this is dangerous: it usually scatters hot wax and may cause clothing or hair to be ignited. A more effective and much safer method is to use a candle-snuffer.

• Wrap a strip of thin aluminium cooking-foil 7 × 15cm round the end of your index finger. Twist the foil so that it forms a small, deep cup with a 'tail'. Bend the 'tail' sideways to make a handle (Fig. 9.1).

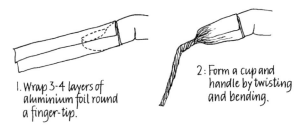

1. Wrap 3-4 layers of aluminium foil round a finger-tip.

2: Form a cup and handle by twisting and bending.

Figure 9.1   Making a candle-snuffer

• Put the cup of the snuffer over the flame: it will go out. (It can be useful to have a second candle burning to save on matches!)
• Experiment with the snuffer, re-lighting the candle and putting it out a few times. Notice that it is not necessary to seal the wick off from the air entirely to put the flame out.

When the snuffer is over the flame, the wick is quickly surrounded by air from which all the oxygen has been removed by burning, so the process cannot continue and the flame goes out, though the wick may continue to smoulder and give off smelly smoke.

What is burning (or, the world's smallest explosion)?
The candle-snuffer is not only useful for putting out the candle safely. Older and more able pupils can use it to find out more about what is burning in the candle-flame.

• Light your candle and let it burn until the flame is steady. Hold a match in one hand and the candle-snuffer in the other.
• Light the match from the candle, then snuff the candle out. Remove the snuffer and immediately move the lighted match towards the wick, watching what happens very carefully. Repeat this a few times till you are sure.

? How does the candle re-light? (It re-lights with a little 'pop' *before the flame from the match touches the wick*.)

This happens because, after the flame has been extinguished, the hot wick is still giving off wax vapour, which is invisible and mixes with the air.The match-flame ignites the vapour-air mixture without touching the wick, showing that the actual fuel for the candle-flame is wax vapour. The 'pop' as the vapour-air mixture ignites is actually a tiny explosion: maybe the smallest explosion in the world!

The structure of a candle-flame

• Look carefully at the candle-flame. It is made up of three zones (Fig. 9.2).

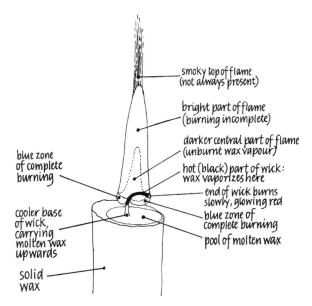

Figure 9.2   A burning candle

The small blue zone at the base has the greatest supply of oxygen and in it the burning is very fast and complete. The dark zone in the middle of the flame is invisible wax vapour which is not burning yet and so does not give out any light. The upper part of the flame is luminous: a strong light source. In this zone there is not enough oxygen to burn the vaporized wax as rapidly as at the base of the flame, so it burns in two stages.

• Hold a strip of *thick* aluminium foil in the bright orange part of the flame for two seconds (not longer), then look at it.
? What has been deposited on the metal? (A layer of soot.)

The first stage of burning produces very small solid particles of soot (carbon). These then burn, glowing as they do so and emitting the orange light we see. Putting the cold metal into this part of the flame hinders the second part of the burning process, causing some of these carbon particles to be deposited rather than being burnt. This is called incomplete burning. Incomplete burning of fuels such as coal, diesel oil and petrol in badly-maintained furnaces and engines produces very small, solid soot particles in the air which are a major cause of air-pollution (see Activity 5.9.1).

9.5: Rusting of iron and steel

Rusting of iron and steel (*9.5) is a very destructive example of metal corrosion which causes enormous amounts of damage and dilapidation every year to machines and installations made of iron and steel (*10.2). Rusting is a complex, irreversible chemical change in which iron metal is combined with oxygen from the air in the presence of water to form a flaky, red-brown material (rust) which chemically is similar to the ore from which much iron is produced by smelting (*10.2).

Activity 9.5.1

Investigating the conditions under which rusting occurs
This investigation is a useful exercise in experimental design and careful execution, as well as having obvious relevance to children's own lives through the need to anticipate and prevent the occurrence of rusting. Having introduced and discussed the scientific view that both oxygen and water are needed for rusting to occur, older and more able pupils may be able to devise and design their own investigation.

Equipment and materials: 12 steel nails; fine abrasive paper; 6 small, dry plastic drink bottles; water and the means to heat it safely; vegetable (cooking) oil; thread; paper towel; grease or petroleum jelly (e.g. 'Vaseline'); adhesive paper labels.

- Clean 12 steel nails with fine abrasive paper until they are bright and shiny.
- Set up 6 test-chambers using small plastic bottles. Put two cleaned nails into each, then set them up as in the following list. Label each bottle as shown in italics:
  - *air and water*: add a little water but not enough to cover the nails completely.
  - *air only*: leave the nails in dry air.
  - *water only*: boil water for 1 minute; leave it to cool for 1 minute, then pour enough into the bottle to cover the nails completely. Immediately add a layer of vegetable (cooking) oil to seal off the hot water and nails from the air.
  - *humid air*: drop water on to a piece of paper towel until it is wet but not dripping. Tie it on to a piece of thread and hang it in the bottle; secure the thread by screwing the top on the bottle.
  - *tap-water*: cover the nails completely with tap-water.
  - *grease*: cover the nails completely with a layer of grease or petroleum jelly, then half-cover them with water.
- Predict the result in each trial, and give a reason for each prediction.
- Look at the bottles every day for a week, then take the nails out, examine them and record how much they have rusted. Compare the results with your predictions.

The expected results and their significance are as follows:

- *air and water*: the nails will rust because both air and water are present.
- *air only*: there is no rusting because there is no water.

– *water only*: there is no rusting because there is no air. Boiling removed dissolved air from the water and the oil layer kept it sealed.
– *humid*: the nails rust because water evaporates into the air from the wet paper and droplets condense on the nails from the humid air.
– *tap-water*: the nails rust because tap-water contains dissolved air.
– *grease*: there is no rusting because the grease-layer protects the metal from both water and air.

This quite detailed and structured investigation can be used as the basis for a discussion, or further work in technology on the problems of rust and its prevention. It is also useful to compare and contrast rusting and burning (*9.5).

10

Obtaining and Making Materials

Investigating the materials which are used in familiar human activities and artefacts provides an opportunity for children to use, consolidate and extend what they have learned about the properties of materials and ways of changing them (Chapters 6–9). It should also make it possible for them to exploit the close links between science, technology and other parts of the curriculum.

In order to work effectively in this area it is necessary to select a group of materials which have particular relevance to children's lives, and whose origins and properties they can understand (see Section 10.2), but as an introduction it is helpful to develop some basic ideas about the origins of materials and the processes used to change them so that their usefulness is increased.

10.1: Natural and man-made materials and objects

In finding out and communicating about the ways in which commonly-used materials are made and obtained, it is usual to distinguish the natural from the man-made; but in order to do this clearly it is necessary also to distinguish between materials and objects shaped or made from them (see also Section 7.1). For example, wool is a natural material, but woollen yarn is made by human activity from that material: it does not occur naturally, and so is a man-made object.

Activity 10.1.1

Sorting natural and man-made materials and objects
Discussion based on a simple sorting exercise is an effective way of making clear the distinctions between natural and man-made materials and objects. The sorting activity itself is an application of setting using a Carroll diagram, with four possible sets. As is usual in such exercises, it is helpful to begin by sorting a range of examples which fall obviously into one of the sets, then progress to considering others which do not. Examples which can readily be assigned to one of three sets are easy to find: populating the fourth may be more difficult.

– *Material and object both natural*: pebble, mineral crystal, shell, bone, feather, fossil, bamboo cane, seed, fruit (including nuts and seed-heads), fleece, raw cotton.

- *Material natural, object man-made*: carved or polished stone, carved or turned wood, woollen yarn or garment, cotton yarn or garment, wood basket (e.g. willow or split bamboo), roof-slate, bottle-cork.
- *Material and object both man-made*: glass bottle and jar, plastic bottle, jar or toy, cardboard box, book, nail, screw, nut and bolt, all-metal or metal-and-plastic tools, brick, tile or any ceramic vessel, garment made of synthetic yarn.

The fourth set includes naturally-formed objects of man-made materials, which are much less common and usually associated with breakdown such as corrosion or attrition. Examples include steel rusted so much that its original shape has been lost, and beach-pebbles of glass, brick and concrete.

Placing objects in the four sets is likely to involve discussion which will show not only how much children know of the origins of materials, but also the extent to which they understand and can use the concepts of 'natural' and 'man-made'. Having succeeded in placing objects in these sets, children can then usefully discover the limitations of these, for example by being presented with objects made of both natural and man-made materials, such as tools and furniture made of wood and metal. These do not fit into the pattern of classification used (a Venn diagram would be needed), but as long as their materials can be correctly identified and their origin understood, this is not a problem: the setting exercise has served its purpose.

Activity 10.1.2

Investigating the origins of materials

Once children can distinguish reliably between natural and man-made materials and objects, they are in a position to investigate the origins of materials. From a scientific point of view (which is likely to be rather different from the technological one), the most informative way of doing this is to trace the changes to which materials are subjected in order to make them usable. Relatively few materials are used by humans with no change or modification (straw or reed for thatching and bamboo are examples), so this approach suggests two main groups: materials modified by physical changes and those made by chemical changes.

Here again a productive strategy is to discuss with children the origins of a range of materials and objects with which they are already familiar and which they can handle and re-examine in the classroom. The following lists may be helpful in making a selection.

Materials modified by physical changes

- *cutting, carving and splitting*: wood, stone and slate;
- *crushing and grinding*: clay, chalk, metal ores, coal, roadstone, foodstuffs (especially cereals and spices);
- *sieving and sorting*: sand, gravel, roadstone, flour (see Activity 6.4.1);
- *sedimentation*: clay for ceramics (see Activity 11.10.2);
- *spinning, weaving and knitting*: cotton, wool, linen, silk;
- *dissolving, filtering and evaporating*: extraction and purification of salt and sugar (see Activity 6.4.2).
- *pulping and sieving*: paper (glue or size is also added).

Materials made by chemical changes

Of the very wide range of chemical processes used to make materials, the following are of great importance:

- *heating or firing*: ceramics (including bricks), glass, plaster, cement (*10.2);
- *smelting from ores*: all metals, including iron and steel (*10.2), aluminium, zinc and copper;
- *synthetic processes*: plastics (*10.2), artificial fibres and yarns.

Once a selection of materials has been made for children to work with, further research may be needed to find out how they are produced. This research is likely to be especially productive if it can be carried out on materials used by local industries and products, and can often be developed into a case-study of the uses of natural and man-made materials as related to their properties (Section 10.2).

10.2: Investigating how materials are obtained and used

The range of materials obtained, modified, made and used by human societies has for thousands of years been very wide. The growth of science, technology and industry has shifted emphasis from natural materials towards man-made ones, but has not markedly increased the diversity of materials used or the complexity of technological knowledge deployed in using them effectively. Faced with such complexity it is essential that some kind of case-study approach (*1.1) should be adopted so that children's attention can be focused on a relatively small group of materials, used for purposes which are of immediate relevance to them. In addition, it is a great advantage if the materials are used in ways that children can see, and whose results are evident in the end-product.

House-building as a case-study

In spite of technological advances and an increased range of materials, houses and even apartment-blocks are still essentially built by hand-craftspeople, in stages which are clearly visible and easily understood. The range of materials used (*10.2) varies with climate, locality and design, and can be linked both to the history and the geography of the region as well as the technology of designing and building structures. Because children live in houses and apartments, they can understand on the basis of first-hand experience the relationships between the properties of materials and their uses.

Building firms and projects will often allow (and even welcome) children on-site in well-planned visits, when they can not only see stages in construction, but also question people who use the materials every day about their properties and the ways in which they are used.

Other industries as case-studies

Other local industries in which smaller ranges of materials are used may also be very productive as case-studies. The important factors from an educational point of view are that children should be able to understand the properties of the materials used, see the processes of making in action and be familiar with the products through personally interacting with them. For example, the properties of materials and chemical changes involved in simple baking are investigated in

Activities 9.2.2 and 9.2.3. This could be extended by studying the work of a bakery or pastrycook. Clothing, footwear and printing are other examples of industries which can give children a significant insight into the importance of understanding the properties of materials, how they are obtained and the ways in which they are used.

11

Earth Science

11.1: The place of Earth science in the curriculum

Investigations into the properties of materials and their origins (Chapters 7–10) make it possible to integrate work in science closely with technology. In a similar way, Earth science is a part of the curriculum in which science and geography meet and interact.

Changes in our environment, whether natural or brought about by human activity, cannot be adequately understood without reference to fundamental ideas on physical and chemical change (Chapters 6 and 9). A useful starting-point is the concept of the Earth as divided into three parts: the atmosphere, hydrosphere and lithosphere (*11.1) which correspond to the three phases of matter: gas, liquid and solid (see Section 6.1). Apart from events such as volcanic eruptions and earthquakes, which have their origins deep inside the Earth, changes in their physical environment which children experience and observe come about when the atmosphere, hydrosphere and lithosphere interact in a variety of ways. Examples of such changes and their results include aspects of the weather and atmosphere (Sections 11.2–11.6), rocks and their weathering (Sections 11.7–11.8) and the properties of soils (Sections 11.9–11.10).

11.2: Temperature

Temperature, measured in degrees celsius (°C, Activity 12.3.2), is a measure of how hot or cold things are. Although water and soil temperatures are of great importance in determining climatic patterns and seasonal plant growth, the environmental temperature which affects children's lives most directly, and which they can most easily investigate, is that of the air around them. It is important always to emphasize that changes in temperature are brought about by heating and cooling; processes which involve the transfer of energy (Section 12.3). This principle affects both how children measure air temperatures and what significance their results have.

Activity 11.2.1

Measuring air temperature
Air temperature can be measured using either liquid-in-glass or digital thermometers, but such measurements must always be carried out in the shade. If a

thermometer is in sunlight, it is being heated by radiant energy from the Sun and so will be at a higher temperature than the air around it (see Activity 12.3.5). A more extreme example of the same effect is the heating of metal objects such as cars by intense sunlight.

By holding a thermometer in a variety of locations, shaded by a piece of card or the observer's own body, variations in air temperature can easily be measured. On their own, however, such measurements are not very productive. Their significance lies in the way in which they can help children to think about ways in which the air around them is heated and cooled. In most cases the causes of variation in air temperature can easily be identified. On a sunny day, for example, air temperature will usually be lower on the shady side of a building than on the sunny side. This is because, although the *thermometer* is in the shade in both locations, the earth or paving in sunlight is being heated much more than that in the shade, and is heating the air above it.

One difference which may puzzle children is that the air temperature just above paving in the sun is usually much higher than that just above mown grass nearby. This is because the evaporation of water from the grass leaves and soil cools the air above them (see Activity 6.3.4). A combination of shaded soil and evaporation means that on a sunny day when the trees are in full leaf, the air temperature in woodland is much lower than it is outside.

These and similar variations are examples of the way in which very localized variations occur in broad climatic patterns. Every locality has in effect its own climate (microclimate) which may be of great importance in agriculture and horticulture, for example in the growing of fruit and vines.

Activity 11.2.2

Making and using temperature records

As well as measuring and trying to explain variations in air temperature at any one time, it is also useful to keep records over longer periods. The simplest way to do this is to use a maximum-minimum thermometer, kept in the same place in constant shade outdoors and read at the same time each day. This measures the highest and lowest air temperatures during the 24-hour period. As with local air temperatures, such measurements help to develop children's understanding only if they are related to possible causes of variation. For example, minimum temperatures can often be related very directly to how clear or cloudy the sky is. Cloud cover reduces the rate at which the land surface is cooled at night, so at any time of the year minimum temperatures tend to be higher on cloudy nights than on clear ones.

Although maximum-minimum thermometers show the range of temperature during a period of time, they do not show a pattern of variation, or the times of day and night when the extremes occur. The recording of air temperature during a 24-hour period provides an excellent opportunity to introduce older pupils to data-logging using temperature-probes and computers. A variety of systems is in use, one of which may be available on loan from a local high-school. The advantage of data-logging is that children can gain experience not only of collecting information, but also of displaying it in a variety of ways which can then be related to forecasts and larger-scale weather features such as fronts and depressions (see Section 11.6).

11.3: Wind

Wind is the name given to any movement of the atmosphere, which can be caused both by large-scale patterns of pressure difference such as depressions and anti-cyclones (*11.6) and local heating or cooling. Children can observe the effects of wind and measure both its direction and speed, but because all their observations and measurements are carried out near the ground, these need to be planned and interpreted in two ways. First, observations are needed which can be related to broad patterns as shown in charts and TV forecasts (see Section 11.6). Such measurements need to be carried out in large open spaces such as playing-fields. Secondly, children need to become aware of local conditions, in which obstacles such as buildings and trees can bring about marked variation in both the direction and speed of the wind, as people on the ground experience it.

Activity 11.3.1

Observing the effects of wind

Children can observe the effects of wind directly. This is most easily done when there is a moderate to fresh breeze, by watching its effects on trees, feeling it blowing on the face and holding up windmills or turbine-wheels made of card so that the moving air can drive them round. This also provides good opportunities to reinforce the idea that air, though invisible, is a real substance because it exerts forces on objects in the path of its movement (see Activity 6.1.3).

Even if wind-speed is not measured, children can learn a lot about the general effects of wind at different speeds by using the Beaufort Scale, modified for conditions likely to be observed on land (Table 11.1). In particular, simple direct comparisons between the wind felt at ground level and the movement of tree-tops can make the important point that both the speed and direction of moving air often depend very much on exactly where one is positioned.

Activity 11.3.2

Measuring wind direction

The direction of the wind is the compass bearing *from which* the wind appears to be blowing so that, for example, an air-stream moving towards the north-east is called a south-westerly wind. The wind direction at any moment can easily be found using a weather-vane (Fig. 11.1) in conjunction with a fluid-filled field-compass (Activity 15.5.1) to determine the bearing. The weather-vane shows the wind direction by pointing in the direction from which the wind appears to be coming. Recording wind direction may not be a simple matter, however, because even in large open spaces it can be very variable, particularly in gentle breezes caused by local heating of the land-surface on sunny days. Watching the vane for one or two minutes will usually give an indication of the overall direction of air-movement and also allow children to comment on its variability.

If weather-vanes or flags on high buildings or poles are visible, these provide a useful check on children's measurements, since wind direction at 10m or more above ground is usually much less variable than that at ground-level.

Table 11.1   Modified Beaufort Scale for estimating wind speed

Beaufort number	Seaman's term	Speed mph (kph)	Observed effects
0	Calm	under 1 (under 1)	Calm; smoke rises vertically
1	Light air	1–3 (1–5)	Smoke drift indicates wind direction; weathervanes do not move
2	Light breeze	4–7 (6–11)	Wind felt on face; leaves rustle; weathervanes begin to move
3	Gentle breeze	8–12 (12–19)	Leaves and small twigs in constant motion; light flags extended
4	Moderate breeze	13–18 (20–29)	Dust, leaves and loose paper raised up; small branches move
5	Fresh breeze	19–24 (30–39)	Small trees in leaf begin to sway
6	Strong breeze	25–31 (40–50)	Larger branches of trees in motion; whistling heard in wires
7	Moderate gale	32–38 (51–61)	Whole trees in motion; resistance felt in walking against wind
8	Fresh gale	39–46 (62–74)	Twigs and small branches broken off trees; progress impeded
9	Strong gale	47–54 (75–86)	Slight structural damage; slates blown from roofs
10	Whole gale	55–63 (87–100)	Seldom experienced on land; trees broken or uprooted; considerable structural damage occurs
11	Storm	64–72 (101–115)	Very rarely experienced on land; widespread damage
12	Hurricane	73 or more (116 or more)	Violence and destruction

Note: Wind speeds are given first in miles per hour (mph), followed by speeds in kilometres per hour (kph) in brackets.

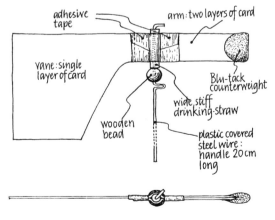

Fold card round the drinking-straw and secure with adhesive tape.

Figure 11.1   A simple weather-vane

Wind direction tends to be much more variable and unpredictable around buildings than in large, open spaces. This can be investigated by making a wind flow-chart. Wind direction is measured in a large number of places round the school on the same day. Each measurement is plotted as it is taken on an outline plan of the buildings, as an arrow pointing *in the direction of the air-flow*, i.e. towards the tail of the weather-vane. The resulting chart will resemble wind-flow charts which children are likely to see in TV weather forecasts (see Section 11.6) and may be complex: it is by no means uncommon to find arrows very near each other pointing in different or even contrary directions! What this shows is that wind-flow between buildings, like water in a rocky stream-bed, moves smoothly in some places but in others forms swirls and eddies which are very unpredictable.

Activity 11.3.3

Measuring wind speed

For scientific purposes measurements of speed are usually given in metres per second, but it is more practical to give wind speeds in miles or kilometres per hour, because these units are used in weather forecasts. They are also likely to mean more to children through their own experience of travelling in cars or trains. Wind speed is measured with an anemometer. The only way to make accurate measurements of wind speed in any situation is to use a portable spinning-cup anemometer. This is an expensive item, but if one can be borrowed it is possible to use it to calibrate simpler anemometers whose use is more limited, but which children can make for themselves.

The simplest and most practical anemometer is the deflection type, in which a pivoted flap is moved upwards by wind-flow. The angle of deflection corresponds to the speed of the air-flow (Fig. 11.2). When using this type of anemometer it is important to keep the flap at right-angles to the wind direction, so it is helpful to have a wind-vane in use at the same time. This also limits its usefulness: deflection anemometers have to be used in large open spaces if they are to be at all reliable.

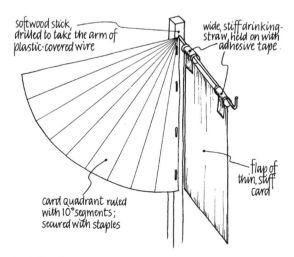

Figure 11.2   A simple deflection anemometer

Deflection anemometers can be calibrated by using them alongside a spinning-cup device, to find the absolute wind speed which corresponds to different angles of deflection. With a lightweight flap a deflection anemometer is very sensitive to light winds. Stronger winds, which blow the flap out horizontally, can be measured by making another anemometer and loading the lower edge of its flap with a 5 or 10g mass held on with adhesive tape.

If the wind-speed is variable, it is usual to record both the 'average' or continuous speed and the highest speed recorded in the most severe gust. It is also very helpful if children can link their measurements of wind-speed both to direct observations of its effects and to the modified Beaufort Scale (Table 11.1).

11.4: Water in the atmosphere

A wide range of visible changes in the atmosphere is connected with water and the ways in which it changes state between liquid, gas and solid. These include cloud, mist, fog, dew, and frost, as well as various kinds of precipitation (Section 11.5). Simple observation and keeping of weather-diaries are useful to focus children's attention on these phenomena and to begin development of the concepts of pattern and cause-and-effect in relation to the weather they experience. In order to gain a deeper understanding, however, it is necessary for the children to begin explaining these observations in terms of their knowledge of melting, freezing, evaporation and condensation of water (see Sections 6.2 and 6.3) as these occur in the atmosphere and at the Earth's surface.

Cloud, mist and fog

Cloud, mist and fog are natural aerosols: suspensions of liquid water-droplets which are so small that they remain suspended in the air and do not settle out (compare Activity 6.5.1). Children are likely to be familiar with the cloud which forms as steam condenses (Activity 6.3.2). Cloud formation in the atmosphere is very similar, except that it occurs at much lower temperatures. Water evaporating from land or sea mixes with the air as water-vapour, just as water from a wet object drying in the classroom does, making the air humid (Activity 6.3.3). If the humid air is cooled enough, some of the water-vapour condenses (Activity 6.3.2) into cloud, mist or fog.

Cloud is produced when warmer, humid air rises and is cooled to the point at which condensation occurs. Cloud formations are very varied and can give a lot of information about conditions in the atmosphere and the weather which is likely to be experienced at ground level (*11.4). Mist and fog form when cool air sinks and becomes colder still through contact with land or water, so that a 'cloud' is produced by condensation at or near the surface. The tiny water-droplets scatter light, as particles in suspension always do (see Activity 6.5.1), so mist and fog reduce the distance we can see clearly. If visibility within this 'cloud' is between 1 and 2km it is referred to as mist; if below 1km, as fog.

Frost

Frost is caused by a kind of condensation children are likely to have seen in freezers and freezing compartments of refrigerators. Air at 0°C can still contain water-vapour, and if it comes into contact with solid surfaces below 0°C, some of this water-vapour condenses as frost, passing from gas to solid (ice) without an intermediate liquid phase. Frost is most likely to occur when the air is still, cold and stable; conditions which are usually associated with clear skies and rapid cooling of the land-surface at night. Observations of frost can readily be correlated with children's own observations, weather forecasts (Section 11.6) and measurements with maximum-minimum thermometers (Section 11.2).

11.5: Precipitation and the water cycle

Precipitation is the general name for water falling on the Earth's surface either as solid or liquid, including rain, snow, sleet and hail (*11.5). Precipitation is for most children the most easily-observed part of the water-cycle, which can be investigated both through direct observations and and by linking these to more fundamental concepts of physical change (Sections 6.2, 6.3).

Activity 11.5.1

Observing and measuring precipitation

Simple observations and descriptive records of precipitation in weather-diaries can readily be linked both to locally-observed aspects of the weather, particularly cloud formations and wind, and to broader patterns as shown by weather forecasts (see Section 11.6). The correlations become much more meaningful if precipitation is measured and records are kept over a period of weeks or months. Rain and hail are relatively easy to measure; snow is more difficult because under many conditions it is drifted by wind so that finding the depth which fell overall requires special techniques.

Making and using a rain-gauge
Rain-gauges have a reputation for being difficult to make and use. This is un-deserved, but there may be difficulty in finding a suitable site in which the gauge will be readily accessible but remain free from interference. A rain-gauge should stand well away from buildings and trees, or on a flat roof. Using the very simple type of gauge described, measurements need be taken daily, to minimize inaccuracies caused by evaporation of water collected.

Equipment and materials: 2-litre plastic drink bottle; scissors; old modelling-clay; measuring cylinder; ruler; graduated syringe or dropper; calculator.

- Screw the cap firmly on to a 2-litre plastic drink bottle. Cut round at the top of the cylindrical sides.
- Trim the rim of the upper part level and turn it upside-down to make a funnel. Embed the cap and neck in a lump of old modelling-clay to keep the funnel upright.

Rainfall is measured in mm; that is, the *depth* of water which has fallen on the area during the day. This can be found by measuring the *volume* of water collected in ml and dividing this by a constant which must be calculated for the particular funnel being used.

Conversion constant = area of the funnel (in sq.mm) ÷ 1000.

For example, if the diameter of the funnel is 100mm (the diameter of a standard 2-litre plastic bottle), its radius is 50mm.

Area of funnel $= \pi \times r \times r$
                        $= 3.142 \times 50 \times 50$
                        $= 7855$ sq.mm
Conversion constant $= 7855 \div 1000$
                        $= 7.855$

This means that, for this funnel, each mm of rainfall will result in 7.85ml of water being collected, so

rainfall in mm = volume of rain in ml ÷ 7.85

- Take measurements of rainfall every day.
- If a large volume of water is collected, pour it into a measuring-cylinder or cup. Small volumes can be measured by drawing them up into a 5 or 10ml graduated syringe, or a 3ml moulded plastic dropper.

Activity 11.5.2

Modelling the water cycle
The water cycle is a large-scale pattern of changes in which water circulates between hydrospere, atmosphere and lithosphere (*11.5). In detail, the water cycle on any part of the planet's land surface is likely to be complex; but in principle it is simple and can be modelled in the classroom. To understand the model and its significance, children must be able to link it to evaporation and condensation (Activities 6.3.2 and 6.3.3). The main events are the evaporation of water from vegetation, land and water surfaces, condensation of water vapour as clouds and the precipitation of rain, snow and hail which returns water to the planet's surface.

The simplest model of this evaporation-condensation-precipitation cycle is similar to that discussed in Activity 6.3.3, except that extra water should be added to form a pool in the bottle. The paper towel represents the land surface and vegetation; the pool of water, the hydrosphere. Clouds do not form, but as warm humid air is cooled at the top of the bottle, water vapour condenses as droplets and 'rain' runs down the bottle sides.

A more developed model is a terrarium in which small non-flowering plants are grown (see Section 5.2). Here real plants are speeding up evaporation into the air, and water condensing on the inside of the plastic sheet cover 'rains' down on to the plants and soil again.

Having established the basic concepts of the water cycle, children should then research the ways in which these affect their own lives by finding out how the water supplies they use are obtained and processed. A wide range of information and learning resources is usually available from companies and agencies responsible for local or national water supply.

11.6: Patterns of weather

Children are likely to see more relevance in daily observations of weather conditions, and to develop a greater understanding of them, if they are linked not only to physical changes such as evaporation and condensation, but also to broader weather patterns and events. These could include depressions and frontal systems, anti-cyclones and thunderstorms (*11.6).

An effective strategy for developing these connections is to make video-recordings of the most detailed weather reports and forecasts available on TV, or print out charts from the internet. Print charts or record reports and forecasts end-to-end for a week, then display or play them through as a sequence and compare them with the children's own weather records for the same period. Two activities can be based on a sequence of this kind. First, how well did the forecasts agree with local conditions as they were experienced? Was the forecasting accurate? Secondly, older and more able children can find out how well the forecasters predicted the overall pattern of weather. Did the depressions, fronts and other weather-patterns develop as they predicted? Simple analytical studies of this kind serve to emphasize that even with modern techniques, the weather over much of the planet is, under some circumstances, highly unpredictable.

11.7: Rocks and their formation

As with any environmental topic, detailed guidance on the identification and study of local rocks is beyond the scope of this book, but some general guidance can be given (see also *11.7). When studying rocks, as when investigating habitats and ecosystems, an effective strategy is to research one's locality in some detail rather than attempt a comprehensive survey. There are two main ways to do this. The first is to find out about the natural geology of the area. Museums and advisory services can usually provide information and exhibits both on the kinds of rock occurring naturally in the locality and the processes involved in their formation. Visits to sites where rocks are exposed always need to be undertaken with care as most of them are potentially hazardous, but are likely to be be very informative if they can be arranged safely.

The second line of enquiry is to look for different rock-types which are used in buildings and memorials, which in many areas are numerous and varied. Granite (igneous), limestone and sandstone (sedimentary), slate and marble (metamorphic) are all easily-recognized rock-types which may be obtained locally or imported. Brick made from clay (*10.2), which is a sedimentary rock, replaces stone as a basic building material in many areas where soft sediments lie at the Earth's surface. Museums, students of local architecture, builders and monumental masons can all provide valuable information on the sources of the rocks and bricks which children are likely to see in their locality, and are usually willing to share their expertise.

Learning about rocks which form and are used in the locality is particularly productive if it is linked to what is known of their physical and chemical properties. Hardness (Section 7.3), porosity (Section 6.6) and resistance to weathering (*11.8) are the most important properties, which determine not only how rocks affect the landscape, but also where and how they can be used as materials and the kinds of soil which are likely to develop above them.

11.8: The weathering of rocks

Weathering is the collective term for the physical and chemical breakdown of rocks. Under natural conditions, weathering can be observed only on exposed rocks, but it is proceeding all the time under the soil layers which cover much of the land surface (*11.8), leading to soil formation (see Section 11.9).

The most frequently-seen examples of weathering are on buildings and walls, where rocks and man-made materials such as bricks and mortar are exposed. Children can observe these and may be able to identify three forms of weathering, caused by frost, acid rain and living organisms (*11.8).

11.9: Weathering and soil formation

Soil is the name given to the complex surface layer which covers much of the Earth's land surface, and in which rocks, weather, plants, animals and other living things interact (*11.9). If a semi-natural habitat such as woodland is accessible, it may be possible to dig a small soil-pit to show the layering (soil profile) in the upper part of the soil. For a profile to be seen clearly the pit needs to be about 60cm square and dug down as far as is practicable. Once dug, cut the sides as cleanly and vertically as possible with a spade or trowel. This should show the surface layer of organic matter and humus, the intermediate layer of mineral soil and, if the pit is deep enough, the upper layers of weathering rock.

Natural, uncultivated soils can usefully be contrasted with cultivated soils in which the upper layers are much less distinct as a result of mixing, both by digging or ploughing and the activity of earthworms (*11.9). Children can investigate local cultivated soils in more detail (Section 11.10).

11.10: The properties of soil in relation to plant growth

Cultivated soils are of great importance because the plants grown on them are the basis of the human food-web (see Activity 5.7.1). Cultivation and high levels of earthworm activity usually mix and aerate the upper layers of cultivated soil, so that they lack the structure and surface layer of organic matter found in many natural soils. This makes it easier for children to investigate and compare their physical properties, which have a significant effect on the ways in which they can be used for farming and gardening.

A good way to investigate soil properties is to obtain samples of two locally-occurring soils which have markedly different textures: a light, crumbly sand loam and a heavy, sticky clay or silt loam are ideal. If possible they should come from places (e.g. the school grounds) which are accessible and where children can try digging the soils for themselves. Squeezing and rubbing a handful of soil, as in the first test, is exactly what farmers and gardeners still do to assess the likely quality of an unknown soil.

Activity 11.10.1

Comparing soil textures

Equipment and materials: A handful of each of the following: damp silver-sand; pottery clay (or natural clay subsoil); two local soils of contrasting texture, damp but not wet; paper towels; plastic bowl with water (for hand-rinsing).

- Squeeze a handful of damp silver-sand in one hand, then put it on to a paper towel. Rinse and dry your hand.
- Do the same with a handful of pottery clay. Compare the properties of the two materials.
- ? What are the main differences? (The sand crumbles apart, whereas the clay clings in a mass.)

This difference is caused by particle size: the clay particles are so small that the water makes them stick together much more firmly than the sand grains can (see also Activity 8.2.1).

- Feel some sand and clay by rubbing them between your finger and thumb. (The sand grains can be felt, but the clay particles are very much smaller, so clay feels slimy, not gritty.)
- Now do the same with two samples of local soils. Compare their properties, and compare both with the sand and clay.

Most cultivated soils have properties which are intermediate between those of sand and clay, because they contain a range of particle sizes (see Activity 11.10.2), but the degree to which they cling together or crumble, and their textures when rubbed, give a good indication of their likely properties in cultivation.

- ? Which soil would be easier to dig? (The one which crumbles easily.)
- ? Does water run through sand? (Yes.) Does it run through damp clay? (No; but if children are uncertain they should make a small cup of damp clay and test it.)
- ? Why is there this difference? (Because sand-grains are much larger than clay particles, they have spaces between them through which water can move. The clay particles cling together so no water can pass through.)
- ? Which soil would dry out more quickly after rain, and why? (The more crumbly one, because water will drain through it faster.)

These simple observations can start to develop the idea that soil texture affects its properties: how easy it is to cultivate and how quickly it will drain. (*11.10).

Activity 11.10.2

Simple soil analysis
Having compared the physical properties of soils with those of sand and clay, children can relate these to the ranges of particle sizes in the soil. This is an example of separation of a mixture made up of solid, insoluble particles, in which sedimentation is more effective than sieving (compare Activity 6.4.1).

Equipment and materials: Glass jars with well-fitting screw-on lids; enough soil to fill each jar one-third full; water; magnifying-glass or hand-lens.

Safety note: In order to see particles at all clearly it is necessary to use glass jars, since plastic ones become scratched. Shaking these has to be done with care, and should be supervised.

- For each sample: Crumble the soil and break up as many lumps as you can. Fill the jar about one-third full of soil, then add water until it is two-thirds full.

- Shake the jar vigorously in both hands for 20s. Leave it to stand for a minute, then shake it again until all the lumps have been broken up.
- Leave the jar to stand for at least an hour (overnight is better).
- After they have settled, examine the samples, looking for visible particles and layers.
? What patterns do you notice? (The particles have settled out in order of size, with the largest at the bottom. There may be some dead plant material on top of the soil particles or floating on the surface.)
- Look at the layers with a magnifying-glass or hand-lens. The smallest particles you can see as separate bits are fine sand; above them are silt and clay which have smaller particles still.
- Compare the two samples. It is usually possible to relate the thicknesses of sand, silt and clay to the physical properties you observed earlier.

Children can learn most from observations of soil texture and particle size if they can see and dig for themselves the soils from which the samples were taken.

12

Energy

12.1: Energy and change

Most of science, and nearly all investigations carried out by children, is concerned with change. Learning and understanding in science mean, with only a few exceptions, finding out how and why things change as they do. Understanding changes at anything more than a superficial level is impossible without the concept of energy. Although it is not always used directly in thinking and communicating about scientific issues, the concept of energy is always there in the background; a kind of unifying and supporting base for a great diversity of investigations and explanations in science.

The basic idea of energy is very simple: it is the property of objects and systems (from atoms, electrical circuits and living things to planets, stars and galaxies) which enables them to change. There are different forms of energy (Section 12.2) which enable systems to change in different ways, and the more energy a system has, the more change it can undergo or bring about in other objects or systems. Any change involves transfer of energy from one part of a system to another, but it is important to understand that this transfer of energy neither causes the changes we observe nor is caused by them: they are simply different aspects of the overall change in the system.

In many investigations it is not at all necessary to refer to energy. Often the idea can remain in the background, to be used if it is needed, and in some cases it may even be unhelpful to introduce it. At primary level, for example, sufficiently detailed explanations of how the movement and shape of objects change can usually be made in terms of forces (see Chapter 14), and to introduce the concept of energy when it is not needed is to risk a great deal of confusion (*14.2). The only scientific investigations at primary level in which energy transfer has to be the central concept are those of heating and cooling (Section 12.3). In most other areas, including electricity (Chapter 13), our first concern is usually with the effects of energy transfers rather than with the transfers themselves.

Even though energy is not a mainstream concept in most of primary science, it still has a role to play. In any scientific investigation it may be useful to think in terms of energy, because it may enable us to help children make connections and begin to see science as an integrated whole rather than, as it often seems to be, a great mass of unconnected pieces of knowledge.

12.2: Forms of energy

The changes which any object or system can undergo or bring about depend upon the amount and forms of energy which it has. As energy is transferred from one part of the system to another, its form may change as well. For example, a 'battery' (dry-cell) has chemical-potential energy which it can transfer to a circuit as electrical energy. If the circuit includes a lamp, this transfers electrical energy to its surroundings as radiant energy (light) and thermal energy. When the dry-cell is transferring energy it is changing (chemical change), but both the energy transfer and the chemical change are aspects of the overall set of changes the system is undergoing.

Of the main forms of energy which affect children's lives, only one (nuclear energy) is not involved directly in any of their investigations. The first four forms of energy discussed are characteristic of systems which are undergoing change: we are aware of them only when they are transferred as changes take place. The other three forms are called potential energy, and are characteristic of systems which, although they are capable of change (because they have energy), are not changing at the moment.

Kinetic energy

Kinetic energy is energy of movement. The kinetic energy of an object is the energy transferred to it in making it move, and is most obvious when something impedes the object's movement, slowing or stopping it. Two ways in which this can occur are friction (Section 14.3) and impact (Activity 14.2.3) in which the kinetic energy is transferred to the object's surroundings as thermal energy. The brakes of a bicycle or car, for example, become hot as they slow the vehicle down. Transfer of kinetic energy as thermal energy can be experienced very easily by rubbing *dry* hands together: overcoming friction forces causes the skin to be heated so it is, and feels, warmer.

When any object is made to move, energy is transferred to it as kinetic energy. The three examples of this which children are most likely to investigate are the transfer of chemical-potential energy as muscles move the skeleton (Activities 3.5.4, 14.4.1, 14.4.2); gravitational-potential energy as objects fall (Activities 14.2.3, 14.3.4) and elastic-potential energy as stretched and squashed objects are released (Activities 7.2.1, 7.6.1, 14.2.1).

Thermal energy

Transfers of thermal energy are investigated and discussed in Section 12.3.

Electrical energy

When electric current is generated (see Chapter 13), energy is transferred to the circuit as electrical energy. The source may be kinetic energy in a generator such as a dynamo, chemical-potential energy as in a dry-cell or battery (*13.4), radiant (light) energy as in solar panels (Section 17.5), or nuclear energy (*12.2).

Radiant energy

Light is the form of radiant energy with which children are most familiar: others include radio waves, microwaves, infra-red radiation and x-rays. Energy is transferred to the environment as light energy and infra-red by devices such as electric lamps (see Activity 12.3.5 and Section 13.7), but chiefly, as far as we on Earth are concerned, by thermonuclear reactions in the Sun (*12.2, *18.5). Light and infra-red radiation are absorbed by and transferred to any material which does not reflect them. In most materials it is transferred as thermal energy so the material is heated, but children are likely to work with two systems in which some of the light energy is transferred either as electrical energy (solar cells, Section 17.5) or as chemical-potential energy (photosynthesis, Section 4.4).

Gravitational-potential energy

This form of energy is determined by an object's position in relation to the Earth. Any object and the Earth interact as a gravitational system. In moving an object upwards, away from the Earth, energy (kinetic energy) is transferred to it and its gravitational-potential energy increases. Any activity which involves raising objects or allowing them to fall (Activity 5.6.2, Chapter 14 and especially Activities 14.2.3, 14.3.4), can be explained partly in terms of changes in gravitational-potential energy.

Elastic-potential energy

When an elastic object (see Section 7.6) is distorted by applying unbalanced forces to it, kinetic energy is transferred to it as elastic-potential energy. This is transferred back as the object is released and regains its original shape. Activities which involve this energy change include both the compression of air and distortion of other objects (Activity 7.2.1; Section 7.6) and the use of elastic bands when investigating forces (Activities 14.1.4, 14.2.1).

Field energy

A situation which is in some ways similar to the behaviour of elastic materials can occur between two magnets. If two magnets attracting each other are moved and held apart, or if two magnets repelling each other are pushed and held together, kinetic energy is transferred to the system as potential energy (sometimes called field energy), which is again transferred as kinetic energy if they are released and move (see Activity 15.4.4).

Chemical-potential energy

Like all changes, chemical changes (see Section 9.1) involve transfers of energy. Materials which transfer energy to the environment as they change have chemical-potential energy. The most obvious examples are fuels (Activity 9.4.1) which transfer thermal and light energy to the environment as they burn, and 'batteries' (dry-cells, *13.4) which transfer electrical energy to circuits as they generate current. When discussing burning, in particular, it is important to distinguish clearly between energy (a property) and fuel (a material which has that property).

Chemical changes in which energy is transferred to the reacting materials result in the formation of substances which have higher levels of chemical-potential energy. The most important example of this kind of chemical change is photosynthesis (*4.4) in which carbon dioxide and water are synthesized into high-energy chemicals such as sugars and starch, the energy source being radiant (light) energy from the Sun, absorbed by chlorophyll.

12.3: Heating, cooling and temperature

Heating is the process by which energy is transferred to a material or object as thermal energy, and which results in a rise in the temperature of the material. The reverse process is cooling, i.e. the transfer of thermal energy to an object's surroundings, resulting in a fall in the temperature of the object and a rise in the temperature of its surroundings.

When investigating and discussing heating, cooling and temperature, it is important to avoid any suggestion that 'heat' is a substance, that an object contains a certain amount of 'heat' or that 'heat' is transferred from one object to another. A good way to do this is to use the word 'heat' as a verb and never as a noun. Objects are heated (and cooled) by transfers of thermal energy: they become hotter (or colder) as a result. Any object has a certain amount of thermal energy, depending on the materials which make it up and its temperature, but to speak of it as having 'heat content' is confusing and misleading.

When investigating heating and cooling, we are concerned both with causes (transfers of thermal energy) and with effects, such as expansion and changes in temperature. As is often the case in science, it is easier to understand the changes taking place if we examine the effects first and then seek their causes. Investigations of expansion (Activity 12.3.1) lead on to work on thermometers and the measurement of temperature (Activity 12.3.2). Children are then in a position to look more closely at how heating and cooling take place by conduction, convection and radiation (Activities 12.3.3–12.3.5), and how they may be slowed down by thermal insulation (Activity 12.3.6).

Heating and expansion

The atoms and molecules which make up all matter (*8.1) are constantly in motion. Atoms and molecules of gases move freely, those of liquids can move slowly between each other, but those of solids are bonded together and can only vibrate (see Activities 8.2.1, 8.2.2). When a material is heated, its atoms or molecules move more, and more violently, than they did before. One result of this is that the volume of the material or object increases: this is known as thermal expansion. Thermal expansion is a physical change which in most materials is completely reversible if the material is cooled.

Thermal expansion occurs in nearly all materials, but in some much more than in others. Among solids, most metals expand on heating much more than other materials do, but even their expansion is difficult to detect without special equipment. Children are likely to be familiar with the thermal expansion and contraction of liquids through the use of thermometers (Activity 12.3.2). It is, however, difficult to show the expansion of liquids such as water with simple equipment, because the situation is complicated by the expansion and contraction of the container as well as the water inside it. Gases, on the other hand, expand on heating much more than either solids or liquids do and children can easily see the expansion and contraction of air as it is heated and cooled.

Activity 12.3.1

Thermal expansion and contraction of air

Equipment and materials: Two plastic drink bottles of similar sizes (2-litre is ideal), one with its screw-top; rigid plastic tube, e.g. barrel of a ball-point pen; Blu-tack; drill and drill-bits; two absorbent cloths about 30 × 20 cm; hot water; ice-water.

- Drill a hole in the screw-top of one bottle so that the rigid tube will just pass through it. Push the tube through to half its length and seal it with Blu-tack (the seal must be gas-tight). Screw the top on to the bottle.
- Cut the top from the other bottle, put water in it and and arrange the two bottles as shown in Fig. 12.1. Do not let the tube touch the bottom of the lower bottle.

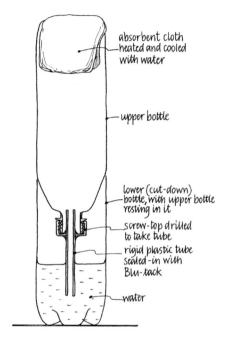

absorbent cloth heated and cooled with water

upper bottle

lower (cut-down) bottle, with upper bottle resting in it

screw-top drilled to take tube

rigid plastic tube sealed-in with Blu-tack

water

Figure 12.1   Observing thermal expansion and contraction of air

- Fold and place an absorbent cloth on the top of the upper bottle (Fig. 12.1): soak it in hot (not boiling) water.
- ? What happens? (Air bubbles out of the tube into the water in the lower bottle.)
- ? Why does this happen? (Because the air in the upper bottle is being heated by the hot water in the cloth, causing it to expand. There is no longer room for all the air in the bottle so some of it bubbles out.)
- When the bubbling stops, remove the first cloth, replace it with the second and soak this in ice-water.
- ? What happens? (Water rises up the tube and then pours into the upper bottle.)
- ? Why does this happen? (The air is being cooled by the cold water, causing it to contract. As its volume becomes less, water flows into the tube and bottle.)

Two points to note are first, that when we say the air is 'being cooled', what we mean is that thermal energy is being transferred from it to the colder water in the cloth (mainly by conduction, see Activity 12.3.3). Secondly, water is not being 'sucked' into the upper bottle as the air inside contracts: it is being *pushed* in by atmospheric pressure, to the point at which air pressures inside and outside the bottle are equal. This activity provides additional evidence that gas fills a container completely (see Activity 6.1.3), since heating at one end of the bottle immediately produces an effect at the other.

Activity 12.3.2

Temperature and thermometers
Temperature is a measure of how hot or cold a material or object is. It is measured using thermometers in degrees celsius (°C), 0°C being the freezing-point of water and 100°C its boiling-point. Children are likely to use three types of thermometer and may use two others, but it is usually worth making a separate activity of using all the available types together in order to compare them and see how they can and cannot be used to measure temperature in different situations.

Liquid-in-glass thermometers
Children are likely to be most familiar with the thermal expansion of liquids through the use of liquid-in-glass thermometers. When the liquid in the bulb is heated it expands, so that its volume increases and it rises up the very narrow bore in the centre of the glass stem. When the thermometer is put in colder conditions the reverse happens: the liquid is cooled, it contracts and the level in the bore goes down. The glass wall of the bulb is very thin, so that the liquid inside will be heated or cooled as quickly as possible when the outside temperature changes.

The most widely used liquid-in-glass thermometers can measure between −10 and +110°C. They are suitable for most applications but the risk of breakage means that they should not be used for the measurement of body and skin temperatures. The level of liquid in the stem shows temperature on an analogue scale, so children may need help in learning to read thermometers of this kind.

Digital thermometers
Digital thermometers measure the temperature at the tip of a metal probe and show this in figures on a liquid-crystal display (LCD). They measure intermittently rather than continuously, and most have a 'rapid' mode in which measurements are made more frequently than in 'normal' mode. Digital thermometers, though relatively expensive, are very useful for many activities, especially for measuring skin and body temperatures (see Activities 3.6.3, 3.9.3) and investigations of air temperature (Section 11.2).

Liquid-crystal thermometers
Children are likely to encounter these in non-scientific contexts. They consist of a black plastic strip in which, at a small range of temperatures, figures or coloured panels become visible. Typical applications include monitoring of temperature in rooms and tropical fish-tanks, and quick checks on body temperature to find out if it is well above normal. These thermometers can be fairly accurate but most have only a very narrow range of measurement and are not generally useful for scientific investigations.

Maximum-minimum thermometers
These thermometers show the highest and lowest air temperatures in the period since their last setting, and are very useful for making ongoing weather records (Activity

11.2.2). Reading and re-setting them requires care but is a useful skill for children to acquire.

Data-logging systems

Logging temperature is carried out by recording data from one or more temperature-sensitive probes using a computer and special software. Systems of this kind are an excellent introduction to the use and potential of data-logging, since they can provide not only a continuous record of temperature but also have the ability to present the data in a variety of ways. They can be used not only for environmental measurement, but also in experimental situations such as the testing of thermal insulators (Activity 12.3.6).

Activity 12.3.3

Heating by conduction

If the rapidly-moving atoms or molecules of a hot material are in contact with those of a cooler material, thermal energy will be transferred from the hotter to the cooler until the temperature of the two is uniform; a process known as thermal conduction. Materials vary very widely in their thermal conductivity. Most metals conduct thermal energy rapidly, whereas non-metals such as wood and plastics are such poor thermal conductors that they are thought of and used as thermal insulators (Activity 12.3.6).

Equipment and materials: Metal spoon, plastic spoon and wooden dowel or lolly-stick, all about the same length; shallow plastic bowl of about the same diameter; Blu-tack; matchsticks; butter or margarine; water and the means to heat it safely.

- Place the spoons and stick in the bowl so that each projects by nearly half its length; fix them to the rim with Blu-tack.
- Using butter or margarine, fix two matchsticks to each object (Fig. 12.2).
- Heat water; carefully pour hot (not boiling) water into the bowl so that the bottom part of each object is immersed.

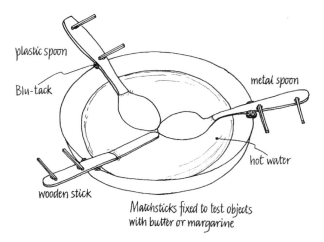

plastic spoon

Blu-tack

metal spoon

hot water

wooden stick

Matchsticks fixed to test objects with butter or margarine

Figure 12.2   Observing thermal conductivity

? What happens? (After a short time the matchstick on the metal spoon near the rim of the basin falls off, as the fat is melted.)

? Why does this happen? (The lower parts of all the objects are heated by the water. Thermal energy is then transferred to the rest of the spoon by conduction, heating it. This in turn heats the fat, causing it to melt.)

? Why does the fat on the plastic spoon and stick not melt? (Both are very poor thermal conductors, so the parts out of the water stay cool even though the parts in the water are heated.)

? The fat on the end of the metal spoon either does not melt, or takes longer to melt. Why is this? (As the metal is heated by conduction, it is itself heating the cooler air around it. The result is that the temperature of the metal at the end of the spoon rises only slowly and often it does not become hot enough to melt the fat.)

This simple investigation shows why wooden or special plastic utensils are used to stir hot liquids in cooking: their very poor thermal conductivity means that one end stays cool even though the other is very hot.

Activity 12.3.4

Heating by convection
When liquids and gases are heated, they expand (Activity 12.3.1), so that a litre of either weighs less when hot than when cold, and will tend to rise through the cooler material around it. A similar movement occurs in reverse if a gas or liquid is cooled. This movement is convection, which speeds up the redistribution of thermal energy throughout systems ranging in scale from a saucepan on a hot-plate to the Earth's atmosphere and oceans heated by the Sun.

Children can easily observe convection currents resulting from localized heating. Room heaters (without hot-air blowers) have convection currents rising from them. Paper spirals or turbine-wheels suspended on threads above such heaters will spin round, impelled by the upward air-currents. Similar air-currents can be seen on sunny days in the air above cars and roads, as a shimmering caused by refraction of light passing through layers of air of differing density (*17.6).

Convection in water can be seen by heating water in a fairly large (2 litre or more) vessel and dropping in a few grains of solid, water-soluble dye so that it sinks to the bottom. The ideal vessel for this is a 2 litre hard-glass chemical beaker which will withstand direct heating. Water heated in a saucepan behaves in a similar way but the currents are much more difficult to see. Water at the bottom is heated and rises, while cooler water in contact with the sides sinks to take its place so that a circulation is set up, caused by convection. This models in a very simple way the kind of circulation caused by heating and cooling in both the atmosphere and oceans.

Activity 12.3.5

Heating by radiation
Any hot object emits a form of radiant energy (*12.2) called infra-red, which behaves like light but which we cannot see. It is this radiation which is detected by night telescopes used (among other things) for filming nocturnal mammals. When

any object absorbs this radiation, it is heated. Children can investigate this effect using a table-light with an ordinary (tungsten-filament) lamp and compare this with an 'energy-saving' lamp.

Equipment and materials: Table-light with reflector hood and 60W tungsten-filament lamp; two liquid-in-glass thermometers; A5 black and white card; (if available: an 'energy-saving' lamp of equivalent light output).

- Take the air temperature of the room; check that the two thermometers show the same reading.
- Place the black and white cards side by side. Place a thermometer on each, parallel to and 1cm away from the edges where the cards meet.
- Adjust the table-light so that it is directly above the bulbs of the thermometers, pointing downwards and as close to them as possible.
- Switch the lamp on and wait for 5 minutes; record the temperatures shown by the two thermometers. (Both will be much higher than room temperature; but the thermometer on the black card will be hotter than that on the white.)
? Why were both thermometers much hotter than the room? (Because they had been heated by the lamp.)
? What caused the difference in their temperatures?

The difference comes about because the white card reflects much more light and infra-red than the black one. Because the black card is absorbing more radiant energy it is being heated more strongly, so its temperature, and that of the air just above it, rises more than that of the white card. A similar effect causes differences in air temperature on sunny days (Activity 11.2.1).

- Switch the lamp on again. Move your hand, palm up, towards the lamp but **do not touch it**.
? What do you feel? (As the hand approaches the lamp, it feels warm.)
? What causes this feeling? (The skin is absorbing and being heated by infra-red radiation, so it feels warm.)
- If you have one, replace the filament-lamp with an 'energy-saving' one, then bring your hand close to it as before.
? What is the difference? (The 'energy-saving' lamp warms the hand much less.)

'Energy-saving' lamps and fluorescent tubes are more efficient because they transfer a much greater proportion of electrical energy as visible light and much less as infra-red than filament-lamps do.

Activity 12.3.6

Thermal insulation
Thermal insulation occurs when materials slow down the transfer of thermal energy from one object or material to another, so tending to maintain the temperature difference between them. Thermal insulation can never be perfect, but in practical terms it keeps hot things hot (and cold things cold) for longer, slowing the rate at which they are cooled (or heated) by the transfer of thermal energy to (or from) their surroundings.

   Children can most easily begin to understand the concept of thermal insulation by investigating one particular kind, the most familiar form of which is their own clothing. Air is a very poor thermal conductor (i.e. a thermal insulator) and our clothes 'keep us warm' by trapping layers of air, so slowing down the transfer of thermal energy by conduction and convection from our warm bodies to their colder surroundings. When an object such as a hot-water tank or a refrigerator is similarly surrounded with layers of fibrous or foam material, it is said to be lagged.

The basic effects of lagging can be very quickly and directly experienced by pouring hot water into two disposable cups of similar size, one of thin plastic and the other of polystyrene foam, then feeling both. The hot liquid is 'lagged' by the foam cup whose external temperature is much lower, whereas the thin cup can be picked up comfortably only if it is lagged with a paper towel or similar insulating material. Children can investigate the same effect more systematically, but still very simply, by wrapping the same number of layers of different materials (held on with elastic bands) round a ceramic mug filled with hot water and explaining the differences they feel. Suitable materials include thin cloth, fur fabric, paper towel, aluminium foil and corrugated cardboard.

Older and more experienced children can design and carry out controlled measurements on the relative effectiveness of different lagging materials. A suggested procedure is given below. Using thermometers, this is most effectively managed by dividing the class into groups, each of which carries out one trial, and pooling the results. If equipment is available, however, this is an excellent opportunity for datalogging with all the trials conducted at the same time.

Equpiment and materials for each trial: 2 plastic bottles with cylindrical sides, one larger than the other (e.g. 2 litre and 500ml); insulating material for test, e.g. paper, plastic foam sheet, plastic foam 'chips', cloth, sand, wood shavings); elastic bands; thermometer; measuring-jug; water and the means to heat it safely.

- Cut the tops off both bottles; if using a sheet material, wrap the smaller bottle so that it and its insulation will just slide easily into the larger one. Hold the layers in place with elastic bands and put the same thickness of insulation under its base.
- If using a particulate material, put a layer into the bottom of the larger bottle, place the smaller bottle onto this and pour or pack material round it.
- Measure 300ml water; heat this to 70°C, pour it immediately into the smaller bottle and take its temperature.
- Continue to record the temperature of the water every 10 minutes until it reaches room temperature. Before each reading, stir the water gently with the thermometer.
- A control should be set up, consisting of two bottles with no lagging material between them, filled and measured in the same way.
- If you can, present all the results on one graph to show visually the patterns of cooling in all the trials.

The most efficient insulator is of course the one which keeps water warm the longest. If children are interested, the same equipment can be used to show that thermal insulation is equally applicable to keeping things cold, by finding out how long (standard size) ice-cubes take to melt completely when insulated by the various materials.

13

Electricity

Socially and technologically the lives of most children are affected more, and more directly, by electricity and its applications than by anything else they learn about and investigate in primary science. Children can carry out a variety of investigations into simple circuits and the properties of materials in relation to them. These are both interesting in themselves and very useful as a foundation on which an understanding of electric current, its effects and control can be built. Although such an understanding is notoriously difficult to develop, children at primary level can make significant progress if they are encouraged to think critically about the simple circuits they build and the ways in which these behave.

13.1: Simple circuits

Representing circuits
Simple (series) circuits are the basic tool for investigating electricity at primary level, and their basic properties need to be understood before attempting to use them to explore further. Fig. 13.1 shows a simple circuit represented by a sketch and a diagram. Younger children may need instructions for circuit-building to be given in pictorial form, but circuit diagrams are much more effective and children should learn to read, use and draw them as soon as they are capable. The symbols most commonly used in primary science are shown in Fig. 13.2. Circuit diagrams show the relative position of different components but not the actual shape and length of the conductors, or how connections have been made.

Basic equipment
Careful selection and matching of components is essential if children are to learn effectively with a minimum of delay and frustration. Some of the main points to note are:

- *cells and batteries:* All investigations should be carried out using low-voltage direct-current (DC) sources such as sealed dry-cells and batteries, which are labelled with the voltage of the current they generate (see *13.5 and Activity 13.3.1). If cells or batteries are connected in line, positive-to-negative (in series), the voltage of the current they generate will be the *total sum* of all their voltages. If

178

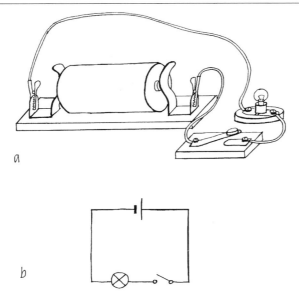

a

b

Figure 13.1   A simple circuit represented by a drawing and a diagram

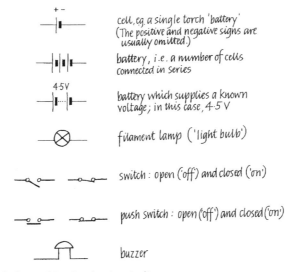

Figure 13.2   Symbols used in simple circuit diagrams

dry-cells are used, a holder is advisable so that connections to them can be made easily (see Fig. 13.1). Rechargeable cells and batteries must not be used, because they may become very hot if short-circuited and leaks are highly poisonous.
– *wires and clips*: All wires should be insulated. Connecting clips such as crocodile ('croc') clips are very helpful, especially for younger children. If bare-end wires are to be used, a pair of wire-strippers will be needed.
– *lamps* ('bulbs'): It is important to begin investigations with suitable lamps. The labelling of lamps can be confusing, because a lamp is expected to work at a

voltage somewhat above its stated 'working voltage'. Thus a lamp labelled '3.5V' is normally used with a 4.5V battery. Lamps of different working voltages are needed for some investigations and it is very useful to identify them with spots of different colours, using model-paints. Lamps should normally be used in holders. Screw-type (MES) lamps should not be screwed in tightly.

– *switches*: Switches should be included in all early experiments with circuits where, apart from reducing wastage, they have a positive role to play. At this stage simple open switches are most useful, but push-switches, which will stay closed, are useful in some later investigations.

Activity 13.1.1

Investigating simple circuits

Equipment: Battery or dry-cell(s) with holder; wires; lamp of suitable working voltage in holder; open-type switch; magnifying-glass or hand-lens.

If a simple circuit is set up as in Fig. 13.1, children can carry out a range of very simple experiments to investigate its properties. These can usefully be thought of in three groups:

1. *Making the circuit work*: All connections have to be in place and the switch has to be closed before current will flow and the lamp will light up.
2. *Changes which prevent the circuit from working*: In the circuit as shown there are six connections. If any is undone there is a gap in the circuit and the lamp will not light up. Opening the switch makes another gap in the circuit, and children should also try the effect of (gently) unscrewing the lamp and screwing it in again.
3. *Changes which have no apparent effect*: Reversing the positions of the switch and lamp, reversing the connections to the battery or using wires of different length bring about no apparent change in the way the circuit behaves.

The main points to be made on the basis of these experiments are that:

– the lamp lights up only while current is flowing;
– a circuit has to be complete before current can flow in it;
– any gap in the circuit will prevent current from flowing;
– a switch is a device which opens a gap in the circuit and so can be used to control it;
– changing the relative position of component parts has no apparent effect (see also introduction to Section 13.9).

Children should also look at the lamp with a magnifying-glass or hand-lens and identify the part which lights up (the filament). Notice that it is a coil of very thin wire: this information will be useful later.

Activity 13.1.2

Finding out more about simple circuits

Equipment: Lamps (without holders) including 1.25V; battery; standard R20 dry-cell; wires; small electric motor; buzzer.

Having made a lamp light up using a holder and a switch, children can learn more by finding out how to do the same using a lamp, two wires and a dry-cell only. This shows first, that to complete the circuit one contact has to be made with the stud at the base of the lamp and the other with the side (Fig. 13.3a). Any other pattern of connection (for example, with both wires in contact with the base or side) will not make a circuit. Secondly, it shows that the terminals of a dry-cell are the metal stud at the top and the metal plate at the base. If in any trial the lamp does *not* light up, the contacts should be broken immediately because the battery may be short-circuited (*13.11). This exercise can be extended by solving simple puzzles, for example making a 1.25V lamp light up using a standard (R20) dry-cell and one wire only; or a battery with both terminals at one end and no wires at all (see Fig. 13.3b,c).

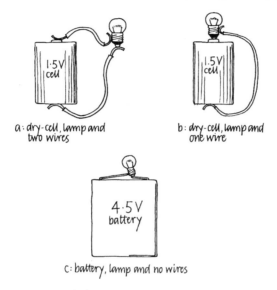

a: dry-cell, lamp and two wires

b: dry-cell, lamp and one wire

c: battery, lamp and no wires

Figure 13.3   Making circuits with fewer parts

Older and more able children can develop their understanding of simple circuits (Fig. 13.1) by using a buzzer or a motor in place of a lamp, having checked that their working voltages are correct. Most buzzers will sound only if they are connected in the right way, i.e. with their red lead to the positive terminal of the battery. This introduces the important idea that the current in a circuit of this kind (DC) has direction, and moves in one direction only, which is determined by how the battery is connected. Moving the buzzer to different positions shows also that the current moves in the same direction all the way round the circuit. An electric motor can make the same point. It will work whichever way it is connected, but if the connections to the battery are reversed, it rotates in the opposite direction.

13.2: Conductors and insulators

Materials which can form part of an electrical circuit are called electrical conductors. Electrical conductivity is an important property of materials which children can investigate in a very direct way.

Activity 13.2.1

Identifying electrical conductors

Equipment and materials: Battery; lamp with holder; piece of soft wood about 10 × 5cm; four wires; two drawing-pins (thumb-tacks); variety of materials, e.g. steel, brass, aluminium, copper, wood, card, plastics, fabrics.

- Construct a circuit as shown in Fig. 13.4, with a gap between the drawing-pins in place of a switch. Test the circuit by connecting the drawing-pins with another wire.

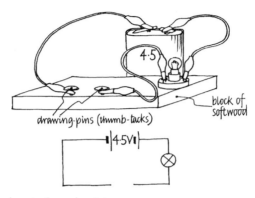

Figure 13.4   Testing electrical conductivity

- Test the electrical conductivity of a variety of materials by placing them across the gap, in contact with both drawing-pins.
- ? If the lamp lights up, what does this tell you about the circuit? (It is complete, because current is flowing in it.)
- ? What does this tell you about the material? (Current can flow through it; it is an electrical conductor.)
- Test all the materials you have available and sort them into two groups: conductors and non-conductors.
- ? What do you notice about the conductors? (All of them are metals, and all the metals are conductors.)

Materials through which electric current cannot flow are called electrical insulators (compare thermal conductors and insulators, Activities 12.3.3 and 12.3.6). They are important because some of them, particularly plastics, are used to cover electric cables and components such as switches, to prevent accidental short-circuits (*13.11) and their effects, especially electric shock and fire (*13.13).

A non-metallic conductor
The only common non-metallic material which is an electrical conductor is graphite, the form of carbon used in the 'lead' of pencils. If pencil-leads are available, their conductivity can be shown by using them to bridge the gap in the circuit, as above. To show the conductivity of the graphite inside a pencil, detach the leads from the drawing-pins, clip or hold one on to the point and press the other on to the exposed 'lead' at the other end. Graphite is not a very good conductor and the 'lead' of soft (B

or 2B) pencils has greater conductivity than that of hard ones (H or 2H), so that the lamp glows more brightly (see next section).

13.3–13.6: Investigating electric current

When devices which form part of an electrial circuit are activated, energy is transferred to them: lamps are heated and light up, motors rotate and buzzers sound. Children usually identify the battery as the source of the energy transferred during these changes. What reaches the devices and causes these transfers of energy is electric current (*13.3,*13.4) generated by the battery. From the activities discussed earlier in this chapter, children can learn a lot about electric current.

– It can flow only when a circuit is complete.
– It can flow only through some materials (conductors) which can form part of an electrical circuit.
– It flows, in the DC circuits we use, in a particular direction, which can be reversed.

Lamps as current measurers
Not only the direction, but the rate at which current flows in a circuit can be changed. In order to develop children's understanding of electric current and the behaviour of circuits, it is necessary to vary and compare current in circuits in a simple way. Exact measurement in amps (A), using an ammeter, is not usually needed at primary level. Simple comparisons are sufficient and can easily be made, because *the greater the current flowing through a lamp filament, the brighter it glows.*

Activity 13.3.1

Changing the current in a circuit
Exactly how this activity is approached will depend on the equipment available. There two ways in which children can change the current flowing in a circuit and they should experiment with both, changing the source of current first and then the lamps used. In all experiments it is very useful to have a second circuit set up as a control, which is similar to the test-circuit, but which is kept unchanged so that the brightness of the lamp in the test-circuit can be compared with it.

Changing the source of current
Children should experiment first with changing the number and type of dry-cells or batteries used to generate current, keeping the same lamp in the circuit throughout. If using dry-cells or batteries together, they must be connected end-to-end with the positive terminal of one connected to the negative terminal of the next (in series). A switch should always be included in the circuit.

In order to see differences in brightness most clearly and to minimize 'blowing' of lamps through current overload, it is prudent to begin with a circuit in which the total voltage of the battery, however it is generated, is less than the working voltage of the lamp. For example, a good combination to begin with would be three dry-cells (output $3 \times 1.5V = 4.5V$) with a 6V lamp. The current can then be varied by reducing or increasing the number of cells or batteries: the higher the voltage of the battery, the more current flows and the brighter the lamp glows. If the voltage of the battery is well above the working voltage of the lamp, it should be switched on only for a second or two.

A similar effect can be observed by connecting a buzzer to batteries of differing voltage. As the voltage is reduced the sound will change, usually becoming lower in both volume and pitch.

Experimenting in this way enables children to see in a very direct way that if everything else remains the same, the current in a circuit depends on the number and type of batteries or dry-cells used. To put it very simply, two similar cells or batteries connected in series will 'push' more current round a particular circuit than one will, and some batteries can 'push' current more than others. The property of a cell or battery which determines the size of the 'push' is properly known as electromotive force (emf), but because this is measured and shown on batteries in volts (V) it is easier to use the commoner term 'voltage'.

Changing the lamp

The second investigation requires more thought and logic. If a circuit is set up and lamps of differing working voltage are tested in it, their brightness will vary. If, for example, a circuit incorporating a 4.5V battery is used to test 12, 6, 3.5 and 2.5V lamps, it will be found that the lower the working voltage of the lamp, the brighter it will glow.

The first step to understanding this result is to remind children that the brightness of the lamp is an approximate measure of the current flowing through it. This test shows that if everything else is kept the same, the battery can cause more current to flow through some lamps than through others, so they glow more brightly. This comes about because lamps (and all other conductors) vary a great deal in how easy or difficult it is to make current flow through them. This property is called the resistance of the conductor. Other things being equal, more current will flow through a circuit with lower resistance than through one with higher resistance. In the context of our experiment, the lamp with the lowest working voltage had the lowest resistance, so the battery could make the most current flow through it and it glowed most brightly. Knowing this, we can investigate an important effect of electric current: the way in which it heats some conductors.

13.7: The heating effect of electric current

When an electric current passes through a conductor, the conductor is always heated. If the current is small and the conductor is a wire of a metal which is a very good conductor of electricity, such as copper or aluminium, the heating effect is very small indeed. If the current is very large, even a copper wire may be heated until it melts, as for example overloaded fuses do (*13.13). However, if a material is a less effective conductor and very thin, as for example the filaments of lamps are, it will be heated strongly even by a small current. As we have seen in Activity 13.3.1, the greater the current passing through a conductor of this kind, the greater the heating effect and the brighter the lamp glows.

With close supervision or as a demonstration, children can investigate the heating effect of current further. The following activity not only shows the heating effect very directly; but also makes the point that a lamp in a circuit limits the current which can flow in it. This is particularly significant when trying to understand how circuits behave when more components are added to them (Activity 13.9.1).

Activity 13.7.1

Observing the heating effect of electric current

Materials and equipment: Battery with 6V–9V output; lamp with appropriate working voltage in holder; 4 wires with 'croc' clips; steel wool (e.g. from a domestic scouring pad).

- Set up an incomplete circuit incorporating the lamp in its holder, with two wires unconnected in the middle (a switch is not necessary). Touch the two unconnected 'croc' clips to test the circuit: the lamp should light up.
- Hold a very small bundle of steel wool strands in one 'croc' clip; touch the steel wool with the other, then take it away again.
- ? What happens? (The lamp lights up.)
- ? What does this tell you? (The steel wool is an electrical conductor.)
- Disconnect the lamp and its holder; join the two wires which were in contact with it together.
- Keeping your hands well away from the end of the wire, touch the free 'croc' clip on to the steel wool again.
- ? What happens? (The steel wool sparks and burns.)
- ? What is causing the steel wool to burn? (It is being heated in air by the electric current passing through it.)
- ? Why did the steel wool not burn when the lamp was in the circuit?

When current is passed through a lamp, it heats up. This shows that the lamp has quite a high resistance (see end of Activity 13.3.1), so it limits the current flowing in the circuit. This small current does not heat the steel wool enough for it to burn. When the lamp is removed the resistance of the circuit is reduced and a much larger current can flow in it, so the steel wool is heated much more strongly, its temperature rises and it burns. Children may be surprised that iron metal can burn, but they have probably seen this happen before, either in fireworks such as 'sparklers' or as sparks fly from steel on a grindstone.

13.8: Cause and effect in changing current

Even without precise measurement, Activities 13.3.1 and 13.7.1 show the logical relationship between voltage (of the cell or battery), resistance (of the lamp and other parts of the circuit) and current. Voltage and resistance are causes, and current is the effect they produce. Voltage and resistance are properties of the circuit: changing either or both will cause a change in the current. Conversely, if the current changes, there must have been a change in the voltage, the resistance, or both. Understanding these simple logical relationships is of great importance because it enables children to interpret the behaviour of a wide range of circuits which they may build experimentally or as part of their work in technology.

13.9: Unbranched (series) circuits

Any circuit in which the components are connected in a single unbranched loop is known as a series circuit: components are said to be connected in series.

It is helpful, before building different circuits, to return to the basic observation that placing the same components in various positions within a series circuit makes no difference to the way in which they behave. In particular, the lamp glows with the same brightness wherever it is placed. This is important because it shows that *the current is the same in all parts of a series circuit.* The significance of this becomes apparent when more lamps and batteries are added.

Activity 13.9.1

The effect of adding components to a series circuit
As in Activity 13.3.1 it is helpful to build a second basic circuit which can be kept unmodified as a control, for comparison.

Equipment: 3 batteries; 3 lamps of suitable working voltage and holders for them; 2 switches; 7 wires.

- Build two basic series circuits as shown in Fig. 13.1. Switch them on together to check that the lamps in both glow with equal brightness.
- Keep one circuit unchanged and use it throughout for comparison.
- Add a second lamp to the test-circuit (Fig. 13.5a) and close the switch.

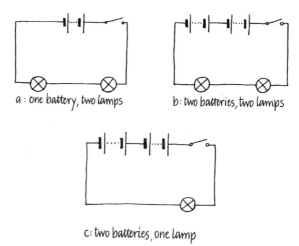

a : one battery, two lamps   b: two batteries, two lamps

c: two batteries, one lamp

Note that these tests can be carried out with any matched batteries and lamps.

Figure 13.5   Adding components to a series circuit

? What effect does the second lamp have? (Both lamps glow, but less brightly.)
? What does the brightness of the lamps tell you about the current flowing in the circuit? (It is less than when the circuit had only one lamp.)

The key to understanding this situation is the point made above, and which children should have observed for themselves, that in a series circuit the current is the same throughout. In particular it is important to avoid any suggestion that the two lamps are 'sharing' the current, and to challenge it if children offer it as an explanation. The scientific view is that a (smaller) current is flowing equally throughout the circuit, including both lamps.

? Why does less current flow when there are two lamps in the circuit?

The heating-up of a lamp shows that it is quite difficult for the battery to 'push' current through it, i.e. it has a fairly high resistance. This has been corroborated by Activity 13.7.1, in which a lamp was shown to limit the current flowing in a circuit. Two lamps make it even more difficult for the battery to 'push' current through the circuit, so less current flows.

- Add a second battery to the circuit (Fig. 13.5b). Before switching it on, predict what the result will be.
? What happens when the circuit is switched on, and why?

Both lamps glow as brightly as that in the control circuit, showing that the current is about the same as it was with one lamp and one battery. Although the two lamps increase the resistance, the two batteries increase the voltage, so the current stays about the same.

- Keeping both batteries, remove one lamp from the circuit (Fig. 13.5c). Switch the circuit on *for a second or two only*: predict what will happen when you do.
? What happens, and why? (The lamp glows very brightly because a larger current than normal is flowing through it.)
? What might happen if the circuit were left switched on? (The filament would probably overheat and break, so the circuit would be broken.)

Activity 13.9.2

A puzzling circuit
This activity is suggested as an example of the way in which investigations of series circuits need to be extended for older and more able pupils capable of developing an understanding of electric current. Solving the puzzle requires them to use most of what they have learned so far on this topic.

Equipment: Small buzzer; lamp of about the same working voltage; range of batteries; switch; 4 wires with 'croc' clips.

Set up the circuit as shown in Fig. 13.6, using a battery whose voltage is a little less than the working voltage of the buzzer (e.g. a 4.5V battery with a '6V' buzzer). Make sure the buzzer is connected correctly.

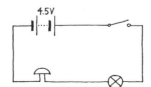

Using a buzzer whose working voltage is 6V, the buzzer will sound but the lamp will not light up.

Figure 13.6 A puzzling circuit

? What happens when the current is switched on? (The buzzer sounds but the lamp does not light up. To arrive at an explanation, go back to first principles.)
? Is current flowing in the circuit? (Yes; because the buzzer sounds.)
? Is current flowing in all parts of the circuit? (Yes. If there is a gap in any part of a series circuit, current will not flow, so current must be flowing throughout this circuit.)
? If current is flowing through the lamp, why is it not glowing? (Because the current is too small to heat it to a high enough temperature.)
? How could you test this idea? (Connect the circuit to a battery of higher voltage: it is usually possible to make the buzzer sound and the lamp glow at the same time.)
• Replace the original battery.
? Why is the current so small using this battery? (The circuit must have a very high resistance, so the battery can 'push' only a very small current round it. The only component which could be causing this is the buzzer.)
? How could you test this idea? (Remove the buzzer from the circuit: the lamp will light up.)
? What does this circuit tell you about the current needed to make the buzzer sound and the lamp light up? (The buzzer will sound with a current which will not make the lamp glow at all, so it must require a much smaller current.)

13.10: Branched (parallel) circuits

If a circuit has two or more routes through which current can flow at the same time (compare Figs. 13.5 and 13.7) it is a parallel circuit, whose components are said to be connected in parallel. Investigations of parallel circuits may not be required at primary level, but can be useful for consolidating very able pupils' understanding of the relationship between voltage and resistance as causes and current as effect (see Section 13.8). When working with parallel circuits fresh batteries should always be used, since those near the end of their working life may not be able to generate a large enough current.

Activity 13.10.1

Investigating parallel circuits

Equipment: 2 similar batteries; 4 similar lamps with holders; buzzer; switches; wires.

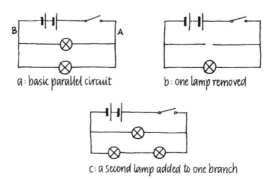

a: basic parallel circuit   b: one lamp removed

c: a second lamp added to one branch

Figure 13.7   Parallel circuits

- Build a basic series circuit (Fig. 13.1) to act as a control, for comparison of lamp brightness.
- Build a basic parallel circuit (Fig. 13.7a) and switch both circuits on.
? What happens? (Both lamps in the parallel circuit glow as brightly as that in the series circuit.)
? What does this tell you about the curent flowing through *each lamp?* (It is the same in both lamps of the parallel circuit and in the series circuit.)
? If the same current is flowing in all three lamps, how big a current is flowing in the unbranched parts of the parallel circuit, i.e. at points A and B in Fig. 13.7a? (Twice as much as in the series circuit.)
? Why is the current in the parallel circuit more than that in the series circuit? (The voltage is the same, so the parallel circuit must have a lower resistance.)

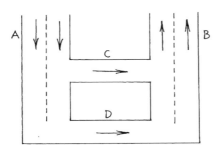

In a crowded one-way traffic system, more traffic can circulate past points A & B if both single-lane roads C & D are open. C & D are like lamps in a circuit, which limit current. Two lamps in parallel allow more current to flow (as at A & B in Fig 13.7a) than one.

Figure 13.8   Modelling current in a parallel circuit

Children usually find it difficult to understand how a circuit with two lamps can have a lower resistance than a circuit with one, but an analogy with (one-way) traffic in a city may be useful. Fig. 13.8 shows a model of current flow. In the model, the two-lane roads represent the unbranched (low-resistance) wires in the circuit; the single-lane roads the (higher-resistance) lamps. In slow, nose-to-tail traffic, will more vehicles be able to pass points A and B if both single-lane roads are open, or if only one is open? Obviously, if both are open; but opening or closing the road at point C will not affect the amount of traffic able to move past point D. If in an electrical circuit there are two lamps through which current can flow, the resistance *of the whole circuit* is lowered and the battery can make more current flow through it.

- Unscrew one lamp in the parallel circuit (Fig. 13.7b). Before switching it on, predict what will happen.
? How does the circuit behave? (The lamp is unaffected: the circuit is now a simple series circuit. If the brightness of the lamp is affected, fresh batteries are needed.)
- Add a second lamp to one branch of the parallel circuit (Fig. 13.7c). Before switching it on, predict what will happen.
? How does the circuit behave, and what does this show?

The single lamp glows brightly, while the two in the other branch behave as we would expect of two lamps in series: both glow, but more dimly, showing that less current is flowing in that branch of the circuit than when there was only one lamp in it. This comes about because the two lamps together set up a higher resistance, so the battery can make less current flow *in that branch* of the circuit. It also shows that the two branches of the circuit behave independently. This can be confirmed by removing a lamp from one branch of the circuit, which leaves the other branch unaffected.

14

Forces and Their Effects

14.1: Forces and change

Scientific concepts of force are used to help us explain and predict the movement and shape of objects, both when these change and when they remain the same. Scientists cannot say what forces are, only what they do, so in order to learn about them, their effects have to be experienced.

Starting points

Children experience forces and their effects from birth onwards, which provides a natural starting-point for developing a more systematic and scientific understanding. A particularly useful starting-point is the idea that forces are pushes and pulls.

At a simple intuitive level children can develop the idea of pushes and pulls in relation to their own bodies and actions in two different ways. First, they can make objects move by pushing away and pulling towards themselves. Secondly, they can change the shape of flexible objects by pushing and squashing, pulling and stretching, or bending them (see Fig. 7.1). Activities of this kind can also be used to start establishing fundamental scientific principles, in particular:

- forces bring about changes in movement, or shape, or both;
- forces have magnitude: they can be bigger or smaller;
- the bigger the force which is applied, the bigger the change it brings about;
- forces have direction;
- changes in shape or movement occur in the direction of the forces
  which bring them about.

These ideas may appear complex; but in fact they are only a summary of everyday experience. A useful strategy is to enable children to gain experience of forces in action through work in other areas of the curriculum, which can be referred to and repeated when forces are being explored in science. Activities 14.1.1 and 14.1.2 are examples of these.

Activity 14.1.1

Forces and movement in physical education (PE)

Equipment: Selection of play-balls; 5 bean-bags; 5 boxes or hoops; safety mats.

Change of movement

- Throwing objects: roll and throw balls with a small push or a large one.
- ? Which makes the ball go further?
- ? Why does it go further? (Because the big push speeds it up more and this makes it go further.)
- Target games, e.g. throwing bean bags into hoops or boxes: each player has 5 bags; top score wins (see Fig. 14.1).
- ? Does it take the same force to get a bag into the 5 point box and the 100 point box?
- Jumping: Standing long (broad) jump on to a safety mat: the bigger the effort (force) you put into the jump, the further you go.

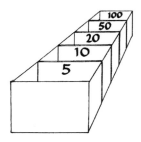

Figure 14.1   Arrangement of target boxes for throwing game: throw from a line 1–3 m from the nearest box (vary according to age and skill of children)

Activity 14.1.2

Forces and change in art

Equipment and materials: Clay, modelling clay or play-dough; boards, rollers, modelling tools, shapes to press in; large paintbrushes, liquid paints, sugar-paper, crayons, pencils.

Change of shape

- *Modelling*: using clay, modelling-clay or play-dough: the bigger the force applied to the material, the bigger the change of shape, e.g. making impressed patterns, rolling out, making thumb pots.
- *Painting*: When using a brush loaded with paint, the harder the brush is pushed down into the paper, the more it bends (changes shape) and the more paint is squeezed out. This can be seen much more clearly with a large brush than with a small one.
- *Drawing*: When a pencil or crayon is pushed or pulled it moves in the direction of the force applied to it. The marks made are a visual record of these forces and movements.

The direction of forces related to change
All the activities mentioned in Activities 14.1.1 and 14.1.2 can be used to establish the idea that changes are brought about in the direction of the forces which cause them, e.g. a ball goes in the direction in which it is thrown (pushed). This is particularly evident in target-throwing games and drawing, in which controlling the direction of the force applied to the object is critical to the result.

Measuring forces
Because forces have magnitude, they can be measured. The unit of force is the newton (N). At primary level the definition of the newton is not important, but it is helpful for children to have experience of forces of known magnitude. This can be done in two main ways: by holding objects and feeling their weight and by using and making forcemeters.

Activity 14.1.3

Experiencing and measuring forces

Equipment: Range of masses 100g–1kg; a variety of objects of known masses up to 5kg; thread and string.

Simply by holding a range of known 'weights' (masses) in the hand, children can gain a direct impression of how large and small measured forces are. The known forces can then be compared with a range of familiar objects.

A 100g mass is pulled down by gravity (i.e. has a weight of) nearly 1N, so holding 100g on the hand and suspended by a thread gives direct experience of how small a force 1N actually is. 1kg has a weight of nearly 10N (9.81N to be exact) so comparisons can be made with a range of objects whose weights are known. For example, if a 3.2kg brick is held on the hand or suspended from a string, it exerts a downward force of 31.4N, (see also Activity 14.5.3)

Forcemeters
Measured forces can also be experienced directly using forcemeters. These are devices in which the force applied changes the shape of an elastic object, usually a spring. Measuring the change of shape gives a reading in newtons for the force applied. Forcemeters are available which measure both pulling and pushing forces.

Measuring pulling forces using forcemeters

Equipment and materials: Forcemeters with differing ranges between 0–10N and 0–50 N; elastic bands, card, paperclips.

The most familiar kind of forcemeter is the spring balance which measures a pulling force applied to a hook which stretches a spring in a cylinder (Fig. 14.2). Different models give different ranges of force measured, (0–10N, 0–20N and so on). Stretching the spring by hand is another way of giving direct experience of what forces of differing magnitude feel like (see also Activity 14.1.4). A common limitation on the use of spring balances is that many are difficult to read. This can usually be

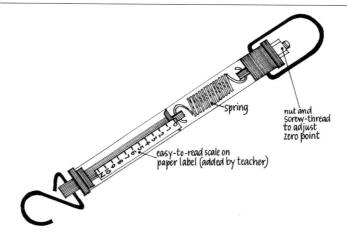

spring

nut and
screw-thread
to adjust
zero point

easy-to-read scale on
paper label (added by teacher)

Figure 14.2   A forcemeter suitable for primary classes

overcome by drawing a simplified but accurate scale on a self-adhesive label and sticking it on to the barrel.

Children can make simple pulling forcemeters for themselves using elastic bands and card scales (Fig. 14.3). These can be calibrated in newtons by hanging masses on to the hook, remembering that 100g has a weight (is pulled down with a force of) about 1N. The elastic band 'push-pull' described in Section 14.2 can also be calibrated for use as a forcemeter for both pulling and pushing forces.

Children can use forcemeters to measure the forces needed to carry out a wide range of familiar activities involving pulling actions, for example: opening a door; pulling out a drawer or lifting a desk-lid; lifting a chair, pulling a trolley loaded with PE equipment. These actions require a large range of forces, so children may need to select different forcemeters for the various measurements they carry out.

Measuring pushing forces using forcemeters

Equipment: Top-pan spring balances (kitchen scale type).

The most convenient ready-made forcemeter for experiencing and measuring pushing forces is the top-pan spring balance, usually seen in the form of kitchen scales. These are usually calibrated in kg and for use as a forcemeter need to be re-calibrated in newtons (1kg on the scale is roughly equal to 10N): small self-adhesive labels are useful for this. The 'push-pull' described in Section 14.2 can be used to measure both pulling and pushing forces.

Using push forcemeters, children can measure the forces needed to carry out familiar activities, such as *closing* a door or drawer and pushing, rather than pulling, a loaded trolley. Do these pushing actions require the same forces as the corresponding pulling actions? Other possibilities include pushing a chair into place and holding up a pile of books (see also Activity 14.5.3).

More about pushes and pulls

Forcemeters are useful not only for measuring forces but also because they can lead directly to a better understanding of pushes and pulls. A very important principle, which needs to be established as early as possible in children's scientific work on

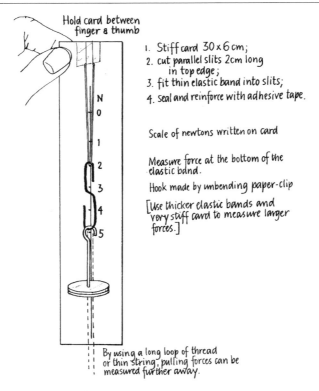

Hold card between finger & thumb

1. Stiff card 30 x 6 cm;
2. cut parallel slits 2cm long in top edge;
3. fit thin elastic band into slits;
4. seal and reinforce with adhesive tape.

Scale of newtons written on card

Measure force at the bottom of the elastic band.

Hook made by unbending paper-clip

[Use thicker elastic bands and very stiff card to measure larger forces.]

By using a long loop of thread or thin string, pulling forces can be measured further away.

Figure 14.3   Making a simple forcemeter

forces (*14.1), is that any pushing or pulling action involves at least two forces. A significant problem for teachers is that in many everyday experiences, e.g. throwing a ball, only one of these forces can easily be identified, so we need to develop ideas about pushing and pulling actions through examples where the effects of both forces can be experienced directly.

Both pushing and pulling always involve a pair of forces acting in opposite directions. If the forces are acting towards each other the action is a push; if away from each other, it is a pull. In developing these ideas it is helpful to begin with body actions which lead to the forces being experienced directly.

Activity 14.1.4

Experiencing pulling and pushing actions

Pulling actions

Equipment: Thick elastic bands (5 for each group); 5mm dowel 10cm long (2 for each group); forcemeters.

- Hold several elastic bands together with two pieces of dowel as handles, as in Fig. 14.4). Stretch the elastic bands a little by pulling your hands outwards, across your chest.

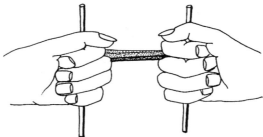

Use 3 or 4 thick elastic bands with pieces of dowel for handles. Hold hands in front of chest and pull them outwards.

Figure 14.4   Experiencing pulling forces

? How hard are you pulling? (The main purpose of this question is to direct attention.)
● Now pull harder.
? When you pull harder, what happens to the elastic band? (It gets longer: another example of 'the bigger the force, the bigger the change'. See also Activity 14.2.3.)
? How do you know, even with your eyes shut, how hard you are pulling? ('I can feel it!')
? Which part of you can you feel it with?

What is likely to emerge from this questioning is that most of the sense of how hard one is pulling comes not from the skin but from the muscles of the upper arms which are actually exerting the pulling forces.

In working out what forces are involved, concentrate on the hands, not the elastic band. Pairs of pulling forces are acting in opposite directions on each hand; the outward force exerted by the muscles of the arm and the inward force by the elastic band. If the hands are still, these forces are in balance (see Section 14.5). If the force exerted by the arms changes, the band will become longer or shorter until the pairs of forces are in balance again.

Pushing actions

Equipment: Plastic play-balls (inflated or foam); well-inflated large balloons; bucket of water; large bowl.

● Hold a large plastic play-ball or a well-inflated balloon between the hands as shown in Fig. 14.5, then push inwards, squashing it.

This requires the use of different muscles from the pulling action in Activity 14.1.7, but the sense of how large a force one is exerting is similar. Children can feel the squashed ball pushing outwards, while at the same time being aware of the inward pushing force they are exerting. This is another useful example of the principle that the shape of an object does not change when the forces acting on it are in balance (Section 14.5). Another way of experiencing pairs of pushing forces, which will be discussed later in the context of floating and sinking (Activity 14.6.2), is to push a play-ball down into a water-filled bucket standing in a bowl (Fig. 14.6).

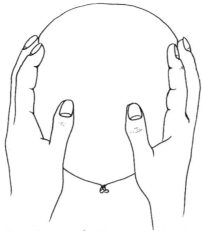

Hold a balloon or ball between your hands, in front of your chest, and push inwards.

Figure 14.5   Experiencing pushing forces

Push down on the ball. As water is displaced and overflows, the remaining water pushes up on the ball.

Figure 14.6   Experiencing pushing forces

Forces in and out of balance

Experiencing pushes and pulls provides a useful beginning to work on forces and their effects, but is limited because in many everyday situations it is not at all obvious that pairs of opposing forces are acting on objects. For example, when throwing a ball, the ball pushes back on my arm with the same force that my arm pushes forward on it, but this is not usually detectable. A solution to this problem is to adopt an alternative approach, based on the idea of forces in and out of balance (*14.1). There are basically only two situations to consider:

1. *forces out of balance*: the movement and/or shape of the object are changing;
2. *forces in balance*: the movement and/or shape of the object are not changing.

This approach emphasizes that it is the *change* in the shape of an object or the way it is moving which tells us most about the forces acting on it; and that the absence of change is just as significant as change itself.

14.2: Forces out of balance: basic investigations

Making some simple equipment

*Materials and equipment: **Pusher** (for each one): softwood 5 × 2.5 × 20cm; 2 round wire nails 5cm long; elastic band. **Push–pull** (for each one): plastic pipe 10cm diameter × 5cm long; wood dowel 0.5cm (5mm) diameter × 20cm long; masking tape; wire paper-clip; elastic band; drill and drill-bit to drill hole with clearance for dowel; hacksaw. **Trolley** (for each one): soft wood 15 × 6 × 1cm; 4 card or moulded wheels, 2 dowel axles to fit wheels 8cm long; 2 plastic straws, diameter wider than axles, 6cm long; hot-melt glue and glue-gun.*

To carry out simple investigations on changes of movement, it is worth making some simple equipment. What is needed is a device to apply forces in a consistent and predictable way, coupled with toys or specially-made trolleys whose movements can easily be observed.

The most easily-made and obtained equipment is a toy car propelled by a simple elastic band 'pusher' (Fig. 14.7). By pulling the car back to different positions this can be used to reinforce the idea that 'the bigger the force applied, the bigger the change it brings about'.

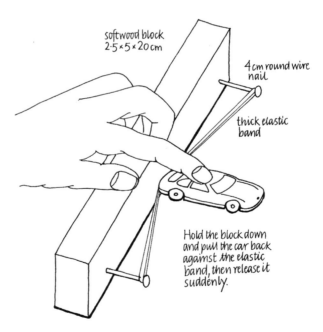

softwood block
2·5×5×20cm

4cm round wire
nail

thick elastic
band

Hold the block down
and pull the car back
against the elastic
band, then release it
suddenly.

Figure 14.7   Toy car and pusher

Slightly more elaborate but with a much wider range of experimental possibilities are the 'push-pull' device and the simple trolley shown in Fig. 14.8. When it is pulled and released the rod springs back, exerting a pulling force at one end and a pushing force at the other. The magnitude of these forces can be changed by moving the sliding rod a greater or lesser amount and by using elastic bands of differing

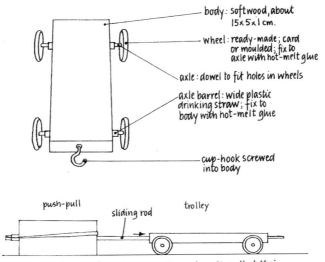

body: softwood, about 15x5x1 cm.

wheel: ready-made; card or moulded; fix to axle with hot-melt glue

axle: dowel to fit holes in wheels

axle barrel: wide plastic drinking straw; fix to body with hot-melt glue

cup-hook screwed into body

push-pull   sliding rod   trolley

Make your trolleys first; then make the push-pulls so that their sliding rods are the correct height to push on the trolleys.

Figure 14.8a   Trolley

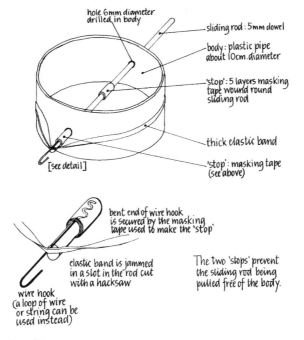

hole 6mm diameter drilled in body

sliding rod: 5mm dowel

body: plastic pipe about 10cm. diameter

'stop': 5 layers masking tape wound round sliding rod

thick elastic band

'stop': masking tape (see above)

[see detail]

bent end of wire hook is secured by the masking tape used to make the 'stop'

elastic band is jammed in a slot in the rod cut with a hacksaw

The two 'stops' prevent the sliding rod being pulled free of the body.

wire hook (a loop of wire or string can be used instead)

Figure 14.8b   'Push-pull'

thicknesses; or kept constant by moving the sliding rod to the same, marked, point
each time before releasing it.

Activity 14.2.1

Investigating changes of movement

Equipment: Push-pull; trolley; variety of toys and movable objects which can slide or roll.

- Use the sliding rod of the push-pull to push the trolley, using different forces.
  Notice that the bigger the force applied, the faster the trolley goes to begin with,
  and the further it travels.
- Pull the trolley using a thin thread looped over the hooks on the trolley and the
  sliding rod of the push-pull.
- Experiment by pushing (and, if possible, pulling) a variety of movable objects,
  including some which move by sliding as well as those which roll.
- ? Why do some go further than others when pushed or pulled with the same force
  on the same surface? (Because the forces slowing them down [friction forces,
  Section 14.3] are different.)
- ? When the trolley is pushed, what force makes it move forward? (The push force
  from the rod, which is itself *pulled* by the elastic band.)
- ? Is there any force tending to prevent the trolley from moving forward from rest?
  (Yes: friction in the wheels and axles.)
- ? When the trolley is rolling forward, is there any force making it move forward?
  (**No**: see next paragraph.)

Children will often explain that 'the object's weight carries it forward' and that it
stops 'because it runs out of push'. Both these explanations are mistaken. There
is no force making the trolley move forward once it has lost contact with whatever is pushing it. The confusion seems to arise because it is common experience
that if we don't keep pushing or pulling things, they stop. But they stop because
forces acting in the *opposite* direction – usually friction – impede their forward
movement.

- ? When the trolley is rolling, is there a force tending to slow it down? (Yes, there
  must be, because it slows down. The force is friction on the wheels and axles.)
- ? In which direction does this friction force act? (Because it slows the trolley down,
  it must be acting in a direction *opposite* to the trolley's movement.)

This activity can also form an introduction to work on friction (see Activity 14.3.3).

Activity 14.2.2

Forces out of balance: changes of direction

*Equipment: Footballs; marker cones (8 for each group); basketball; 'Unihoc' or similar sticks, with
ball or puck; volleyball (with net if available).*

When a force acts on an object in a direction different from that in which it is
travelling, the direction of its movement will be changed. This is experienced in most

ball games, in which the magnitude and direction of the force applied to the ball is critical.

Examples of activities which can usefully be analyzed include:

- Controlled 'dribbling' of the ball between and around marker-cones, either in the context of football (soccer) or hockey;
- controlled running and bouncing with one hand, for example with one bounce every two strides, as in basketball;
- playing volleyball, if necessary in a simplified form;
- 'one-touch' passing in any game.
[● Activity 15.2.2 is also useful.]

Activity 14.2.3

Forces out of balance: changes of shape

Equipment: Shallow container, silver sand sufficient to make a layer 2cm deep in it; metre stick; glass marbles; modelling clay (warmed); scales to weigh 100g; paint and brushes; sugar-paper.

If unbalanced forces act on a flexible object, they will change its shape if they are large enough. This is what happens when plastic and elastic objects are squashed and stretched (see, for example, Sections 7.5, 7.6 and 14.1). These examples can be used to demonstrate the principle that 'the larger the force, the larger the change it brings about', which can be further reinforced in significant ways by investigating changes of shape which occur when falling objects hit the ground.

When a falling object hits the ground it is brought to rest more or less suddenly. This event is called impact. The force which stops the object must act in a direction opposite to its movement, i.e. *upwards*. The magnitude of this force, and therefore the violence of the impact, depends on the mass of the object, how fast it is travelling and how rigid the surface is.

Sand splashes
- Put a layer of dry silver sand 2cm deep into a shallow container.
- Drop glass marbles of the same size into the sand from differing heights and compare the sizes of the splash craters produced.

The size of the splash crater is a measure of the 'change of shape' brought about in the sand, and can be related to the length of fall and the force of impact. On a small scale, the impact of the marble on the sand is a very violent event. This activity can be used to emphasize that the faster an object is travelling, the more violent the impact will be if it is stopped suddenly, and the more damage this will do: a significant point in road safety.

Dropping modelling clay
Modelling clay such as 'Plasticene' is an almost perfectly plastic material (Activity 7.6.1) which when warmed is very easily shaped and squashed.

- Weigh out 100g pieces of modelling clay and shape them into spheres.
- Drop the spheres from differing heights between 0.5 and 2m on to a smooth, rigid surface. The impact will produce a flat face on the sphere. The size of this flat face

is a measure of the change of shape undergone and therefore the magnitude of the impact force and, indirectly, the speed of fall at the moment of impact.

- An alternative is to use the same sphere dropped from different heights, re-shaping it for each trial. The size of each impact face can be recorded by brushing paint onto it and printing it. This gives a very clear visual comparison.

The flattened impact face on the sphere of clay shows clearly that the force which stops its fall is an *upward* one. If the children are doubtful about this, ask them to try to reproduce the flat face by squashing with their hands and see which in direction they have to press! Discussing the implication of this with more able pupils, it may be useful to compare this with the friction forces exerted by the brakes of a bicycle or car: they too act in a direction opposite to the movement of the vehicle, i.e. backwards.

14.3: Friction

Friction is a force which tends to impede the movement of objects and materials past each other, regardless of whether they are solids, liquids or gases. Most children can readily develop and use the concept of friction as a force which slows down moving objects and makes things difficult to move (see Activity 14.2.1). More difficult, but equally necessary to an understanding of movement in everyday life, is the idea of friction which prevents movement in one way and so makes it possible in another.

Activity 14.3.1

Static and limiting friction

Equipment: As shown in Fig. 14.9, with a variety of surfaces, both on the 'sliders' and the base-board. These could include plain wood or chipboard, fine and coarse sandpaper and carpet.

Basic understanding of friction as a force which impedes movement of surfaces past one another can be developed using simple equipment as shown in Fig. 14.9. As the bucket is loaded (with sand or known masses) the pulling force on the string and the 'slider' increases, and so does the friction (static friction) between the 'slider' and the base-board. At this point the two forces are in balance, so the 'slider' stays still. When the pulling force is greater than the friction between the 'slider' and the surface it is resting on, the forces are no longer in balance so that the bucket, string and slider will move.

The greatest static friction which there can be between two surfaces is known as the limiting friction, which can be measured using a forcemeter. Once the 'slider' is moving, the pulling force needed to keep it moving will usually be less than the limiting friction, because the moving surfaces cannot grip together as firmly as they can when they are stationary. Children can usefully experiment with a variety of surfaces, as listed above and try to explain the differences between them. The 'sliders' can also be loaded with masses or bricks: this will increase the limiting friction by pressing the two surfaces more closely together.

The direction in which static friction acts
When the string on the slider is pulled, it tightens, showing that the friction force is acting *in the opposite direction* from the the pulling forces which are tending to

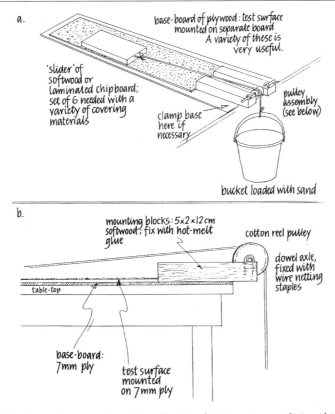

Figure 14.9   Simple equipment to investigate limiting friction: a) general view; b) detail of pulley

make the slider move. This is true generally: friction acts in the opposite direction from the movement of the object which is experiencing it, so that it always tends to slow a moving object down.

Activity 14.3.2

Friction and walking
Friction is often thought of as a nuisance, a force which slows things down, but without static friction most forms of movement on foot and in vehicles would be impossible. When walking, for example, the sole of the foot and the floor are pressed firmly together so the limiting friction between them is very high. If possible it is useful to carry out the following observations both barefoot and with shoes on.

- Stand with both feet flat on the floor. Without lifting your body weight from either foot, try to slide one foot forwards, backwards or sideways. (On surfaces which are safe to walk on, this cannot be done because the limiting friction is too high.)
- Transfer more of your body weight on to one foot and try to move the other sideways. (Only when the load on one foot has been significantly reduced will it be possible to slide it across the floor.)

- Working in pairs, watch your partner's feet carefully as (s)he walks past slowly.
? When do the feet move forward? (The feet move forward only when they are lifted from the floor.)

When walking, the leg pushes backwards on the foot. Static friction between the foot and the floor prevents the foot from sliding back, so the body is pushed forward as the leg straightens. It may be easier for children to see this when their partner is barefoot. They may also be able to feel the pushing action of their own legs more readily if they walk backwards. If the limiting friction between foot and ground is lessened, for example on ice or a slippery wet floor, normal walking is impossible and dangerous falls are likely to occur.

Activity 14.3.3

Sliding and rolling friction

Equipment: Base-board and 'slider' (Fig. 14.9); forcemeter; a long narrow tray about 60 × 15cms covered with glass marbles, all of the same size, leaving enough room for them to move around freely; a set of eight cylindrical rollers 10cm long and all of the same thickness (these can be made from 20mm diameter dowel or a broom handle).

Although friction is necessary for some kinds of movement such as walking (and for wheeled vehicles), there are many situations where it is a disadvantage and can usefully be reduced. One way of doing this is to eliminate sliding between surfaces and substitute rolling movement.

- Using a plain wood 'slider' with a brick on it and pulled by a forcemeter, find the limiting friction between the slider and the base board as described in Activity 14.3.1.
- Now place the the tray of marbles on the base-board. Put the loaded 'slider' on to the marbles and again find the limiting friction.
- Alternatively, use the rollers. This requires co-operative work in a team of three. One person reads and pulls the forcemeter, a second takes rollers from behind the 'slider' as it moves, while a third places rollers in front of it. Start with the 'slider' on three or four rollers, pull the forcemeter until it starts to move and then keep it moving slowly so that the rollers can be taken up and replaced.

Comparing the forces needed to move the load shows clearly that rolling friction is much less than sliding friction.

Activity 14.3.4

Solid-air friction and parachutes

Equipment and materials: A variety of fabrics, including woven cloth and plastic sheet; thin string; yogurt pots; 20g masses or weighed modelling clay; scissors; metre sticks.

When an object is moving through air, friction forces are set up between them which tend to slow the movement of the object. Taken together these friction forces are known as air resistance or drag. The design of cars attempts to minimize drag so that fuel consumption is reduced, but in some circumstances drag can be very useful. One of these is when objects are falling from a great height and there is a need to slow them down so that the impact when they hit the ground (see Activity 14.2.3) is minimised. The device most often used to achieve this is a parachute.

When investigating parachutes it is often helpful to give the children a definite task: for example, to make a parachute which will lower a load of 20g as slowly as possible from a height of 2m. It may also be helpful to place restrictions on the size of the canopy to be used, for example, not more than 25cm across in any direction. This still leaves many variables for the children to explore:

- shape of canopy;
- number of strings;
- length of strings;
- type of material used;

as well as the problem of how to attach the load to the strings and the strings to the canopy. Questions of fair testing may also arise; for example, should a parachute be dropped with the canopy open, or rolled up?

If the parachutes swing a lot they can usually be made more stable by cutting one or more holes in the centre of the canopy to allow a flow of air through. This can lead to further enquiries: for example how big the holes can be without reducing the performance of the parachute.

The behaviour of parachutes is complex and difficult to explain in detail, but the basic principle of the way they work is not. When an object falls it speeds up because it is acted on by the Earth's gravitational force (i.e. its own weight). To reduce the speed of its fall it is necessary to apply a force in the opposite direction, i.e. upwards. In the case of the parachute this upward force is drag generated by the canopy as it is pulled down through the air. Many fruits and seeds also have 'parachutes' which help their dispersal (Activity 5.6.2).

14.4 Forces and machines

A machine is a device which, by applying and transferring forces, enables a person to do something which they cannot do unaided. Most simple hand tools are machines which enable the user to bring about changes in movement (e.g. screwdriver, claw-hammer, nut and bolt, spanner) or shape (scissors, pliers, garlic press, can opener) and which therefore work when unbalanced forces are applied to them.

All simple machines work by transferring a force applied by the user (the effort) to a point at which it acts to overcome some kind of resisting force (the load). The force can be a force resisting movement, usually friction or weight; or a resistance to change of shape, which is a measure of the strength and stiffness of the object (Sections 7.5, 7.7). When investigating how simple machines work it is important that children identify the effort and the load in each case. In nearly all the machines children are likely to work with the effort is a small force operating over a large distance, which the machine changes into a much larger force operating over a much smaller distance, in order to overcome the load. Because of this, these machines are sometimes called force-multipliers.

Activity 14.4.1

Simple levers: removing a can lid

Equipment: Empty cans with tightly-fitting lids; old screwdrivers (this activity can easily ruin a good screwdriver!)

- Use the screwdriver to remove the lid of the can (Fig. 14.10a). To try again, tap the lid on *gently* with a light hammer, or push it on firmly with the sole of your shoe.

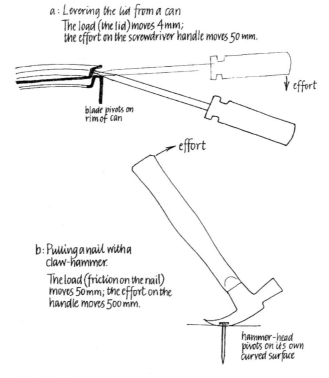

a: *Levering the lid from a can*
The load (the lid) moves 4mm;
the effort on the screwdriver handle moves 50 mm.

blade pivots on
rim of can

effort

effort

b: *Pulling a nail with a claw-hammer.*
The load (friction on the nail) moves 50mm; the effort on the handle moves 500 mm.

hammer-head pivots on its own curved surface

Figure 14.10 Two simple lever systems

? What is the load? (Friction between the lid and the can.)
? What is the effort? (Downward push force applied by the hand to the screwdriver handle.)

The screwdriver is acting as a simple lever, which pivots on the outer rim of the can.

? How far does the effort move? (Measure movement of the screwdriver handle.)
? How far does the load move? (Estimate how far the can lid is lifted before it becomes free.)

Notice how much further the effort moves than the load. This gives a rough guide to how much the lever is multiplying the force of the load. If, for example, the effort moves 50mm and the load moves 4mm, the lever is multiplying the force by 50÷4, i.e. the load is 12.5 times greater than the effort.

Activity 14.4.2

More simple machines

Children can find out more about how simple machines multiply forces by experimenting with a claw-hammer pulling nails out of wood (Fig. 14.10b), nuts and bolts turned with a spanner holding pieces of wood together (Fig. 14.11) and scissors cutting card (Fig. 14.12).

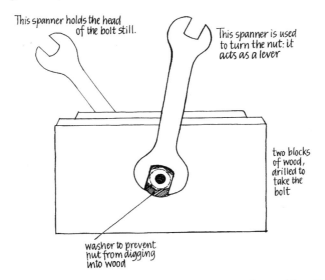

This spanner holds the head of the bolt still.

This spanner is used to turn the nut: it acts as a lever

two blocks of wood, drilled to take the bolt

washer to prevent nut from digging into wood

Figure 14.11   Using nut, screw-thread and spanners as a simple machine. Both the spanner (lever) and the screw-thread are force-multipliers. Together they make the nut and bolt exert a very large (compression) force on the wood

Activity 14.4.3

The bicycle: a more complex machine

Equipment: Bicycles.

The bicycle is a complex system which is in effect an assembly of simple machines. Many of these can be understood in terms of basic ideas on machines and friction. Some of the simpler ones which could be investigated are:

- *brakes*: levers; cables to transfer forces by pulling; high friction between brake-blocks and wheels;
- *wheels*: held in place by screw-threads and nuts on the spindles; low-friction bearings in hubs (ball-races and grease);
- *cranks, chain and gears*: cranks are levers, chainwheel and gears are cogs; force from cranks is transferred by chain being pulled forwards by chainwheel; low-friction bearings in bottom-bracket; friction between chain and cogs reduced by oil.

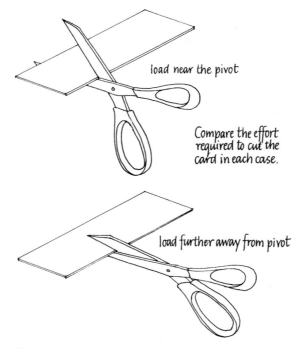

load near the pivot

Compare the effort
required to cut the
card in each case.

load further away from pivot

The nearer the load (resistance of card) is to the pivot, the
greater the (shear) force exerted by the blades.

Figure 14.12   Scissors as a lever system

14.5: Forces in balance

If the movement or shape of an object are changing, the forces acting on it are out of
balance. If the movement or shape of an object remain unchanged, the forces acting
on it are in balance. Pulling and pushing actions using elastic objects are useful
introductory examples (Activity 14.1.4). One mistaken idea which it is necessary to
avoid, or overcome when it appears in children's explanations, is the belief that if
movement and shape are not changing, no forces are acting on an object. This may
be particularly difficult for children to understand when there are no changes to be
observed and the forces acting are not at all obvious.

Activity 14.5.1

Beam balances

Equipment: Simple beam balances (preferably a range of different types); masses ('weights');
objects to weigh; modelling clay.

The beam balance has a great advantage as a starting-point for systematic investigations into forces in balance. Forces (weights) are clearly acting on it, but the beam
will stay still and level only when these are balanced exactly.

- Use known masses ('weights') to check that the balances are correctly adjusted both when empty and when loaded.
- Balance the beam with masses, objects or pieces of modelling clay.
? What do you know about the weights (forces) on the two pans? (They are in balance: equal and acting downwards.)
- Add a small piece of modelling clay to one pan. Observe and describe what happens.
? How does this change the forces acting on the beam? (They are out of balance.)
? What is the result? (The pan with the larger weight acting on it moves down but stops when it comes to rest on the frame of the balance.)
- Add modelling clay to one pan until the beam is level and balanced again.
? To which pan did you have to add the modelling clay? (The one with the smaller weight acting on it.)
? How much did you have to add? (The same amount that was added to the other pan when the balance was upset.)
- Particularly with younger children, repeated trials both adding material and taking it away can be a useful way of developing the ability and willingness to predict the results of actions.

Throughout investigations using beam balances it is helpful to keep reinforcing the idea that it is forces out of balance which cause *change* of movement (in this case, movement from rest). If nothing is changing, the forces acting on the system are in balance.

Activity 14.5.2

Experiencing forces in balance
Children throughout the primary age range are more likely to develop scientific concepts of force and use these consistently if they are used to explain what they experience with their own bodies. Two ways of experiencing forces in balance are set out in Activity 14.1.4.

Activities as part of PE can also be useful and it may be helpful to begin work on these some days before the topic of forces in balance is introduced in science.

Equipment: Thick soft rope (for a tug-of-war).

- Balance and body control: ask children to balance on one foot, in any position. This can be achieved only by balancing the weight of the body around the foot on the ground and staying still.
- Now move one arm or leg.
? What happens? (Either you move another part of your body to compensate and stay in balance, or you fall over!)
- Tug-of-war: try contests with randomly selected teams. Notice that when the pulls are equal, neither team moves.
? If teams are not equal, which way do the teams move? (In the direction of the bigger pull.)
- Now try with the six smallest children in the class against the six largest.
? Who wins? (The largest children.) Is it a fair contest? (No.) Why not? (Because the forces cannot be balanced.)

Activity 14.5.3

Forces in balance: object stationary

Equipment: Bricks or other objects of similar mass (about 3 kg): top-pan spring balances (kitchen scale type).

For many children (and not a few adults) the most puzzling case of forces in balance is that of an object at rest, as when a book rests on a table. The difficulty is usually to convince children that any forces at all are being exerted by a passive surface such as a table or floor, which isn't 'doing' anything. One strategy to overcome this is to combine physical, hands-on experience with questioning in quite a structured way. What follows is one example of a possible sequence.

- Put a brick on a table.
? What would happen if the table were not there? (The brick would fall.)
? Why doesn't the brick fall? (The table is stopping it or holding it up.)
? How is the table preventing the brick from falling? (Answers to this should reveal something of the children's own ideas; the remainder of the activity is aimed at finding a scientific answer.)
- Hold out your arm, half-bent with the hand flat, palm up. Place a brick on your hand.
? Why doesn't the brick fall? (Your hand is supporting it.)
? How is your hand able to support the brick? (Because your arm is pushing up on it.)

This makes the point that an object at rest does not fall because it is being supported by an *upward* force equal to its own weight. The two forces are in balance so the movement of the object does not change, i.e. it stays still. The same principle of a balanced supporting force is essential to an understanding of floating (see Section 14.6).

- To measure the upward force which is preventing the brick from falling, place it on a top-pan balance.
? What happens, and why? (When the brick is put on the pan, forces are not in balance, so it moves down until the upward force from the spring inside the balance is equal to the weight of the brick. This should be measured in newtons, not kilograms, see Activity 14.1.3.)

Activity 14.5.4

Forces in balance: object moving

Equipment: Parachutes (see Activity 14.3.4); small gliders or paper aeroplanes.

A stationary object is perhaps the most obvious example of something whose movement is not changing; but this is also true of an object which is moving in a straight line at a constant speed. If movement of this kind is observed, it implies that the forces acting on the object are in balance. It is difficult to demonstrate this principle convincingly in the primary classroom because speed cannot be measured accurately, but interesting examples can arise in play with parachutes and small model gliders.

- When a stable parachute has been made (see Activity 14.3.4), observe changes in its speed as it falls.

As it begins to fall the parachute will speed up until the drag on the canopy (upward force) is equal to the weight of the parachute and its load (downward force). The forces on the parachute are in balance, so its movement does not change: it is moving in a straight line, vertically down, and at what appears to be a constant speed.

- Use or make a small glider or paper aeroplane which will glide *slowly* from a very gentle launch.

The fall of a glider is slowed not by drag, as a parachute is, but by lift. This is an upward force exerted on the wing as it slices through the air (see also Activity 5.6.2). When the glider is in a straight-line slow glide, all the forces acting on it are in balance so that its movement does not change perceptibly, either in speed or direction.

14.6: Floating and sinking

Although most children experience floating and sinking very early in their lives through play, developing a scientific understanding of it is far from easy. Simple activities such as the classification of materials and objects into 'floaters' and 'sinkers' are useful at any point in the primary age-range as an introduction to more systematic investigations.

When an object floats in a liquid, or in air as a hot-air balloon does, it neither rises nor falls, so the forces acting on it must be in balance. Since gravitational force (the weight of the object) acts downwards, there must be an equal force acting upwards. This upward force is known as upthrust. When starting to develop a scientific understanding of floating and sinking, therefore, the first idea to establish is that an object floats because it is prevented from falling.

Activity 14.6.1

Floating as arrested fall

Equipment: Large plastic bowls; buckets; water; table-tennis balls.

- Hold a table-tennis ball over an empty plastic bowl. Predict what will happen if the ball is dropped. (It will fall and hit the bottom of the bowl.)
- Half fill the bowl with water and hold the ball over it. Predict what will happen if the ball is dropped. (It will fall to the surface of the water and float.)
- ? Why doesn't the ball hit the bottom of the bowl when there is water in it? (It is stopped by the water.)
- ? A force must have acted on the ball to stop its fall. In what direction did this force act? (In the direction opposite to the ball's movement, i.e. upwards, see Activity 14.2.3.)
- Try to make the ball sink by pushing it under the water. Predict what will happen when you let it go. (It will come up to the surface again.)
- What makes the ball come up? (An upward force on it from the water.)

- Fill a bucket nearly full of water. Push the ball down to the bottom. Predict what will happen when it is released. (The ball will usually come up so fast that it shoots out of the water.)

The last two observations show that water can exert large upward pushing forces on objects. This force is called upthrust.

Activity 14.6.2

Displacement and upthrust

Equipment: Inflated play-ball; bucket of larger diameter than ball; large bowl; water.

This activity investigates the way in which water exerts upthrust and it is also a good way of experiencing pushing action (see Activity 14.1.4).

- Stand the bucket in the bowl and fill it completely with water.
- Float the play-ball on the water, then push it down a little, gently.
- ? What do you observe? (Water overflows from the bucket into the bowl, see Fig. 14.6.)

As the ball is pushed down, it pushes some of the water aside and occupies space within the bucket. There is not enough room in the bucket for the ball and the water, so the water overflows. This is called displacement. The more the ball is pushed down into the bucket, the greater the displacement and the resulting overflow of water.

- Push the ball further down into the water, then hold it down.
- ? What force do you have to exert on the ball to keep it from rising up? (A downward push force.)
- ? While you hold the ball down, it does not move, so the forces acting on it must be in balance. What force is balancing your downward push? (The upward push of the water on the ball, i.e. upthrust.)
- Push the ball down even further into the water and hold it down.
- ? As you push the ball deeper into the water, what changes are there in the amount of water displaced and the force needed to hold the ball down? (Both become greater.)

This investigation shows that, as more water is displaced, the upthrust on the ball increases (see also Activity 14.6.3).

Activity 14.6.3

Floating and sinking

Equipment and materials: Blocks of softwood about 20 × 10 × 2.5cm; range of masses ('weights') 10g–100g; modelling clay; elastic bands; bowls; water.

Any object can float only if it can displace enough water to generate upthrust equal to its own weight. This means that if the weight of a floating object is increased, it must displace more water in order to stay afloat. If its weight is increased so much that it cannot displace enough water, it will sink.

- Float a block of wood on water. Measure how much is above the water.
- Put a load on the block so that it still floats level. The load has to be *under* the floating block, or it will turn over. Hold the load on with elastic bands.
? What happens when a load is added to the block? (It sinks deeper in the water.)
? Why does this happen? (The weight of the block plus load has been increased, so a greater upthrust is needed to balance it. Upthrust can be increased only if more water is displaced, so the block sinks lower, pushing aside more water.)
- Carry on loading the block, keeping it level, until you find the load needed to make it sink.
? Why does the block eventually sink? (It sinks because it cannot displace enough water to generate a big enough upthrust to balance its weight. The forces acting on it cannot be balanced, so it keeps on moving downwards, i.e. it sinks.)

Activity 14.6.4

Making a 'sinker' float
A material which will sink when in a lump may float if its shape is changed so that it displaces more water.

Equipment and materials: Bowls; water; modelling clay; rectangles 10 × 5 cm of thick aluminium foil (e.g. from food trays).

- Make a solid ball of modelling clay about 5cm diameter; find out if it sinks or floats. (It sinks.)
- Try to think of a way to change the shape of the modelling clay so that it will float. (Two ways are: make a flat rectangular sheet and pinch it into a boat shape; or press into the ball to make it hollow, then keep moulding and pinching to make a hemispherical cup shape.)
? Why will your shape float, when the same material in a lump will not? (Its shape, a hollow shell filled with air, means that it can displace more water than a solid lump and so gain enough upthrust to balance its weight.)
- Try the same experiment with aluminium foil.

This investigation shows why it is possible to make ships from dense materials such as steel.

- Now make a hole in the bottom of your floating shape of modelling clay and try to float it again. (It will sink.)
? Why does the shape sink when it has a hole in it? (As it fills with water, upthrust is reduced. When the upward force is too small to balance the weight of the clay, it sinks.)

This shows why steel ships sink if they have a hole in the bottom.

15

Gravity and Magnetism

15.1: Action-at-a-distance

Both gravity and magnetism result in forces being exerted on objects. Ideas about forces as pushes and pulls, which may be in balance or not (*14.1), apply to all forces, but gravitational and magnetic forces are mysterious because they can be exerted by objects which are not in contact with one another. This is called action-at-a-distance (*15.1). It may be useful, particularly with older and more able children, to introduce the idea of action-at-a-distance before beginning more detailed investigations on gravity and magnetism.

Activity 15.1.1

Action-at-a-distance by a magnet

Equipment: One or more 'strong' magnets; small plain steel paper-clips; thin thread; Blu-Tack or similar material; sharp scissors.

- Tie 30cm thread to a paper-clip; fasten the other end to a table or desk with Blu-tack. Use the magnet to lift the paper-clip and thread until the thread is vertical and taut.
- Now carry on lifting the magnet very slowly.
- ? What happens? (The paper-clip becomes detached from the magnet and 'floats' in mid-air at the end of the thread; see Fig. 15.1.)
- ? What is holding the paper-clip up? (A magnetic pulling force.)
- ? What is holding the paper-clip down? (Its own weight and the pull of the thread.)
- ? How is the pull force exerted by the magnet different from that exerted by the thread?

The thread can pull (mechanical force) only when it is attached to the clip. The magnet can pull (magnetic force) even when it is not in contact with the clip. This is an example of action-at-a-distance.

If children are doubtful about the pull of the thread holding the paper-clip down against the upward pull of the magnet, make the clip 'float' in mid-air as shown in Fig. 15.1. Ask them to predict what will happen if the thread is cut with sharp

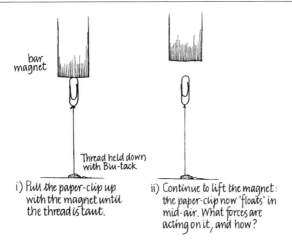

i) Pull the paper-clip up with the magnet until the thread is taut.

ii) Continue to lift the magnet: the paper-clip now 'floats' in mid-air. What forces are acting on it, and how?

bar magnet

Thread held down with Blu-tack

Figure 15.1 Action-at-a-distance by a magnet

scissors, then see if their predictions are correct. (The clip, now free to move, will move *upward* and attach itself to the magnet.)

Activity 15.1.2

Action-at-a-distance by gravity

Equipment: Table-tennis or other lightweight play-balls; thread; Blu-tack.

Several of the activities on forces discussed in Chapter 14 make use of and illustrate this action, e.g. 14.2.3, 14.3.4, 14.5.4, 14.6.1.

- Fasten 30cm thread to a table-tennis or other lightweight ball using Blu-tack. Hold the thread with the ball suspended.
- ? What forces are acting on the ball? (The ball remains still, so the forces acting on it must be in balance [*14.1, *14.5]. The downward force is gravitational, i.e. the weight of the ball; the upward force is the pull of the thread.)
- ? If the ball were released by cutting the thread, what would happen? (It would fall.)
- ? What makes it fall? (Gravitational force.)

Gravitation is an example of action-at-a-distance, but because we all experience it all the time it is difficult for children to understand it as a force which acts on objects even when they are not in contact. The key to understanding its significance is the realization that objects do not 'just' fall. As with any other change in movement, an object held up and then released falls only because unbalanced forces are acting on it (see *14.1 and Section 14.2). The idea of gravitation as action-at-a-distance under-lies all our understanding and predictions of, for example, how galaxies, stars, planets and satellites move in space (see Chapter 18).

Gravitational and magnetic fields

A scientific approach to gravity and magnetism can be made much easier by develop-ing a simple idea: the concept of *field*. A field is, simply, a zone around an object (e.g.

a magnet or the Earth) in which another object experiences forces, *whether or not the two are in contact*. Children may well be familiar with this idea in a fictional form ('force-fields') through watching science-fiction on TV. Pointing out that gravity and magnetism involve real 'force-fields' that we can investigate can be a useful motivating strategy at the start of work on these topics.

15.2: Gravity

All objects have gravitational fields, but unless the object is very massive, e.g. the Sun, Earth or Moon, this field is so weak that it can be detected only by very sensitive measuring methods and has no effect on human activities. An object in a gravitational field experiences a force which tends to make it move towards the (larger) object creating the field. We call such a movement falling and the gravitational force which causes it is the weight of the object.

Experiencing gravity
Children need to experience freely-falling and suspended objects in a wide variety of ways in order to develop and reinforce the basic ideas that:

i) the change in movement of a falling object is an example of action-at-a-distance (see Activity 15.1.2);
ii) objects fall first, because a force (gravitational force) acts on them, and secondly because this force is not balanced by other forces. If gravitational force is balanced by another force, such as an upward push from whatever is supporting it, the object will not fall: see Activities 14.5.3, 14.6.1, 14.6.3);
iii) gravitational force always acts in the same direction (vertically downwards);
iv) the gravitational force acting on an object is always the same if the object remains unchanged and in the same place. For example, if an object is hung from a forcemeter for days or weeks it can be seen that its weight does not change unless the object itself is changed by adding material or taking it away (i.e. by changing the mass of the object).

Activity 15.2.1

Simple investigations with falling objects

Equipment: Selection of play-balls and other non-fragile, soft or lightweight objects, e.g. unifix cubes, small plastic toys, lolly-sticks; in boxes or bags, one for each working group.

The idea that gravity affects all objects near or on the Earth can be developed simply by holding up a range of objects and releasing them.

- Hold up each of the things in your box or bag in turn and let it go. Watch what happens. (Unless there is good reason to do otherwise it may be prudent to limit dropping experiments to a fall of 1m on to a soft surface, e.g. carpet.)
? Are there any things in your box or bag which *didn't* fall when you dropped them? (No.)
? Which way did they fall? (Straight down.) Did they all fall the same way? (Yes.)

? Are you affected in the same way? How do you know? (Yes: if we jump off things we fall and hit the ground. Also we are held down on to the ground all the time: if we jump up, we're pulled back down again.)

Notice that up to this point the term 'gravity' has not been used or needed at all: this would be an appropriate point to introduce, or re-introduce, it. The force which makes things fall and holds them down on the ground is gravitational force. The Earth has a gravitational field around it. Anything in that field experiences gravitational force and is attracted towards the Earth. Activity 14.2.3 can be used to reinforce this idea.

Some children may point out that there are objects which do not fall when they are released, e.g. balloons filled with hot air or certain gases (usually helium). These are a special case because they are so light in relation to their volume that they float in air (*14.6), but if the hot air cools down or the helium escapes the balloon falls just as any other object does.

The direction of gravitational force
Like all forces, gravitational force is a vector quantity: it has both magnitude and direction. The fact that gravitational force always acts vertically downwards (i.e. towards the centre of the Earth) has profound significance for our technology. For example, a weight freely suspended on a string will always hang so that the string is vertical when the weight is still, and the plumb-line is one of the oldest and most widespread measuring devices. It has been used for thousands of years in building, where walls are built and supports set up vertically in order to mimimize bending forces and make the best use of materials which are stiff and strong in compression (*10.2).

Activity 15.2.2

Changes of direction in falling

Equipment: Table-tennis or other lightweight balls; stiff lightweight boards or thin books, about A4 size.

If an object is held still and released, and no other forces are acting on it, it will always fall vertically; but our common experience is that objects do *not* always fall vertically. If an object is not falling vertically, other forces must be acting on it from other directions. An obvious example is a parachute falling in a cross-wind or with a tilted canopy. Less spectacular but more familiar is the path of an object which is moved out of its vertical fall by a sideways force.

- Work in threes. One person holds a ball up, head-high, between finger and thumb. The second holds a board or a thin, stiff book at about 45° to the vertical directly under the ball (Fig. 15.2), so that when the ball is dropped it will hit the board. The third person stands to the side to observe the path of the ball.
- Take turns to observe the fall of the ball. Draw a simple picture to show its path as it falls and bounces, then check your picture by looking again carefully at the ball as it falls.

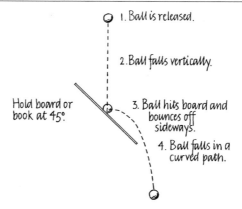

1. Ball is released.

2. Ball falls vertically.

Hold board or book at 45°.

3. Ball hits board and bounces off sideways.

4. Ball falls in a curved path.

Figure 15.2   Change of direction in falling

? What happens when the ball is dropped? (The ball falls vertically until it hits the board. It bounces off to one side and falls in a *curved* path (Fig. 15.2).
? When the ball was released, what made it fall vertically? (Gravitational force.)
? What made it change direction? (Hitting the board; more exactly, a sideways push force from the board as the ball bounced.)
? Why did the ball fall in a curved path after it bounced? (Because it was moving sideways at the same time that gravitational force was pulling it down.)

If an object is moving sideways at the same time that gravitational force is pulling it down, its path will always be curved. This kind of movement occurs in any sport which involves kicking, hitting or throwing flying objects, but can be seen most clearly when the object moves fairly slowly, as in football, netball, badminton and shot-putt. A different kind of fall in a curved path is seen in a pendulum (Activity 15.2.3).

Activity 15.2.3

Investigating pendulums

Equipment: Spherical objects 2–3cm in diameter (small 'power-balls', wooden spheres or large steel ballbearings are good, otherwise make spheres of modelling clay); thin thread; lolly-sticks with a narrow notch cut in one end; Blu-tack; adhesive tape; stop-clock or other timer for 1 minute.

A pendulum is a special example of an object which is prevented from falling in a straight line. A simple adjustable pendulum can be made as shown in Fig. 15.3. It is worthwhile taking trouble to find or make a spherical weight or bob as this makes measuring the length of the pendulum much easier.

When a pendulum is at rest it hangs with the thread vertical. When the bob is moved to one side and released it is higher than its rest point. Gravitational force is still acting downwards, but the pull of the thread is now partly sideways (towards the rest position) as well as upwards, so that when released the bob is made to swing in an arc towards its rest position. There is no force acting on it to make it stop there, so it swings past its rest position and upwards in an arc on the opposite

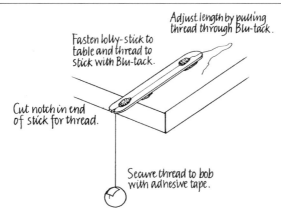

Figure 15.3   A simple adjustable pendulum

side. This movement is then reversed and repeated as the pendulum swings or oscillates.

The movement of the pendulum is opposed by friction forces (air resistance, friction between fibres of the thread and between thread and beam) so that the speed of the bob at the mid-point and the arc of swing (amplitude) will gradually be reduced. However, *the time taken for a complete swing will remain constant,* at least within the limits we can measure in the classroom. When measuring and comparing times the arc of swing (amplitude) should be kept narrow: not more than 10° on either side of the vertical. If this is done, only the length of the pendulum affects the time of swing: changing the weight will have no effect unless the bob is made big enough to set up significantly greater air resistance.

The length of a pendulum should be measured from the point of suspension to the *centre* of the bob, which is much easier if the bob is spherical. To be exact, the time of swing is proportional to the square root of the length. In practical terms this means that to double the time of swing the pendulum has to be four times as long. As a rough guide it will be found that a pendulum 25.5cm long makes one complete swing in 1s, so for a 2s swing it has to be 102cm long.

15.3: Magnets and magnetic materials

Magnets have the property that they create around themselves a magnetic field (*15.1). This is a zone within which objects made of certain materials (magnetic materials) experience forces, while other, non-magnetic materials are unaffected. From the outset it is important to distinguish clearly between magnets and magnetic materials.

A magnetic material has no magnetic field of its own: it is said to be unmagnetized. A magnetic material within the field around a magnet experiences a (magnetic) pulling force, sometimes called magnetic attraction, which tends to make it move towards the magnet, even when the two are not in contact (action-at-a-distance, Section 15.1). Magnetic attraction is further explored in Section 15.6. A magnet is always made of magnetic material, but has been magnetized (Activity 15.6.2) so that it has a magnetic field of its own.

Activity 15.3.1

Sorting magnetic and non-magnetic materials

Equipment: Magnets, preferably in a variety of shapes (bar, disc, ring, horseshoe); a range of small objects in a wide variety of materials, e.g. wood, plastic, card, fabrics, brass (screws), aluminium (foil), copper (thick wire), steel (paper-clips, nails, screws, wire, bolts, nuts), in bags or boxes.

- Test each of the materials in your bag or box with a magnet. Sort them into two sets: those which are attracted to ('stick' to; can be picked up by) the magnet, and those which are not.
- Now test your materials with another magnet of a different shape.
- ? Are your results the same in each case? (Yes.)
- ? What does this tell you? (That magnets of different shapes attract the same things.)

The objects attracted by the magnet are made of magnetic materials. Those not attracted are made of non-magnetic materials.

- Sort all your materials into two new sets: separate the metals from the non-metals. Re-testing if you need to, answer these questions:
- ? Are any of the non-metals magnetic? (No.)
- ? Are all the metals magnetic? (No.)
- Sort the metals into two sets: magnetic and non-magnetic. If you can, identify the metals in each set.

The only magnetic material commonly met with is iron. Nearly all the iron we use is in the form of its harder alloy, steel (*10.2). Most steels are magnetic but some stainless steels are not. Although the non-metals tested by the children are non-magnetic, non-metallic magnetic materials do exist, for example those used to make black 'ceramic' magnets (Section 15.7).

Children may come across objects which look as if they should be non-magnetic but which are attracted to magnets. The commonest ones are screws, hinges and other hardware made of steel thinly coated with brass ('electro-brass') and British 'copper' coins minted after 1992, which have a steel core. In both cases the outer part of the object is non-magnetic but this is no barrier to the influence of a magnet on the steel inside (see also Activity 15.3.3).

Activity 15.3.2

Observing magnetic fields

Equipment: Magnets; thin white card; powdered iron ('iron filings') in a sprinkler-pot; modelling clay.

Magnetic fields are usually invisible, but they have shape and direction. These properties can be made visible by placing a sheet of thin card horizontally over a magnet, where necessary supporting it with modelling clay. Sprinkle a *thin* layer of powdered iron ('iron filings') on to the card and then tap its edges gently with a pencil. The iron particles are magnetic and as the card is tapped they move to form lines which show not only the shape of the magnetic field but also its direction (Fig. 15.4) and thus the

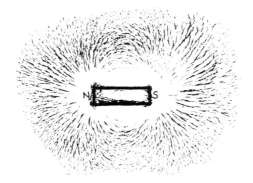

The lines of iron particles show the shape of the field and the direction of magnetic forces in it. These forces act towards the poles of the magnet.

Figure 15.4   Observing the field of a simple bar-magnet

direction of the magnetic force within the field. Because of this, the shape of magnetic fields is often described by drawing imaginary 'lines of force'.

Testing different magnets in this way will show that their fields are differently-shaped. This is particularly useful in understanding how some ceramic magnets behave (Section 15.7) and also shows that some plastic-covered 'bar' magnets are not simple bar-magnets at all, but are made up of small ceramic magnets assembled end-to-end in a plastic case.

Powdered iron needs to be kept dry and handled with care. The best kind of container is a plastic pepper-pot with a screw-on lid. When not in use, cover the holes with Blu-tack or masking tape to prevent spillage. The powdered iron can with care be tipped back into the pot and re-used. If it gets on to magnets it can be removed by wiping and dabbing with small pieces of Blu-tack. Care is needed to prevent it getting on clothes because it will rust very quickly (in hours) and will stain fabrics indelibly.

Activity 15.3.3

Barriers to magnetic fields
Do magnets 'work' only in air? The simple answer is, no; but children can usefully be given the opportunity to find out whether magnets attract magnetic objects through other materials.

Equipment and materials: Magnets; small magnetic objects (e.g. plain steel paper-clips); sheets of a variety of materials, e.g. paper, card, thin plywood, plastic, fabrics, aluminium foil, steel lids from jars or tins (check for sharp edges), plastic cups, water.

For young children, a memorable way of showing that magnets 'work' through some solids and liquids is to find out how to remove a paper-clip from a plastic cup filled with water without getting one's hands wet! For older and more able children, a more systematic approach is helpful:

- Hold a sheet of card flat in one hand. Place a paper-clip on it. Now put a magnet underneath and move it around, touching the card. See if you can make the paper-clip 'follow' the magnet as you move it.
? Does the magnet still attract the clip through the card? (Yes.)
? Does the card act as a barrier to the magnetic field? (No.)
- Repeat your observation with sheets of other materials, e.g. paper, plastic, fabrics, aluminium foil, lids from tins or jars.
? Could the magnet make the clip move through all these materials? (Usually the answer is, no: the clip is attracted only slightly through steel.)
? Was the clip attracted *at all* through steel? (Usually the answer is, yes; because the steel next to the magnet itself becomes magnetized, see Activity 15.6.1.)

As this activity indicates, magnetic fields are unaffected by non-magnetic materials. Children may find out that magnets do not appear to attract magnetic objects through thicker layers of material such as table-tops or books, but this is a result of the distance between magnet and object. As one moves away from a magnet, the intensity of the magnetic field rapidly decreases. This means that the force of attraction between magnet and object becomes so small that it may be difficult to detect.

15.4: The poles of magnets and their behaviour

When sorting magnetic and non-magnetic materials (Activity 15.3.1), children are very likely to observe that in at least some of the magnets they are using, magnetic attraction is not equally strong over the whole magnet. This is seen most clearly with a bar-magnet: the ends (poles) attract magnetic materials most strongly whereas the middle does not attract them at all. This often gives rise to a very common intuitive hypothesis, which appears to explain what is observed but is entirely false: that the poles of the magnet are somehow 'stronger', more highly magnetized or magnetically active than the remainder of it. To understand why this appears to be so, we need to return to the idea of the shape of the field around a bar-magnet (Activity 15.3.2, Fig. 15.4). The pattern of iron particles in the magnetic field shows that at the poles, magnetic force acts *towards* the magnet, whereas in the middle it acts *along* the magnet. The result is that magnetic objects are pulled *towards* the poles and cling to them, but *along* the middle, to which they will not cling, towards one pole or the other.

Activity 15.4.1

Magnetic poles and north-south polarity

The poles of a magnet are those parts at which magnetic force acts directly towards the magnet. The poles of bar and horseshoe magnets are at their ends, whereas those of disc- or ring-shaped magnets are their faces rather than their edges (see Section 15.7).

Since ancient times it has been known that if a long, thin magnet is free to swing it will come to rest pointing in a particular direction. This can easily be shown by suspending a bar-magnet from a thread, but it must be done some way (at least 1m) away from magnetic materials such as the steel frames of furniture. In school buildings with steel girder frames it may be necessary to carry out observations out of doors.

Equipment: Bar-magnet; thread; Blu-tack; some means of suspension (e.g. a wooden rod or cane between two wooden chairs or tables).

- Attach a bar-magnet to the thread with a small piece of Blu-tack, so that the magnet will hang level (horizontally).
- Tie the thread to a support so that the magnet can hang and swing freely. The magnet should be at least 1m away from magnetic materials such as steel-framed furniture.
- Hang the magnet with the thread vertical, so that it does not swing like a pendulum, and let it go. The magnet will nearly always begin to turn to and fro, clockwise and anticlockwise (horizontal oscillation).
- Gradually the magnet will move less and less. When finally it comes to rest, make a note of the direction in which it is pointing.
- Now turn the magnet away from its direction at rest and let it go again.
- ? What happens? (The magnet oscillates and again comes to rest, *pointing in the same direction as before*).
- ? In what direction is the magnet pointing when at rest? (If free from the effect of other magnetic materials, it will point north-south.)
- Find out which end is pointing north, and which south. (This is a good opportunity to remind children that at mid-day the Sun shines from the south in the Northern Hemisphere and from the north in the Southern Hemisphere, see Activity 18.2.3.)
- Mark the end of the magnet which points north with a small piece of Blu-tack. Turn the magnet round so that the marked end is pointing south and let it go.
- ? Will the magnet stay in this position? (No.)
- ? What does this show? (That the magnet not only comes to rest in the same direction each time, but also that its two ends [poles] behave differently.)

The end of the magnet which comes to rest pointing north is called the north-seeking pole or simply the north pole; the other is the south pole.

? What is making the swinging magnet line up north-south? (The magnetic field of the Earth.)

This property of magnets is used in magnetic compasses. These are investigated further in Section 15.5.

Activity 15.4.2

Attraction and repulsion of magnets
Experimenting with a swinging bar-magnet shows that its two poles behave differently. This is a particular example of a general and very important property of magnets: that if two magnets are near each other, their behaviour depends on which poles are brought together.

Equipment: Pairs of bar-magnets, as similar as possible.

- Place one magnet on the table and the other, lined up with it, about 30cm away. Move one closer to the other until *either* they are attracted and come together end-to-end, *or* one moves away from the other.

- Turn one magnet round and try again.
? What happens? (If at first the magnets were attracted, the second time they will push away from one another, and *vice versa*.)

This activity shows the important property of magnetic repulsion, caused by a pushing force between the magnets which tends to keep them apart, in contrast to the pulling force of magnetic attraction which tends to draw them together.

- Label your magnets 1 and 2. Find out which are their north and south poles and mark these.
- Now make the magnets attract and repel each other: there are four different ways to do this. Results can be set out in a table, like this:

Magnet 1	Magnet 2	Attract or repel?
north	south	attract
south	north	attract
north	north	repel
south	south	repel

? What do you notice about the results? (When two north or two south poles are brought together, the magnets repel. When a north and south pole from either magnet are brought together, they attract each other.)

Observations like this give rise to the familiar saying that 'Like poles repel; unlike poles attract', which is a useful aid to remembering what to expect.

- Keep the labels on your magnets: they will be useful for other activities.

Activity 15.4.3

Testing for magnetism
In developing an understanding of magnetism, an important distinction is that between magnets and magnetic materials (*15.3). If an object is attracted to a nearby magnet it must contain magnetic material, but it may be unmagnetized. If two objects a little way apart are attracted to each other, at least one must be a magnet, but without further tests there is no way of telling which is a magnet, or if both are.

The critical test of a magnet is that it can be *repelled* by another magnet: if two objects repel each other, *both* must be magnets. If the magnets are strongly magnetized, detecting this presents no problem: the force of repulsion is sufficient to be felt or to push the two magnets apart.

Equipment: As many different magnets as are available, together with some unmagnetized objects, e.g. large steel nails.

- Try to make as many magnets as you can repel each other. If you know which pole is the north pole of one of your magnets, use the 'like poles repel' rule to find the north poles of the others. (Some magnets, especially black ceramic disc or ring types, have poles at their faces, not their edges.)
- Now try the same test with other objects such as steel nails.
? Are they magnetic? (Yes, because they are attracted to the magnets.)
? Are they magnets? (No, because they are not repelled by the magnets.)

If an object is very small or very weakly magnetized, however, the force of repulsion will be too small to be felt and showing repulsion can be more difficult (see Activity 15.6.3).

Activity 15.4.4

Comparing the 'strength' of magnets

Magnets vary greatly in their 'strength', i.e. the force with which they attract magnetic materials towards them or repel other magnets. This reflects the intensity of the magnetic field, which is determined both by the material of which the magnet is made and the degree to which it is magnetized (*15.3). Three simple activities for testing the 'strength' of magnets are suggested: two using attraction and one, repulsion.

Testing by attraction

Equipment: A selection of magnets; a large box of small plain steel paper-clips; large sheet of paper.

- Put the paper-clips in a heap on the sheet of paper.
- Dip one pole of each magnet in turn into the paper-clips and lift it out. Count how many clips each picks up. The more clips a magnet picks up, the 'stronger' it is.
- A more accurate comparison can be made by hanging a line of (unlinked) paper-clips end-to end from the poles of each magnet. Again, the more clips that can be hung in a line like this, the 'stronger' the magnet.

Theoretically, any magnet should support equal numbers of clips at each pole. Plastic covered composite magnets, however, may have different 'strengths' at either end because each one is made of several separate magnets.

Equipment: A selection of magnets; 15cm pieces of string; adhesive tape; forcemeters (check that the range measured is appropriate).

- Work in pairs. Use a bar-magnet as your constant testing magnet. Tie 15cm string into a loop and fasten this to one end of your testing magnet with adhesive tape.
- Set up the two magnets and forcemeter as shown in Fig. 15.5.

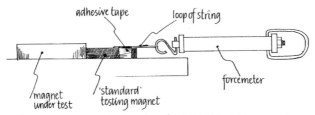

Hold the magnet under test down firmly. Pull the testing magnet slowly with the forcemeter. The force exerted just before the magnets are pulled apart is the force of attraction between them.

Figure 15.5   Comparing the 'strength' of magnets: attraction

- By pulling the forcemeter and testing magnet away slowly, find the greatest pulling force which can be exerted before the two magnets come apart. This is the force of attraction between them. The greater this force, the 'stronger' the magnet tested.

Testing by repulsion

Equipment: A selection of magnets; trolley (see Fig. 14.8) or toy truck; metre stick; Blu-tack; elastic bands; large sheet of paper.

- Choose one magnet, preferably lightweight and 'strong', to be the constant testing magnet. If using a disc- or ring-magnet, fasten it to the front of your trolley or toy truck with Blu-tack. If using a bar-magnet, fasten it on top using elastic bands as well if necessary (Fig. 15.6a).

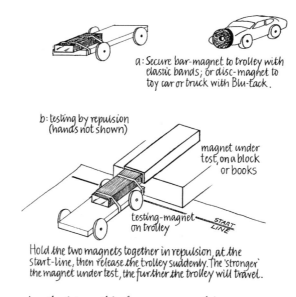

a: Secure bar-magnet to trolley with
elastic bands; or disc-magnet to
toy car or truck with Blu-tack.

b: testing by repulsion
(hands not shown)

magnet under
test, on a block
or books

testing-magnet
on trolley   START
                    LINE

Hold the two magnets together in repulsion, at the
start-line, then release the trolley suddenly. The 'stronger'
the magnet under test, the further the trolley will travel.

Figure 15.6   Comparing the 'strength' of magnets: repulsion

- Bring the magnet being tested up to the trolley as shown in Fig. 15.6b, so that the two magnets are held together while repelling each other.
- Let the trolley go *suddenly*, so that it is pushed and rolls away. Measure how far each magnet being tested pushes the trolley. The one which pushes it furthest is the 'strongest'.

15.5: The earth's magnetism

This section follows on from the last part of Activity 15.4.1. The earth itself is a huge magnet and any magnet on its surface, if free to move, lines up with its magnetic field. This effect has for centuries been used for direction-finding with magnetic compasses. Modern magnetic compasses which can easily be used by children are the fluid-filled field compasses ('Silva' type), but these need handling with care. They are fairly robust, but should not be played or experimented with using very 'strong' magnets, as it is possible to demagnetize or reverse the magnetism of the needle.

Activity 15.5.1

The magnetic field compass

Equipment: Fluid-filled field compasses ('Silva' type).

- Stand well away from large magnetic objects such as steel-framed furniture. Hold a field compass flat in your hand. Note the direction in which the needle points.
- ? Which end of the needle is pointing north? (Usually, the red end.)
- Turn through 90°.
- ? What happens to the compass needle? (It continues to point in the same direction. It is free to swing because it is mounted on a small spike.)
- ? Why does the needle always point in the same direction, even if you turn round? (Because it is a magnet and it is lining up with the Earth's magnetic field.)
- To find out more about how the compass works, turn the compass in your hand very quickly, carefully watching the needle.
- ? How does the needle move? (It moves with the whole compass as it is turned, then slowly swings back to point north-south.)
- ? Why does the compass needle not swing about as a magnet on a thread does?

Children may not have realized that the chamber is filled with fluid. Friction forces between the needle and fluid slow down the movement of the needle. It can move freely, but only slowly. When it swings to its rest position it is moving so slowly that it goes only a little way past, if at all. This is called fluid damping.

15.6: Magnetic attraction, temporary magnets and magnetizing by induction

A magnetic material is attracted to a magnet because, when it is in a magnetic field, it is itself magnetized (*15.3) and so becomes, if only temporarily, a magnet. This is called magnetic induction. It is investigated in Activity 15.6.1.

Activity 15.6.1

Magnetic attraction and temporary magnets

Equipment: Two bar-magnets; two steel nails about 5cm long.

- Hang one nail by its point from the north pole of a bar-magnet (Fig. 15.7a)
- Now hang another nail beside the first (Fig. 15.7b).
- ? How does the direction of the first nail change when the second is added? (When it is on its own the first nail hangs vertically. After the second has been added, neither will hang vertically.)
- Gently press the heads of the two nails together and let them go again.
- ? What happens? (The nails move apart again and will not stay together.)

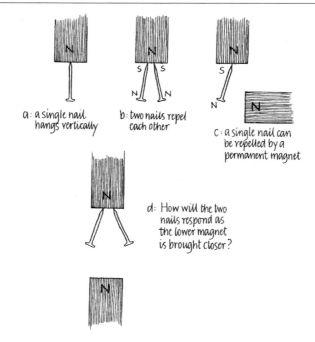

Figure 15.7 Experimenting with temporary magnets

? Why will the nails not hang vertically or stay together? (They are repelling each other, so both must have become magnets.)

This shows that when objects are attracted to magnets, the objects themselves become magnetized and behave as magnets.

● Take the nails from the bar-magnet. Try to make them attract or repel each other.
? Do they appear to be magnetized? (Usually not; but they may be weakly magnetized, see Activity 15.6.3 for testing methods.)

This shows that the nails are temporary magnets. Any magnet which remains magnetized when removed from other magnets, such as the bar-magnets being used here, are permanent magnets.

● Hang one nail by its point from the north pole of a bar-magnet, then bring the second bar-magnet slowly closer to the head of the nail (Fig. 15.7c).
? What happens, and why? (The head of the nail is repelled by the north pole of the second magnet. This shows that it is itself a north pole.)
● Now hang two nails from the bar-magnet as before. Slowly bring the north pole of a bar-magnet closer to them as shown in Fig. 15.7d. Predict what will happen, and why. (The heads of the nails will move further apart because they are being repelled both by the second magnet and by each other.)

Activity 15.6.2

Making small permanent magnets by induction

Equipment: Plain steel paper-clips; pliers; Blu-tack; and 'strong' magnet (bar or horseshoe shape).

Steel becomes temporarily magnetized when in contact with a magnet but when it is removed most, though not all, of this effect will be reversed. Steel can be magnetized more permanently by stroking it with a 'strong' permanent magnet, which is another example of magnetic induction. The magnets made in the following activity will, however, need careful testing to confirm that they are magnetized and what their polarity is (see Activity 15.6.3)

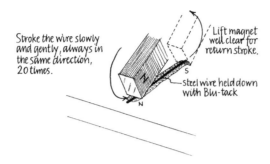

Figure 15.8   Making a permanent magnet by induction

- Make a straight steel wire about 10cm long by straightening out a paper-clip with pliers.
- Hold the wire down to a table-top with a small piece of Blu-tack near either end.
- Find out which is the north pole of your 'strong' magnet.
- Stroke the steel wire about 20 times slowly with the north pole of the magnet, as shown in Fig. 15.8, to magnetize it. This will be more effective if you:
  - stroke slowly and gently;
  - make sure you always use the same pole of the magnet;
  - always stroke in the same direction;
  - lift the magnet well clear when returning it for another stroke.

If the north pole is used for stroking, the north pole of the magnetized wire will be at the end where the stroke started.

- You now need to test the magnetism of the steel wire (see Activity 15.6.3).

Activity 15.6.3

Testing 'weak' magnets

Equipment: Magnetized wire or other 'weak' magnet; permanent magnet (a bar-magnet is best); discs 5mm thick cut from wine corks; Blu-tack or adhesive tape; plastic bowl; water.

- Half-fill the bowl with water. Fasten the magnetized wire to a *dry* cork disc with a little Blu-tack or adhesive tape.
- Float the disc and wire in the middle of the bowl; allow them to come to rest.
- ? Does the wire point north-south? (Usually it does, but this is not the critical test.)
- Try to repel one *end* of the wire by bringing the bar-magnet closer to it slowly. If the wire is attracted, try moving the other pole of the magnet closer to the same end of the wire.

If one pole of the bar-magnet will repel the wire, the wire is itself magnetized. This test uses a model of the kind of floating compass used since ancient times by Chinese, Greek and Viking explorers and navigators.

It is worth asking very able pupils to explain why this test shows the wire to be magnetic when less sensitive tests do not. The answer is to be found by thinking about the forces involved. Because the wire is only weakly magnetized and there is quite a large distance between it and the testing magnet, there is only a very small force of repulsion between the two. If the wire were lying on a table, the friction forces between it and the table-top would be much greater than this force, so the wire could not be moved by repulsion. The friction forces between between the cork and the water are very small; so small that they can be overcome even by the tiny repulsion force between wire and magnet.

15.7: Non-metallic magnets

Many modern magnets, sometimes known as ceramic magnets, are made of a non-metallic material known as magnadur. These are hard and very permanent, but also brittle, so they are likely chip or shatter if dropped. They can be made in a wide range of shapes, including cuboids, discs and rings. Plastic covered composite magnets are usually made up of three ceramic magnets end-to-end in a tough case.

Before using ceramic magnets for investigations it is always advisable to find out how they are polarized. To do this, repeat Activity 15.3.2, testing both the edges and the faces of each magnet. Fig. 15.9 shows a typical result. The idea that the poles are the parts at which magnetic forces act directly towards the magnet is particularly useful here. It shows, for example, that the ring-magnet is *face-polarized*: its poles are its faces rather than its edges.

Face-polarization makes it possible to use ring-shaped ceramic magnets to carry out a striking demonstration of magnetic repulsion, as shown in Fig. 15.10. The magnets are stacked on the dowel with like poles opposed. The dowel is only slightly smaller in diameter than the holes, so the magnets cannot twist or tilt much. As a result they hover with no visible means of support. If they are pressed down and released they are pushed up again and bounce; the pushing action of the repulsion forces in the magnetic field mimics the elastic forces of a compressed spring. Very able pupils may be encouraged to ponder why, if two magnets are stacked in this way and a third is added, the middle magnet moves down, closer to the bottom one.

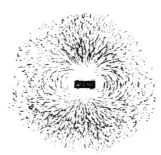

Field of a ring-shaped magnet standing on its edge. Its poles are its faces (contrast Fig. 15.4 a). Cuboid ceramic magnets may be face- or end-polarized.

Figure 15.9   Field of a ceramic magnet

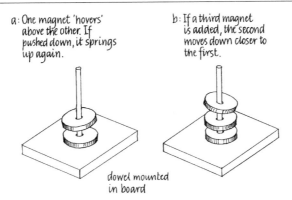

a: One magnet 'hovers' above the other. If pushed down, it springs up again.

b: If a third magnet is added, the second moves down closer to the first.

dowel mounted in board

Figure 15.10   Repulsion by face-polarized ring magnets

16

Sound

When investigating sound in the primary classroom there is much common ground between science and music, not only in developing concepts such as vibration, pitch and loudness, but also in vocabulary, skills of manipulation and discrimination, understanding of causes and effects and, not least, an enjoyment and appreciation of the huge range of sounds we make and hear.

16.1: Sound, vibration and waves

Sound is generated by objects which are moving to and fro very rapidly; the kind of movement usually called vibration. In establishing the causal link between vibration and sound it is helpful for children to play with and learn from a range of examples. The following suggestions are only three of the many possible, which have proved particularly effective in practice.

Activity 16.1.1

Investigating vibration and sound

Rice on a drum

Equipment: The largest drum available (if there is a choice, use a drum whose head is not very tight); beater; price.

- Put the drum level on a table or stand so that you can look horizontally across the 'skin' (head). Scatter a few grains of rice on the head and strike it *gently*. The rice grains bounce up and down because the drum-head is moving up and down very quickly. This is called vibration and it is this vibration which causes the sound you can hear.
- Remove the rice from the drum-head. Look horizontally across the drum-head and strike the drum fairly hard, making sure that the beater or stick bounces off the drum-head and does not rest on it. It is usually possible to see the drum-head vibrating (it may look fuzzy), though the movement is very small and fast.
? Why should the drum-stick not be allowed to rest on the drum-head? (Because it will stop the drum-head vibrating and deaden the sound).

Guitar string

Equipment: Guitar, preferably with nylon rather than steel wire strings.

- Sit with the guitar on your lap as if you were going to play it. Find the thickest string, which makes the lowest sound.
- Pluck the thickest string with your thumb. You will be able both to hear it make a sound and see it vibrate (it looks fuzzy).
- Even if the vibration is difficult to see, it can be felt. Pluck the thickest string, then touch it lightly with a finger-tip. You will feel the vibration and hear the sound change as the string buzzes on your finger. If you touch the string too hard you will stop it vibrating so the sound will stop.

Tuning-fork

A tuning-fork is used as a standard to make sure that instruments are playing the right notes. When it is struck and makes a sound a tuning-fork vibrates, but unlike the drum and the guitar string, it is very difficult to see this happening. This is also true of many other sound sources. This activity shows in three different ways that the tuning-fork is in fact vibrating, and when you have learned to strike it properly, it can be used for a lot of investigations on sound.

Equipment: Tuning-fork; wine-cork; Blu-tack; shallow plastic dishes (e.g. Petri-dishes); dry silver-sand; water; washing-up liquid.

- To use a tuning-fork you need to learn to strike it. Fasten the cork to the table with two pieces of Blu-tack. Hold the tuning-fork between finger and thumb below the 'fork' and hit one prong *hard* on the cork (Fig. 16.1). Put tuning-fork upright with its base firmly on the table; its note will then be heard clearly. *Never strike a tuning-fork on to any hard material!*

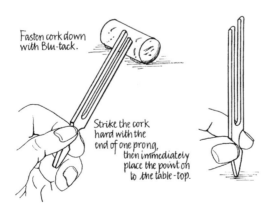

Fasten cork down with Blu-tack.

Strike the cork hard with the end of one prong, then immediately place the point on to the table-top.

Figure 16.1   Striking and sounding a tuning fork

- Strike the tuning-fork, then place one prong very lightly on a finger-tip. You will feel the vibration and hear the sound.
- Put a very thin layer of sand into a shallow plastic dish; hold this flat in one hand. With the other hand, strike the tuning-fork and touch one prong on to the

underside of the dish. This will make the dish vibrate and cause the sand-grains to jump up and down as the rice did on the vibrating drum-head.
- Put a shallow layer of water in a plastic dish on a table. Strike the tuning-fork and touch the surface of the water with one prong. The vibration will make ripples on the water and, with practice, you can usually make spray fly up and droplets run across the surface. The droplet effect can be made more obvious by dissolving a drop or two of washing-up liquid in the water.

Activity 16.1.2

Transmission of sound

Sound, unlike light, has to have a material medium to carry or transmit vibrations. We can hear music and noises only because sound waves are transmitted to our ears through some material from whatever is vibrating. Most often the material which carries the sound waves to us is air, so it may come as a surprise to learn that air is not an efficient transmitter of sound: liquids and solids are much more effective. The transmission of sound is also investigated in Activity 16.4.1 in the context of soundproofing.

The following experiments are perhaps less familiar and more open to testing and questioning than such well-tried favourites as yogurt-pot and hosepipe 'telephones', though these could well be used in addition. Any of the activities can be extended through structured questioning or made more open-ended.

Tuning-fork in air

Equipment: Tuning fork; wine cork; Blu-tack.

- Strike a tuning-fork (Fig.16.1) and hold it at arm's length until you can no longer hear it.
- Now bring the upper part of the tuning-fork very close to your ear.

With the fork close to your ear you will hear the sound quite loudly. This is because air does not transmit sound very efficiently, so the shorter the distance the sound waves have to travel through air, the louder and clearer the sound will be.

Tuning-fork and ruler

Equipment: Tuning-fork; wine cork; Blu-tack; 30cm ruler.

- Hold a ruler with one end pressing on to your head just in front of one ear.
- With the other hand, strike the tuning-fork as before and hold it at arm's length. When you can no longer hear the sound, put the base of the tuning-fork on to the end of the ruler: the sound will then be heard clearly.
- To show that the ruler really is transmitting the sound, take the tuning-fork off the ruler and replace it a few times, listening carefully.
- A similar effect can be heard by asking a partner to sound the tuning-fork on one end of a long table while you press your ear flat to the other.

All these effects are heard because the sound is being transmitted to your ear through solids (the ruler or table and your head) rather than through air.

Tuning-fork and balloon

Equipment: Balloon, inflated with neck tied; tuning-fork; wine cork; Blu-tack.

- Hold the balloon firmly pressed to one ear. Strike the tuning-fork as before and bring the vibrating fork near the side of the balloon away from your ear. Finally, touch the balloon with the tip of one prong.

Even before the fork touches the balloon you will hear the sound, because vibrations travelling a very short distance through the air are making the rubber vibrate, and it is transmitting these vibrations. (Compare bringing the tuning fork very close to your ear, as discussed above.) When the fork touches the balloon and vibrations are transferred directly to the rubber, the sound will be heard much more loudly.

Wire coat-hanger and thread

Equipment: Plain twisted-wire coat-hanger; 1m thin thread.

- Tie the thread to either end of the coat-hanger, so that it can be held with both hands, hanging level with the hook downwards.
- Let the hanger swing gently and touch a table or chair. A very faint sound may be heard, but this soon fades.
- Standing up, pass the thread behind your head and over your ears. Press the thread into both your ear openings with your index fingers (as if 'putting your fingers in your ears'). Lean forward and let the hanger touch the furniture again. A musical, bell-like sound will be heard.

Even when the wire hanger vibrates very slightly it makes a sound, but this is so faint that it is quite inaudible through air. It can, however, be heard clearly when transmitted to the ear through solid materials: the thread, pulled slightly taut by the weight of the wire, and the bones of the skull.

16.2: Differences between sounds: pitch and loudness

Since sounds are produced by vibrations, it follows that if the character of the vibrations is changed the sound we hear will be changed accordingly. There are three main ways in which sounds can be altered: pitch (how 'high' or 'low' the sound is), loudness, and quality or timbre. Of these properties, sound quality, such as the difference between a violin and a trumpet playing the same notes, is too complex to be investigated in the context of primary science, though it should be explored musically. The other two properties are direct extensions of the basic concept of sound as the product of vibration and so need to be investigated.

Any vibration can be basically described in terms of two properties. *Frequency* is a measure of how many times the to-and-fro movement is repeated in one second. The more times the movement is repeated in each second, the higher the frequency. *Amplitude* is a measure of the distance over which the movement occurs; in other words, the violence of the vibration. When a vibration generates sound, the higher the frequency, the higher the pitch of the sound we hear. This is investigated in Activities 16.2.1–16.2.3. The larger the amplitude, the louder the sound; this is investigated in Activity 16.2.4.

Activity 16.2.1

Pitch and frequency

The results and learning from this activity depend significantly on the combination of elastic bands and boxes used, so it is worth taking trouble to select those capable of giving vibrations which can be clearly seen and felt, especially in the low-frequency range. Throughout, it is important that the term 'frequency' should be used only when referring to vibration and 'pitch' only when referring to the sound which is heard.

Equipment: Rectangular card tray or shallow box (the lid to a box of A4 copier paper is ideal); selection of elastic bands, including some long thick ones.

- Place two different elastic bands widthways round a cardboard tray or shallow box. Try to find one long, thick band which is only slightly stretched and another, thinner one which is stretched a little more tightly.
- Pluck the two bands and watch them vibrate.
- ? Does one band vibrate 'faster' than the other? Can you feel the vibrations with your fingers?

The more tightly-stretched band will vibrate 'faster': this may be an appropriate point to introduce the term 'frequency'. If the slightly stretched band is not too tight its vibration will be obviously 'slower' (of a lower frequency) and will be felt more distinctly.

- Hold up the tray and press your ear flat to the back of it. Pluck the two bands again, lightly. Concentrate on the sounds you can hear and any vibrations you can feel.
- ? How are the sounds and vibrations different? (The tighter band produces a higher sound and its vibrations are felt as a buzz. The slightly stretched band produces a low sound and vibrates so slowly that individual vibrations can be felt. This may be an appropriate point to introduce the term 'pitch' and to distinguish it from frequency.)

The slightly-stretched band is likely to be the more difficult to adjust and children may need help with this. The ideal is a frequency low enough so that individual vibrations can be felt, and high enough so that a distinct, though very low-pitched, sound can be heard.

- With the tray on the table, try pulling and holding the bands to stretch them more, and plucking them with your other hand. Listen for changes in the pitch of the sound produced by each band.
- ? What pattern do you notice between the amount a band is stretched and the pitch of the sound it produces? (The tighter the band, the higher-pitched the sound.)
- If you have one, try putting a very thin elastic band round the tray. Compare the pitch of the sound it makes with that of thicker bands.
- ? How is the thickness of a band related to the pitch of the sound it makes? (It may be difficult to separate the effects of thickness and tension here, but in general thin bands make higher-pitched sounds.)

Activity 16.2.2

Controlling pitch in strings

Elastic bands over a carboard tray can produce a range of differently-pitched sounds but the pitch is hard to control and predict accurately. Stringed instruments are designed to allow for precise control of pitch. The most useful one for children to investigate is the guitar.

Equipment: Guitar, preferably with nylon rather than steel wire strings.

- Hold the guitar on your lap as if you were going to play it. Notice that it has six strings made of two different kinds of material and of different thicknesses.
- Find the tuning-peg to which the thickest string is tied. Pluck this string and, as it sounds, turn the peg *half a turn* (not more) and listen for a change in the sound. (The pitch will either rise or fall.)
- Pluck the string again and turn the peg half a turn the other way, i.e. back to where it was, again listening for a change in the sound. (The pitch falls or rises.)

The tuning-pegs show, in a much more precise way, what was found with the elastic bands (Activity 16.2.1): that the tightening or slackening of a vibrating string raises or lowers the pitch of the sound it produces.

The second way of changing pitch is to change the length of a string by fingering.

- Hold the guitar as if you were going to play it. Pluck the thinnest string and listen to its sound.
- Now press the string on to the fingerboard just behind one of the metal bars (frets) on the fingerboard and pluck it again, listening for any change in the sound. This is called fingering the string. Try fingering the string in different places to make different lengths of vibrating string, listening all the time for differences in the sound.
- ? What do you notice? (The shorter the string, the higher-pitched the sound it makes.)
- Try fingering and plucking all the strings in the same way. (They all show the same effect; this is how different notes are made when playing the guitar.)

We can now summarize the relationship between the vibrating string and the pitch of the sound it produces. There are three factors we need to consider: the thickness of the string, its length and how tightly stretched it is. If everything else stays the same:

- the thinner the string, the higher-pitched the sound;
- the longer the string, the lower-pitched the sound;
- the more tightly-stretched the string, the higher-pitched the sound.

Children's understanding of the relationship between length and thickness of the vibrating object and the pitch of the sound produced needs to be consolidated by playing other instruments. Two very useful activities are to play a range of tuned percussion instruments; and to take the front off a piano, play a range of notes and see which strings are struck to make them.

Activity 16.2.3

Variable sounds made by blowing

Both the woodwind and brass 'families' of instruments are made to produce sounds by causing a stream of air to vibrate in a variety of ways. Children can investigate the production of sound and variation in pitch by blowing across the rim of a plastic bottle, and use this learning to understand more about simple woodwind instruments such as the recorder.

Musical bottles

Equipment: Plastic drink bottles with tops removed (1 litre are ideal); water in jug; funnel; waterproof marker pen; piano or other fixed-pitch instrument (if available).

Safety note: As with any shared equipment where there is mouth contact, bottles and instruments must be washed and disinfected before being used by another pupil. 'Milton' is a suitable disinfecting agent.

- Blow across the top of a plastic bottle. Rest your lower lip below the rim and arch your upper lip slightly over it. Blow gently until you learn to make a musical note.
- Hold the body of the bottle lightly with your finger-tips as you blow. You will feel the vibration which is making the sound you hear.
- Half fill the bottle with water. Predict whether it will now make a higher or a lower-pitched sound when blown, and then find out whether your prediction is correct. (The pitch is higher.)

The bottle makes a sound because, as the air-stream is blown over the rim, the air in the bottle and the bottle itself vibrate strongly (resonate,*16.3). The smaller the volume of air in the bottle, the higher the frequency at which resonance occurs and the higher the pitch of the sound heard. Children may notice that they have to blow more gently with an empty or large bottle than with a small or nearly full one. This is because the lower-frequency vibrations with which the bottle will resonate can be produced only by a slower air-stream.

A similar but much more precisely-controllable effect is heard when playing a woodwind instrument such as a recorder: the longer the vibrating air-column, the lower-pitched the note.

Activity 16.2.4

Loudness and energy

Making any object move which was stationary involves transferring energy to it as kinetic energy (*12.2). The greater the energy transfer, the greater the change in movement. In the case of vibration, the more energy transferred to the vibrating object and the air around it, the greater the violence (amplitude) of the vibration and the louder the sound which is heard.

Children can experience the causal connection between greater energy input and greater volume of sound with a wide variety of percussion instruments, simply by striking them softly and hard and listening to the sounds produced. To understand it in terms of greater amplitude, however, they need to be able to see the vibration which their action produces. For this, both the elastic bands stretched over a card tray (Activity 16.2.1) and the guitar (Activity 16.2.2) are very effective. In both, it can be seen that plucking an elastic band or string hard causes it to vibrate over a much greater distance than plucking gently, and this is readily correlated with the loudness of the sound produced.

16.3: Musical instruments

The basic concepts of sound (vibration, frequency, pitch, amplitude and loudness) can all be consolidated and reinforced by an exploration of musical instruments; an area in which music and science can be combined to the benefit of both.

Any exploration of musical instruments has to be adapted in detail to make the most of the resources available, but it is useful to adopt a general, overall strategy of investigation and questioning so that widely-differing instruments may more readily be compared, contrasted and understood. A suggested sequence of 'starter' questions is given here:

1. What first makes the vibrations when the instrument is played? (This is usually a part of the instrument, but in brass it is the lips of the player.)
2. Does this vibration make the sound we hear directly, or does it make another part of the instrument vibrate? (Some percussion instruments, e.g. tambour, cymbals and bells, make the air vibrate directly; most instruments can make loud sounds only by setting up resonance in a tube [woodwind, brass] or hollow body [strings].)
3. Can the instrument make a continuous sound as well as repeated sounds? If so, how is the vibration sustained? (E.g. air-stream [woodwind, brass] and bowing [strings].)
4. Does the instrument have to be tuned to make sure it is playing at the correct pitch? (Most tuned percussion and free-reed instruments such as accordions have fixed pitch and cannot be tuned. The piano is tuned, but not by the player.)
5. If the instrument is tuned, how is this done? (E.g. changing tension on strings; sliding joints in or out in some brass and woodwind.)
6. How is pitch varied when the instrument is being played?
7. Can the instrument play more than one note at the same time?
8. How is loudness of sound changed and controlled when the instrument is being played?
9. What range of sound quality (timbre) can the instrument produce and how is this done?

16.4: Noise pollution and sound insulation

Noise polution is a serious problem in homes, schools, workplaces and the environment generally (*16.4). Noise pollution is most effectively solved by preventing it and this may be achieved in many ways, including actual noise reduction and sound insulation ('soundproofing') of noisy machines. Investigations into sound insulation and its effectiveness can usefully be undertaken in two phases, first observing the children's own working environment; secondly carrying out controlled experiments with a noise generator and a variety of materials.

Activity 16.4.1

Observing sound insulation in the classroom

Sound insulation involves setting up barriers which will prevent transmission of sound (Activity 16.1.2). Walls, doors and windows do this with varying efficiency. Observing noise levels closely also gives the opportunity to raise the issue of the class as a *source* of noise pollution within the school environment.

- Sit in your classroom with all doors and windows shut and without making a sound. Listen carefully for two minutes and try to identify all the sounds you can hear. Very quietly, make two lists: one of sounds inside the classroom, the other of sounds coming into the classroom from outside. When everyone is ready, listen in silence again to check your lists and note any new sounds.
- ? From your lists, select the sounds which you think are loudest. Are these sounds ever a nuisance in the classroom? See if everyone agrees on this.
- Open one (or more) windows and listen again for the sounds you identified with the windows shut, and any new ones.
- ? When the windows are opened, what happens to the number and loudness of the sounds coming in from outside? Are these sounds a nuisance?
- Close the windows. Open your classroom door and listen again.
- ? How do the sounds you hear change when the door is open? Are these sounds a nuisance?
- ? Does the class need the windows and doors shut as a means of sound insulation? How effective is sound insulation in your classroom? How could you as a class reduce the level of noise in your classroom? Who might benefit if you did?

Activity 16.4.2

Comparing materials as sound insulators

This investigation is usually most effective outdoors on a quiet day. It depends on a small noise generator with a constant output in term of loudness and frequency. The most easily-used is a small electric buzzer. Most of these require a 6V battery which must be connected correctly within the circuit, i.e. with the red lead to the + (positive) terminal, or they will not sound.

Equipment: Small electric buzzer; small plastic bag; adhesive tape; battery; leads; switch; card box with lid (about 20 × 12 × 12cm, preferably not larger) and a small hole in the middle of one side; elastic band to hold lid on; material for packing (e.g. dry silver sand, shredded paper, plastic packing 'chips', fabrics, carpet offcuts); surveyor's tape or metre trundle wheel.

- Work in a group of four (or more).Wrap the buzzer in a small piece of the plastic bag, secured round its leads with adhesive tape. (This prevents dust and sand particles getting into the buzzer.) Use the leads to connect the buzzer to the battery and switch in a simple circuit and test it (red lead of buzzer to + terminal of battery).
- Using an agreed, simple repeated signal find the greatest distance at which the buzzer can just be heard, measure it with a tape or trundle wheel and write down the result. (This may be quite a long way: 30m is not exceptional!)

- Repeat this with the buzzer in the empty box, then in the middle of the box, packed round with each of the test-materials in turn.
? Compare your results. Which was the most efficient sound insulating material ? (The one with which the just-audible distance was shortest.)
- Compare your box and materials with structures such as doors and windows. Ask one partner to sound the buzzer just inside a closed door or window while you are outside. Walk away and again find the distance at which you can just hear the buzzer. Testing a double-glazed window in this way is particularly useful.

The box test usually produces some surprises; for example that packed shredded paper makes very little difference to the noise level. Sand is usually the best sound-insulator, though fabrics and carpet offcuts may also be effective if well-packed. None, however, is usually as effective as a well-fitting double-glazed window. Following the buzzer tests it is interesting to find out how much children's awareness and attitudes to noise pollution and sound insulation have changed and developed.

17

Light

Investigations of light at primary level are aimed at laying the foundations for an understanding of two of its fundamental properties. The first is that light is a form of energy which we can see, and which travels in particular directions. This leads to concepts such as darkness, light, transmission and direction, shadows, absorption, refraction, reflection and scattering. The second is that visible light varies not only in quantity or intensity, but also in kind or quality, leading to the concept of colour.

17.1: Light and vision

As a starting-point for investigations into light, it is usually necessary to explore children's own theories as to how we see things.

Activity 17.1.1

Finding out about children's theories of vision

Equipment: Copies of a simple sketch (e.g. Fig. 17.1) on which children can write or draw how they think they can see a distant object.

The generally-accepted scientific theory of vision is that light emitted by or reflected from objects travels to and enters the eyes, stimulating both them and the brain (*3.10). Light emitted from light sources (see Activity 17.2.1) travels to and enters the eye directly. It also travels to other objects such as walls and clocks and is reflected from them into our eyes. In both cases it is light entering the eye which enables us to see. Children and many adults, however, are likely to hold alternative, intuitive theories of vision, the most commonly-held being that light is sent out from the eye and then comes back to it, carrying information about what is seen.

Children's existing theories of vision can usually be assessed by asking them to explain, through drawing and writing, how a person sees objects, and following this up by directed questioning and discussion. To do this it may be helpful to give each child a copy of a simple sketch (Fig. 17.1) on which to draw and write their ideas. Having begun to establish what theories of vision children have, simple experiments with a dark-box can be used both to question and challenge intuitive theories (especially the 'light-from-the-eye' idea) and put forward the scientific view.

242

This boy is reading in a library. Outside, it is dark.
Explain how you think he can see: the light above him;
his book;
the clock on the wall.
Draw on the sheet if it will help you to explain.

Figure 17.1 Assessing children's theories of vision

Activity 17.1.2

Theories of vision: darkness and light

Equipment: Dark-box (see Fig. 17.2).

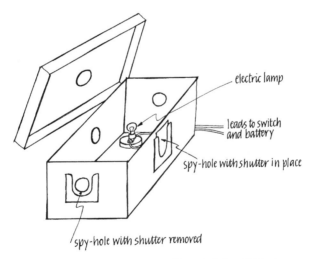

electric lamp

leads to switch
and battery

spy-hole with shutter in place

spy-hole with shutter removed

The inside of the box and lid should be painted matt black.

Figure 17.2 Dark-box

The dark-box
The dark-box (Fig. 17.2) is a simply-made model of a darkened room, based on a shoe or similar box with a well-fitting lid. It may be helpful to use the dark-box in a dimly-lit room to minimize unwanted light 'leaking' in.

- Remove a shutter and look into the dark-box through one of the spy-holes.
? What can you see? (If the lid and shutters fit well, nothing.)
? Why can't you see anything? (Scientific view: because no light is entering the eye. Children with alternative theories may think up quite ingenious explanations, such as, 'In the dark my eye switches off'.)
- Switch on the light in the box.
? What can you see now? (The lamp and the inside of the box.)
? Why can you see things now when you couldn't before?

The scientific view is that light emitted by the lamp enters the eye and so enables us to see it. Children with the 'dark switches my eyes off' and related intuitive theories may now say, 'I can see because the light switches my eyes on', which is at least partly correct in that light does stimulate the eye.

The key to developing (or reinforcing) the scientific view here is the concept not of light, but of darkness. It is important to use the dark-box to establish first, the concept that *darkness is the absence of light*, and secondly the explanation that we cannot see in darkness because there is no light to stimulate the eyes.

Once it is accepted that we can see anything only because light from it enters our eyes and stimulates them (or, more simply, 'makes them work'), the question must be asked, how light reaches us, since some of the things we see are a long way away.

Activity 17.1.3

The dark-box and the movement of light
In order to understand how we can see objects which are distant from us, it is necessary to establish the idea that light travels. In this investigation, we are modelling a very common experience: walking into a dark room and switching the light on.

Equipment: Dark-box (see Fig. 17.2).

- Open a shutter and look into the dark-box.
? What can you see? (Nothing, because no light is entering the eye.)
- Close the switch to turn the light on.
? What can you see now? (The lamp and the inside of the box.)
? Because you can see something, light must be entering your eye. Where did the light come from? (The electric lamp.)
? What made the lamp light up? (Closing the switch, allowing current to flow in the circuit through the lamp.)
? The lamp is some distance from your eye. How can you see light from it? (The light must travel from the lamp to the eye.)

This may seem a very laborious way to make a very simple point, and so in a way it is; but in order to be convinced that light does indeed travel from a source to the eye, children have to be able to see the logic of the situation. Darkness is the absence of light; in darkness the eye can see nothing. But when light is generated in the dark-box, the lamp is some way away from the eye, so the light must *travel* from whatever emits it to the eye, and this can happen only when the switch is closed and current flows in the circuit, making the lamp light up. Any light source seen at night, from vehicle and street-lights to aircraft and the stars, makes the same point: light is being generated some way away from us, and yet we can see it, so it must travel from its source until it reaches our eyes.

17.2: Sources, reflectors and transmission of light

All objects we see can usefully be thought of as being in one of two groups: those which are sources of light and those which are not. A light source is luminous: it emits light. In contrast, any object which is not a light source is visible only when it is illuminated by light from a source and some of this light is reflected from the object into the eye (*17.2). Children may not realize that not only shiny surfaces but any visible object is reflecting light, though dull or matt surfaces scatter as well as reflect it.

Activity 17.2.1

Finding sources of light
Distinguishing between objects which are visible because they emit light and those which reflect or scatter it is not always easy. The key idea, as so often when thinking about light, is that *darkness is the absence of light*. If possible, place objects under test in a dark-box or a blacked-out room. If not, carry out a thought-experiment: '*If this object were in a completely blacked-out room, would it still be visible?*' If it can be seen in an otherwise dark room or box, the object must be a light source.

- Draw the curtains or blinds in your classroom so that the light is very dim.
- ? If the room were in total darkness, which objects in it could you see? (None: if there is no light you can't see anything.)
- ? If the room were blacked-out completely, with no light at all coming in from outside, which objects in it could give light in the darkness? (Likely examples include electric lamps, TV or computer monitor screens.)

Any object which gives out light is called a *light source*.

- ? What other objects in school can be light sources? (Examples include: slide and overhead projectors, small electric lamps and torches, matches and candles.)
- ? If all the other things in the room are not light sources, how do we see them? (Light from light sources bounces off [is reflected and scattered from] them and travels to our eyes.)
- ? If in a blacked-out room the curtains or blinds are opened, the room is lit up. What is the source of the light? (The Sun, either directly if it is shining into the room, or indirectly from light scattered by the sky [*17.8] if it is not.)

This introduces the important idea of the Sun as a light source for the Earth (*18.1), which is also relevant to work on photosynthesis (*4.4) and forms of energy (*12.2).

Activity 17.2.2

Transmission of light through different materials
The fact that light reaches us from the Sun shows that, unlike sound (see Activity 16.1.2), light does not need a material through which to be transmitted. Light can

pass through a wide variety of materials, but most affect light falling on or passing through them. They can be roughly classified into three groups according to the effect they have.

1. *Opaque* materials and objects allow no light to pass through them.
2. *Transparent* materials allow a distant object viewed through them to be seen clearly.
3. *Translucent* materials allow some light to pass through, but scatter light so that distant objects cannot be seen clearly when looking through them, though objects in contact with the translucent sheets can be.

These three 'classes' are useful but not exact: there are no sharp distinctions between them so that, for example, materials could well be described as 'almost opaque' or 'not quite transparent'.

Equipment: Opaque cardboard tubes 15–20cm long; variety of transparent, translucent and opaque materials in sheet form, e.g. plastics, card, plywood, paper, in pieces large enough to cover the end of the tube and in a range of colours.

Safety note: If the Sun is shining, make sure you do **not** look directly at it.

- Hold or fold a sheet of a material over the end of the card tube so that it fits on as closely as possible. Hold the tube up to the window and look through the other end.
? Does any light come through the material? (If none does, the material is opaque.)
? If some light comes through the material, look to see if you can see clearly through it. If you can, it is transparent, as air and glass are. If you can't, it is translucent.
- Look at all the available materials in this way and divide them into three groups: transparent, translucent and opaque.

In sorting the materials into three groups, children may be confused by colour. In particular they may not think of clear, coloured plastic (e.g. cut from bottles) as being transparent. Transparent coloured materials are also used in Activity 17.8.4. Translucent sheets may give rise to questions. Distant objects cannot be seen through them because the sheets scatter light. Pressing a translucent sheet on to an object, as when using tracing-paper, greatly reduces the effect of this scattering, so the object can be seen more or less clearly.

17.3: The direction in which light travels

The observation that light travels away from its source is one of the two basic principles which underlie any understanding of how light behaves. The other is that light travels in a straight line *unless it is prevented from doing so*. Much of the work needed to understand how light affects our lives, on shadows (Section 17.4), bending of light by refraction (Section 17.6) and reflection (Section 17.7) depends on this basic principle, so it can be useful, especially with older and more able children, to make it explicit through first-hand observation.

The fact that beams of light appear to travel in straight lines is a matter of common experience. Light beams can sometimes be seen from the side because they illuminate and are partly scattered by solid or liquid particles suspended in the air, such as water droplets (mist), smoke and dust (see also Activity 6.5.1; Section 11.4).

Examples include sunbeams through gaps in cloud, car headlights in fog and beams from projectors or lights in cinemas, discos and theatres. If a slide projector and a well blacked-out room are available, it may be possible to set up a simple demonstration of this effect in school. The straight-line path of light can also be shown by making a version of the pin-hole camera to look into, rather than to take photographs.

Activity 17.3.1

Making a pin-hole viewer

Materials: Two card tubes of the same diameter (preferably about 6 cm), 10cm and 40cm long; thin black card; good quality tracing-paper; a needle about 1mm in diameter; adhesive tape.

Safety note: At no time should the viewer be pointed directly at the Sun.

● Make a pin-hole viewer, as shown in Fig. 17.3a.

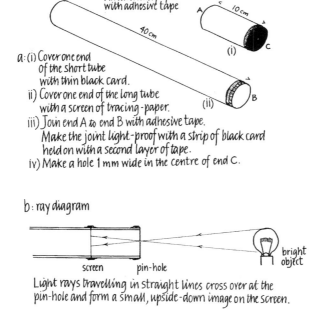

Figure 17.3 A pin-hole viewer

● With the needle, carefully make a hole about 1mm in diameter in the centre of the black card covering the end of the tube.
● Hold the open end of the viewer up to one eye, cupping your hands over both eyes and the end of the viewer to exclude as much light as possible. Point the viewer at a brightly-lit window or a tree or building seen against the sky. Watch the screen for 2 minutes to allow your eye to adapt to the dim light.

? What do you see? (A bright spot of light, which is the pin-hole seen through the tracing-paper screen, surrounded by a dimmer image of the scene which is being viewed.)

? What do you notice about the image? (It is upside-down and left-right reversed.)

It is the reversal of the image which shows that light travels in straight lines (Fig. 17.3b). Light-rays from the top and bottom parts of the scene being viewed, travelling in straight lines, cross over as they pass through the pin-hole so that light from the top part of the scene forms the bottom of the image and *vice versa*. It is useful to compare this mode of image formation with the projection of an image using a lens (Activity 17.6.2).

17.4: Shadows

A shadow is part of a surface which is less brightly illuminated than other areas near it, because light which otherwise would have reached it has been interrupted or diverted in some way. When investigating shadows, children need to observe and understand four properties: size, shape, depth or intensity and sharpness.

Activity 17.4.1

Shadow formation using a point source of light

*Equipment: Room with effective blackout; white wall or screen (pinned-up paper is adequate); small electric lamp in holder, with battery, switch and wires as required (a hand-torch is **not** suitable); variety of card shapes.*

● In the blacked-out room, place the table about 2m away from the screen.
● Connect lamp, wires, battery and switch to make a working circuit. Place the lamp near the edge of the table facing the screen (Fig. 17.4a).
● Switch on the battery lamp, then switch off all the room lights. Avoid looking at the lamp for 1–2 minutes: this will enable your eye to become dark-adapted (Activity 3.10.1).
● Hold up a card shape between the lamp and screen at right angles to the light. Look at the shadow cast on the screen.
? Is the shadow sharp-edged or fuzzy? (It is sharp-edged.)
? Keeping the card at the same angle to the light and not moving the lamp, how can the shadow be made bigger? (By moving the object nearer to the lamp.)
? Again keeping card angle and lamp position the same, how can the shadow be made smaller? (By moving the object away from the lamp.)
? When the shadow is made bigger or smaller, does its edge become any less sharp? (No. The significance of this observation will become clear in Activity 17.4.2.)
? How can the shape of the shadow be changed? (By turning the card shape so that its angle to the light is changed.)

Light travelling outwards in straight lines and in all directions from the lamp is intercepted by the card shape and the resulting shadow corresponds exactly to this shape (Fig. 17.4a). Turning the card shape changes the shape of light intercepted and so alters the shape of the shadow cast. Moving the card nearer to or further away

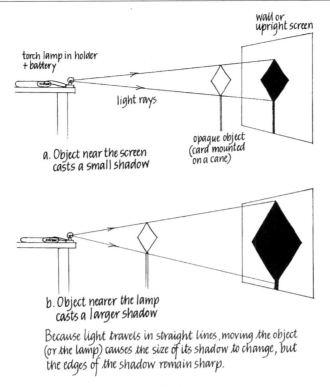

a. Object near the screen
casts a small shadow

b. Object nearer the lamp
casts a larger shadow

Because light travels in straight lines, moving the object
(or the lamp) causes the size of its shadow to change, but
the edges of the shadow remain sharp.

Figure 17.4 Shadows from a point source of light

from the lamp (Fig. 17.4b) without changing its angle makes it intercept a greater or lesser part of the lamp's output and so cast a larger or smaller shadow.

Activity 17.4.2

Shadow formation using an extended source of light
Any light source significantly larger than a point source is called an extended source.

Equipment: Room with effective blackout; white wall or screen (pinned-up paper is adequate); domestic electric lamp (not clear glass) in holder, preferably screwed to a base-board for safety and with lead and plug; variety of card shapes.

- Set up the table, lamp and screen as in Fig. 17.5a, with at least 2m between them. Plug the lamp into the mains electricity supply, switch it on and then switch off the room lights.
- Hold a card shape very near the screen and look carefully at the shadow cast to see how big and sharp it is.
- ? What do you observe about the shadow? (The shadow is very slightly bigger than the card shape and its edges are very slightly fuzzy; but children will probably report it as being the same size and sharp-edged.)
- Move the card shape away from the screen and towards the lamp, watching all the time to see how the shadow changes.

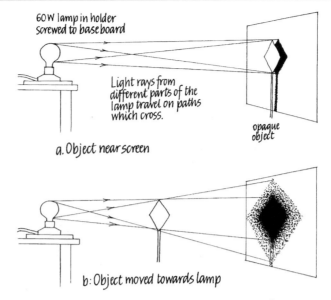

When the object is near the screen there is little room for light rays to cross before they reach the screen, so the shadow is fairly sharp. When the object is further away the shadow is larger. There is much more room for the crossing rays to move apart, so the shadow is fuzzy. The full shadow is surrounded by a zone of part-shadow.

Figure 17.5   Shadows from an extended source of light

? How does the shadow change? (It becomes larger and its edges become more fuzzy as the card is moved away from the screen.)

Light travels outwards in straight lines in all directions from all parts of the lamp, so light rays from different parts of the lamp are on crossing paths (Fig. 17.5a). Usually we do not notice this, but when the light is interrupted to form a shadow there is a zone round the shadow's edge which can be reached by light from part of the lamp but not the whole, so it is neither fully illuminated nor fully in shadow. This zone forms the diffuse or fuzzy edge round the full shadow (Fig. 17.5b). The further the object is away from the screen, the vaguer the shadow's outline.

Activity 17.4.3

Shadows in sunlight

Equipment: Screens (e.g. large sheets of white paper pinned on boards); card shapes.

- Work on a clear, sunny day, outdoors and around the middle of the day if possible. Set up the screens, oriented and tilted so that they are approximately at right angles to the Sun's rays.
- Hold a card shape near the screen and look carefully at its shadow.
? What kind of shadow is cast on the screen? (The same size and shape as the object, with sharp edges.)

● Move the object away from the screen, watching to see how the shadow changes.
? How does the shadow change? (Its edges become slightly fuzzy but it *stays the same size*.)

As the previous two activities show, the kind of shadow formed depends not only on the size and position of the object casting the shadow, but also on the size and position of the light-source. The Sun is very distant, but so large that to us on Earth it is an extended light source, not a point source. This means that light from different parts of the Sun reaches the Earth at slightly different angles (Fig. 17.6a), so that when a shadow-forming object is moved away from the screen a partly-illuminated zone occurs around the full shadow, giving the shadow a fuzzy edge (Fig. 17.6b). However, the Sun is so far away that light rays from any part of it are travelling on almost parallel straight-line paths when they reach the Earth, not diverging as rays from a nearby lamp are (compare Figs. 17.5b and 17.6b). The result is that, as an object is moved away from a screen in sunlight, the size of the full shadow does not change.

Activity 18.2.3 investigates the variation of sun-shadows at different times of the day and year.

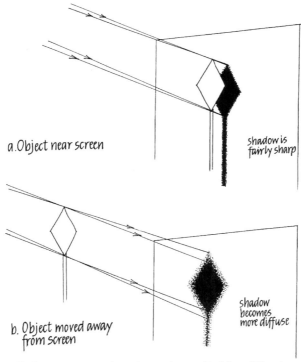

a. Object near screen

shadow is fairly sharp

b. Object moved away from screen

shadow becomes more diffuse

The Sun is very distant but also very large, so light from different parts of it reaches the Earth at slightly different angles. This means that the Sun is an extended light source, not a point source. As the object is moved away from the screen, the size of the full shadow does not change, but the part shadow caused by crossing light rays makes a diffuse zone round it.

Figure 17.6   Shadows in sunlight

17.5: Absorption of light

Light is a form of radiant energy (*12.2). When light falls on a material it may be transmitted through the material (Section 17.6), reflected from it (Section 17.7) or absorbed by it. When most materials absorb light, all the radiant energy is transferred as thermal energy, so the material is heated and its temperature rises (Activity 12.3.5). This effect is particularly noticeable in cars on sunny days, when the internal temperature can rise very sharply and be lethal to animals trapped inside without ventilation. In some systems, however, light energy is transferred in other forms. Children will be familiar with two of these: plants and solar cells. Plants absorb light and transfer part of the radiant energy as chemical-potential energy in the process of photosynthesis (*4.4); solar panels transfer about 10% of the energy falling on them as electrical energy. Children are likely to be familiar with very small-scale solar panels in watches and calculators. They may also have seen roadside weather-recording stations and (on TV) space-stations and the Hubble space telescope, all of which use solar panels as their main energy source.

17.6: Refraction

Transparent materials such as glass and water transmit most of the light falling on them but if light passes from one transparent material to another of different density, for example from water to air, it is bent out of its straight-line path; a process known as refraction. The most obvious results of refraction are the distortion and displacement of images. We usually interpret what we see *as if* light always travelled in straight lines, so that when light is diverted from its straight-line path by refraction (or reflection, 17.7), there is a mismatch between what is seen and what, through other means, we know to be the case: we 'see' things whose shape, size or position appear to be other than what we know them to be in reality. This effect underlies some interesting illusions (Activity 17.6.1) and some effects of lenses (Activity 17.6.2).

Activity 17.6.1

Refraction between water and air: illusions

Equipment: Cuboidal fish-tank or transparent plastic box; water; thin, straight stick.

The 'bent-stick' illusion

- Fill the tank or box with water. Put the stick into the water at an oblique angle, resting on the bottom and side. Look at it from the side, then look down the length of it.
- ? What do you see? (The two parts of the stick in air and in water appear straight, but the stick appears to be bent at the water surface.)

Even though we know the stick is not bent, we cannot avoid seeing it as if it were, because light from it is bent out of its straight-line path by refraction as it passes from water to air (Fig. 17.7). The only position in which the stick does not appear bent is when it is upright in the water.

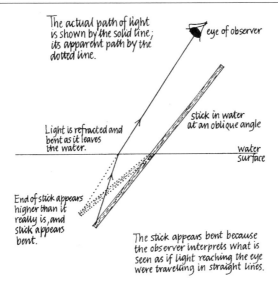

Figure 17.7   The 'bent stick' illusion

The 'double stick' illusion

- Put the stick obliquely in the water so that its lower end end rests in a corner of the box or tank. (Ask a partner to hold it if necessary.)
- Stand so that the outside angle of the corner is facing you (as in Fig. 17.8) and look at the stick.

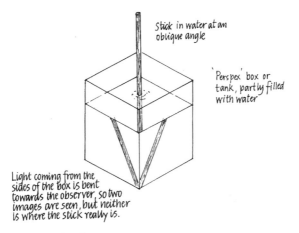

Figure 17.8   The 'double stick' illusion

? What do you see? (If the stick is bisecting the angle of the corner and the observer is looking back along the same line, as in Fig. 17.8, there will appear to be two sticks in the water.)

We do not see the stick where we know it really is. Instead we see a double image, as light travelling from the stick to *both* sides of the tank is refracted towards our eyes as it enters the air. We interpret these images as if the light were still travelling in straight lines, so we 'see' two sticks.

Activity 17.6.2

Refraction between glass and air: lenses

Lenses are pieces of transparent, usually colourless, plastic or glass which are shaped to bend light by refraction in various ways. The most familiar lens is the simple circular magnifying-glass which is biconvex (both faces bulge outwards). Large lenses of this kind (diameter 8cm or more) are good for children to play with and observe, but need handling with care, since glass lenses may shatter if dropped and plastic ones are very easily damaged and rendered useless by scratching.

Using a lens to project an image

Equipment: Magnifying glass (large if available); white paper fixed to board for a screen.

- Work on a bright day in a room with the lights switched off and a brightly-lit view from a window.
- Go as far away from the window as possible while still facing it. Hold your screen so that it is directly facing the window.
- Hold your lens so that it is parallel to both the screen and the window, about 30cm away from the screen. Gradually bring the lens closer to the screen until a clear, sharp image of the window and the scene outside is projected on to it.
? What is the image 'like? (It is upside-down, in colour and much smaller than the window.)

The image projected in this way has much in common with the image seen in a pin-hole viewer (Activity 17.3.1), though it is much brighter: it is small and reversed. The reason for this reversal is shown in Fig. 17.9: light-rays from the object (the window and what is visible outside it) are bent inwards by the lens, so that they cross over between the lens and the screen (compare Fig. 17.3b).

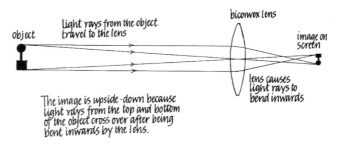

Figure 17.9   Using a lens to project an image

Using a lens as a magnifying glass

Equipment: Magnifying glasses (a variety is useful); pages with small print; small natural objects with a lot of detail, e.g. flowers, feathers, mosses and shells.

● Hold the lens as near to your eye as you can. Keeping the lens still, hold a printed page or one of the objects in the other hand and move it until you can see it clearly.

When using a lens as a magnifying glass it should always be held near the eye, wherever possible moving the object rather than the lens to obtain a clear image. Fig. 17.10 helps to explain how a lens works as a magnifying glass. Light from the near object is bent inwards and projected into the eye, which focuses it to form an image on the retina (*3.10). The brain interprets this image as if the light were travelling to the eye along straight-line paths, so the image appears much larger than the object does to the unaided eye.

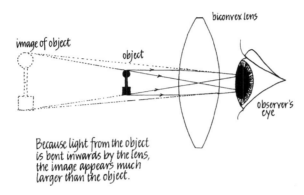

Figure 17.10   Using a lens as a magnifying-glass

17.7: Reflection

Objects which are not light sources (Activity 17.2.1) are visible only when light is reflected from them into the eye. Very smooth, shiny surfaces such as glass, water or polished metal reflect light in a mirror-like way (regular or specular reflection), but it is important to emphasize that shiny surfaces are not the only ones to reflect light. Dull or matt surfaces also reflect light, but in a diffuse or non-specular way. The difference between the two kinds of reflection comes about because matt surfaces, however smooth they may appear, are minutely rough and furrowed so that as well as reflecting light falling on them they scatter it in many directions. Shiny, mirror-like surfaces scatter light very little, so an image can be seen in them.

Mirrors
Most of the investigations into reflection which children are likely to carry out involve regular reflection and the use of flat (plane) mirrors. Glass mirrors are the best in terms of quality (lack of distortion) and resistance to scratching, but must be made safer by covering their backs and edges with self-adhesive plastic sheet.

Flexible plastic mirrors are safer than glass ones but they are likely to bend in use and can very easily be scratched and rendered useless by careless handling. When supplied, plastic mirrors usually have a thin protective film over each surface, which must be removed before use.

To work with mirrors in a controlled and precise way, it is necessary to have some means of holding them upright on tables. This can be done with a bulldog-clip, but more effectively by using a wooden block with a vertical slot cut in one side, in which the mirror can rest (Fig. 17.11).

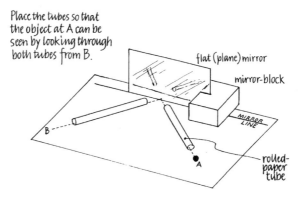

Place the tubes so that the object at A can be seen by looking through both tubes from B.

flat (plane) mirror

mirror-block

MIRROR LINE

B

A

rolled-paper tube

Figure 17.11   How a mirror changes the path of light

Activity 17.7.1

How a mirror changes the path of light
Light normally travels in straight lines (Activity 17.3.1), but when light strikes a mirror its path is changed.

Equipment: Flat (plane) mirror and holder; two straight rolled-paper tubes about 1cm in diameter and 15cm long (roll paper round a felt-tip pen and fix with adhesive tape); A4 white paper; pencil; ruler; small coloured object (e.g. toy or pen-top).

- Put a piece of A4 paper on your table; draw a line parallel to one long side, 1cm from the edge. We will call this the *mirror-line*. Place your mirror, held upright by its holder, on this line near the middle (Fig. 17.11).
- Place a paper tube on the paper, about 5cm from the mirror and at an angle to it.
- Place a second paper tube on the paper and look through it into the mirror. Move the second tube until you can see through it and, in the mirror, straight through the first tube as well (Fig. 17.11).
- Put a small coloured object near the end of the first tube (as at point A in Fig. 17.11) and look through the end of the other tube (from point B). You will see the object at A.
- ? If you can see the object at A when looking into the tube at B, light must be travelling from A to B. What path does the light follow? (From point A, through the first tube towards the mirror, then away from the mirror through the second tube to point B.)
- Try to draw the path of the light on the paper. (This can best be done by marking where the ends of each tube rest on the paper, removing the tubes and mirror, then ruling lines through each pair of points to the mirror-line.)
- Experiment with the tubes at different angles to the mirror. Each time you have the tubes lined up so that you can see through both of them, plot the path of light

towards and away from the mirror. If you can, draw each pair of lines in a different colour.

If the plotting has been done very accurately, the straight lines will join at the mirror-line.

? Light normally travels in straight lines. What does the mirror do to the light? (It changes the direction of the light falling on it. Our straight tubes show that light travels in straight lines towards and away from the mirror, but when light strikes the mirror, the mirror makes it go off in a different direction.)

Older and more able children can measure the angles at which light travels to and is reflected from a mirror. These angles are always the same.

Activity 17.7.2

Seeing round corners
Because the angles at which light travels to and from a mirror are always the same, reflection from a flat (plane) mirror is very predictable. This helps us use mirrors to look at things from otherwise difficult or impossible angles, for example when a dentist uses a small mirror to see all round our teeth and a driver uses rear-view mirrors to look backwards without having to turn round. Mirrors can also enable us to see round objects which are obstructing straight-line vision. One way of doing this is to construct a periscope.

Making a mirror periscope
A periscope is a device which enables the viewer to extend her or his viewpoint to one which is higher, lower or further sideways than is possible with normal viewing. If children cannot make a periscope for themselves it is well worth making one for them so that they can observe its effects both through play and more systematic investigation.

*Equipment and materials: Fairly thin but stiff card (**not** corrugated box-card) size A3 (420 × 296mm); two plastic mirrors, each 75 × 100 mm (cut to size); PVA (white) glue; craft knife; cutting mat; metal ruler or straight-edge.*

- A plan for cutting and folding the card is given in Fig. 17.12. Divide the card into five strips longways as shown; score the lines and fold the card into an open-ended box 70 × 70 × 420mm. Open the card out again.
- Draw the four slits for the mirrors as shown, exactly at 45°. Cut the slits so that the mirrors will slide into them easily but are not loose. (If the mirrors are held tightly they will be distorted.)
- Draw and cut the two viewing ports as shown. Cut out the two shaded portions from the end-flap as shown; this is to accomodate the mirror-slits.
- Fold the card again into an open-ended box. Glue the flaps down on the outside of the box, using your ruler or straight-edge *inside* to help press the edges down.
- Slide the mirrors into the slits so that they project a little on each side.
- Hold the periscope upright and look into the lower mirror. The periscope enables you to see as if you were taller than you are. Look for things which you can see

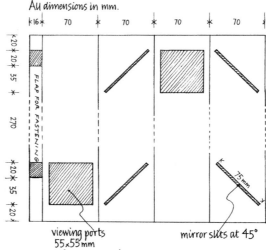

All dimensions in mm.

Use A3 size card (420 x 296 mm); all shaded areas to be cut out;
use flexible mirrors cut to 100 x 75 mm.

Figure 17.12   Making a mirror periscope

with the periscope which you cannot see without it: this is an example of mirrors enabling you to see round corners.

By experimenting with the periscope, children will find that it can be used to see over, round and under obstacles. Because the angles at which light strikes a mirror and is reflected are the same (Activity 17.7.1), a mirror at 45° changes the path of light through 90°. It is also noticeable that the image in the periscope is not a mirror-image of the usual kind. The reason for this is discussed at the end of Activity 17.7.3

Activity 17.7.3

Reflection in mirrors: images
When we look in a mirror, what we see and how we see it is so familiar that it may seem to need no explanation, but mirror-images are far from easy to understand, either for children or adults (*17.7). To explore this in detail is beyond the scope of this book, but the following activity may help older and more able pupils to think about and understand more of mirror-images.

Mirror-images: front-to-back, not left-to-right

Equipment: Mirror with holder; white A4 paper; clear acetate sheet (e.g. OHP writing film) about 10 × 5cm and a pen which will write on it.

- On the acetate sheet, write the word LIGHT and draw a spiral which goes clockwise as you move out of it.
- Put the acetate sheet flat on white paper in front of an upright mirror.
- ? What do you see in the mirror? (The word LIGHT appears reversed and upside-down [inverted]; the spiral appears to run counter-clockwise out from the middle.)

- Now move the acetate sheet so that it appears exactly as its image did in the mirror, and the image appears exactly as the sheet did. (Hint: this cannot be done keeping the sheet flat!)
? How did you have to move the acetate sheet? (Turn it over towards or away from yourself, but *not* left-to-right.)

This shows how the mirror produces a reversed image. The reversal is neither left-to-right nor up-to-down, but front-to-back, i.e. at right angles to the plane of the mirror.

- Now hold the acetate sheet upright quite close to the mirror so that you can see the word LIGHT the right way round, and its mirror-image.
? What is the mirror-image like, and how do you explain it?

The mirror-image of LIGHT looks exactly like the writing seen on the acetate sheet. This is usually a surprise! It happens because the mirror is reflecting the *reversed* letters seen on the back of the acetate sheet, i.e. what you would see if you were looking *in the opposite direction*. The mirror, however, only reverses the direction in which the letters are viewed: it does not reverse them left-right, as you would do if you walked round the table to look at them. The result is that the image appears 'the right way round'.

A similar effect is seen in the periscope (Activity 17.7.2): the first mirror produces an apparently inverted and reversed image; the second repeats this effect so that the image we see appears the right way up and the right way round.

17.8: Colour

When investigating light we have up to this point been concerned with different amounts of light, how light interacts with materials, the direction in which it is travelling, how this can be altered and what we see as a result. When investigating colour we are concerned not with quantity but with quality of light. White light (e.g. sunlight or sky-light) is often said to be made up of different colours, but this can be misleading. It is more useful to think of sunlight as being a band of radiant energy (*12.2) which, when analyzed and spread out, can be separated into narrower bands which we perceive as colours.

Activity 17.8.1

Dispersion and the spectrum
The process by which white light is analyzed and spread out into bands which we can perceive as colours is known as dispersion. The range of colours which we see is a spectrum. The simplest way to investigate dispersion is to use a 60° prism.

Prisms
The best prisms are made of optical glass with ground and polished faces. For general use in primary schools a triangular prism with 60° angles between its faces is best, and a small one (2.5cm high) is quite adequate, but is relatively expensive. It is sometimes possible to obtain 90°-45°-45° prisms by dismantling old, disused 'prismatic' binoculars. These are usually small but of excellent quality. If using them,

work with two faces at 45° where the following instructions call for using two faces at 60°.

Observing the spectrum directly

Equipment: Prism; piece of thin, opaque card 10 × 5cm with a slit 1mm wide and 4cm long cut in it (use craft knife).

- Hold up a prism by its ends (triangular faces) between finger and thumb, quite close to one eye. Look through two sides (square or rectangular faces) at a window.

Notice that in order to see the window through the prism you cannot look directly at it: you have to turn and look well to one side. This is because light from the window is bent out of its straight-line path by refraction as it passes through the prism (compare Activity 17.6.1).

? What is different from normal about what you see through the prism? (The edges and bars of the window have bright colours around them: red and yellow on one side, blue and violet on the other.)

The coloured fringes are very easy to see, but they do not represent the complete spectrum.

- Stand or sit facing a brightly-lit window, but not in direct sunlight. Hold the prism up as before. In your other hand, hold up a piece of card with a narrow (1mm wide) slit cut in it, so that you can see the brightly-lit sky through the slit. Now look through two sides of the prism at the slit in the card. You should be able to see a full spectrum of colours where light comes through the slit.
? Which colours can you see? (Most people see red, yellow/orange, green, blue and violet.) What colour is present in the spectrum which you could not see in the coloured fringes you saw before? (Green, which is in the middle of the spectrum.)

On a sunny day it is possible to project a spectrum. Hold a prism in full sunlight with its triangular ends parallel to the Sun's rays and with one edge (60° or 45°) pointing downwards. A spectrum will then be projected more or less horizontally. This will be seen best if it is projected on to a white card or screen more than 3m away.

Rainbow colours
Colours in rainbows, water spray and dewdrops are all produced by dispersion of white light as it refracted through more or less spherical drops of water lit by the Sun. These effects will be seen only when the observer is facing directly away from the Sun and towards the water-drops lit by sunlight.

There are many examples of objects which appear 'rainbow-coloured' but which create a spectrum in different ways. Examples include oil-films on water, soap-bubbles, the feathers of some birds, bodies and wings of some insects, hologram pictures and CD discs. In all these examples, light rays are reflected from the object in complex ways so that they interact (a process called interference), producing the coloured light we see.

Activity 17.8.2

Colour mixing: paints and dyes
Coloured objects are obviously different from prisms and CDs: they are as it were coloured in themselves. This is because they absorb some parts of the white-light spectrum falling on them and reflect others (*17.8). Colour mixing is complex, but a useful start towards understanding it can be made by finding out what happens when primary colours (reds, blues and yellows) are mixed to make secondary ones (oranges, greens and violet-purples).

   No paint or dye is a 'pure' colour: each reflects a range of colours in different amounts, though we see it as a single hue. For example, a blue paint reflects blue most strongly and this is the colour it appears to us; but different blues also reflect differing amounts of violet and green, though we cannot see them. The usual way in which we become aware of the range of colours reflected by paints and dyes is by mixing different colours together. For example, when blue paint or dye is mixed with yellow, a green colour becomes visible. How this happens is summarized in Fig. 17.13. Blues absorb red, orange and yellow very strongly whereas yellows absorb red, violet and blue. The only colour that both reflect at all strongly is green, so when blue paint or dye is added to yellow, the mixture looks green. Mixing blue and yellow does not 'make' green; but it does make visible the green which both are reflecting all the time.

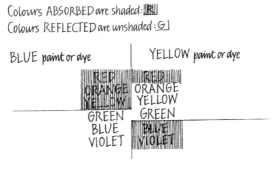

Figure 17.13   Colour mixing by subtraction

   Because a mixture of pigments or dyes produces different colours by absorbing and so removing light from the white light falling on it, this process is called colour mixing by subtraction. This is in contrast to what happens when coloured lights are mixed (Activity 17.8.3).

Mixing paints

Materials and equipment: Paints: a violet-blue ('brilliant blue' or ultramarine); a greenish blue (cobalt blue or turquoise); a warm, orange-yellow ('brilliant yellow'); a cool, lemon yellow; an orange-red ('brilliant red' or scarlet); a violet-red (crimson); white paper; palette; brushes; water-pot.

- Work with fairly thick paint to obtain intense colours: if the paint is ready-mixed, do not dilute it. Paint sample squares of the two blues and two yellows for reference.
- Mix the blues and yellows in two pairs: greenish-blue with lemon yellow and violet-blue with orange-yellow. Add blue to yellow gradually (not the other way round) to keep control of the mixing process, until you have a mid-green. Paint sample squares of the two greens alongside each other and leave them to dry.
- Which pairing makes the more vivid green? (Greenish-blue and lemon yellow.) What is the other green like? (Usually, dull and greyish.)

The quality of green obtained by mixing depends on the ranges and amounts of colours reflected by the blue and yellow paints. Lemon-yellow and greenish-blue both reflect green strongly, so when they are mixed they reflect a lot of green light and we see a vivid colour. Violet-blue and orange-yellow both reflect green much more weakly, so when they are mixed they appear much less intensely coloured, i.e. more dull and greyish.

- Try similar experiments with the other paints: they will also make pairs of bright and dull secondary colours.

Children can also experiment with subtractive mixing with layers of transparent colour, superimposing one colour on another. Felt-tip pens give interesting results, but always put the lighter colour on first (e.g. yellow before blue) and allow each layer to dry thoroughly before putting on the next. The results can be compared with similar inks analysed by chromatography (Activity 6.6.2). If coloured filters are available these give even more spectacular mixtures simply by overlaying them and looking through two or more at once (see also Activity 17.8.4).

Activity 17.8.3

Mixing coloured lights
If coloured lights are added together, for example by shining two spotlights on to the same area of stage or wall, the results are different from those obtained by mixing paints or dyes. The simpler aspects of mixing coloured lights can be investigated using familiar classroom equipment.

Equipment: Microcomputer with colour monitor; art software running a program which can produce a range of colours on screen; large hand magnifying glass.

The screen of a colour TV monitor is a light source (Activity 17.2.1), which emits light in fine vertical lines in three colours: red, blue and green. These are the primary colours when mixing coloured lights (contrast mixing paints and dyes, where the primaries are red, blue and yellow, Activity 17.8.2). The computer and art software are used to control the monitor and put areas of different colours on screen, which can then be examined with a magnifying glass to see which of the three primary colours is being emitted.

Safety note: This method of studying colour mixing requires children to examine a TV screen closely, but only for very short periods of time. This does not present a hazard, but they should not be allowed to look at the screen closely without a magnifying glass, or for longer than necessary, as this may cause headaches.

At least to begin with it is helpful to restrict the range of colours observed. The simplest combinations are:

- *primaries*: red, blue and green;
- *secondaries*: greenish-blue (green + blue, called cyan); pink (blue + red, called magenta); yellow (red + green);
- *white*: red + blue + green.

Children are often very surprised to find white as the sum of adding the three primaries, and yellow as the sum of adding red and green.

These simple observations enable us to develop two significant points. The first is that this method of producing colour effects does not actually consist of mixing colours in the way that mixing paints and dyes does, but unless the observer is very near the screen and using a magnifying glass the individual lines are too small to distinguish, so the eye and brain interpret them as a single area of colour. More subtle colour differences are produced by varying the intensity with which the three primary light-emitters are made to glow.

The second significant observation is that when mixing coloured lights, different colours are produced by *adding* light to the image (additive colour mixing), so that white, which is the lightest 'colour' of all, appears when all three coloured lights are emitted at full intensity. It is also noticeable that a secondary colour (e.g. cyan, produced by adding green and blue) is lighter or paler than either primary colour on the screen. It is useful to contrast this mixing of coloured lights with the effect of looking through two colour filters at once; an example of colour mixing by subtraction (Activity 17.8.2). Blue and green still give blue-green, but it is *darker* than either of the single filters used to produce it.

Activity 17.8.4

Coloured lights and coloured objects

The colour which an object appears to be depends on the colour of the light reflected from it into the eye. If the light falling on the object is white, we will see the object in what we think of as its 'true' colours. If the light falling on an object is itself coloured, for example by passing through a colour filter, the colour of the object may appear to change completely.

Making a colour-box

Equipment and materials: Cardboard box about 35 × 20 × 10cm with a removable lid (a shoe-box is ideal); red, green, blue and yellow colour filters at least 10 × 15cm (other colours useful but not essential); selection of small coloured objects; felt-tip pens in a range of colours; white paper; craft knife; Blu-tack.

- Make a colour-box, as shown in Fig. 17.14.
- Place a colour filter over the window in the box lid; press it lightly on to the Blu-tack to keep it in place; replace the lid on the box so that the colour window is at the far end from the viewing-port.
- Place the colour-box near a brightly-lit window but not in full sunlight, with the viewing-port facing away from bright daylight.

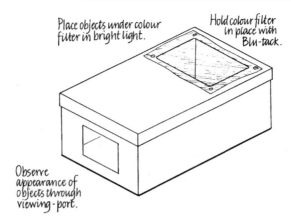

Place objects under colour
filter in bright light.

Hold colour filter
in place with
Blu-tack.

Observe
appearance of
objects through
viewing-port.

Figure 17.14   Making a colour-box

- Place one or more coloured objects in the box, under the colour window. Always include a black and a white object with the coloured ones, for comparison. Replace the lid, look through the viewing-port and observe the colours which the objects appear to be.

Trials using different filters with the same range of objects show clearly how colours appear to change in coloured light and what confusion this can cause. Children can also carry out tests of their own by writing and drawing on white paper with felt-tip pens in a range of colours and viewing these in the colour-box or simply looking at them through colour filters. They can very usefully be encouraged to predict what each colour will look like under coloured light before looking at it. This activity gives excellent opportunities for assessing children's willingness and ability to predict, because each test can be repeated as often as necessary and results are seen very quickly.

18

The Earth in Space

18.1: The Solar System

The planet we live on, which we call Earth, is one of nine planets in orbit round a star which we call the Sun. The Sun, its planets, their satellites (moons) and other smaller bodies such as comets and asteroids, make up the Solar System. With very minor exceptions such as artificial lights and volcanoes on Earth, the Sun is the only light source (*17.2) in the Solar System: we can see our own satellite (the Moon) and other planets only because they reflect light from the Sun into our eyes.

In attempting to develop an understanding of the Solar System we have two main problems. The first is sheer scale: the Solar system is so large in relation to ourselves that it is very difficult to gain any realistic notion of it. To us the Earth seems enormous, but in relation to the Solar system it is tiny. The second major problem is that without specialized equipment, long-term observation and complex calculations the Solar system is very difficult to observe and learn about. The solution to both problems at primary level is to use the information gained by other scientists to develop simple models. These can then be used both to interpret the changes and events which children experience, and help them understand in the future how their lives are affected by the movement of the Earth and Moon around the Sun.

Activity 18.1.1

Modelling the Solar System
One way to gain at least a simple idea of how large the Sun is in relation to the planets, and how far apart the planets are in relation to their sizes, is to make a scale model. The scale is enormously reduced: five thousand million times smaller than reality!

Equipment and materials: Each group needs: 1 play-ball 280mm diameter; modelling clay; 2 small glass marbles each 10mm diameter; poppy seeds; mustard seed; peppercorns; metre trundle-wheel or surveyor's tape.

- Work in groups of six or more, on a large, flat playing-field. Start from one edge of the field; ask one partner to hold the 280mm play-ball. This represents the Sun.
- The four planets nearest the Sun can now be modelled by holding different sized seeds at the right distances:

- Mercury: poppy seed (1mm) at 12m;
- Venus: peppercorn (2.4mm) at 22m;
- Earth: peppercorn (2.5mm) at 30m;
- Mars: mustard seed (1.3mm) at 45m.
- If you had a really large field to work on, the remaining planets would be model-led like this:
  - Jupiter: make a clay ball (28.5mm diameter) at 156m;
  - Saturn: make a clay ball (24 mm diameter) at 285m;
  - Uranus: glass marble (10.3mm) at 574m;
  - Neptune: glass marble (10mm) at 900m;
  - Pluto: poppy seed (0.5mm) at 1,180m.

In most situations the children are likely to have to imagine the modelling of the outer planets, but even so this activity does give quite an accurate and graphic impression of how far apart the planets are and how small they are in relation to the Sun.

18.2: The Earth in orbit

The earth's orbit round the Sun is nearly circular and it travels at very high speed: about 107 000 km each hour, or nearly 3 000 km each second. We are quite unaware of this because we are carried along with the Earth and have no nearby stationary object with which to compare our movement. However, the Earth stays in orbit only because it is prevented from moving away from the Sun. We can make a simple model of the moving Earth and the forces acting on it which helps to show how this happens.

Activity 18.2.1

Modelling the earth in orbit

Equipment: A light, soft play-ball; 2m thread or very thin, light string; adhesive tape.

- Work outside, or in a large room or hall; you need at least 2m clear space all round you. Fasten the thread to the ball with a piece of adhesive tape.
- Hold the string about half-way along. Lift the ball off the floor and start to swing it in a circle around you, with your arm above your head. Only your arm should move: keep your head and body still.
- As the ball starts to swing faster, gradually let the thread run out through your fingers until you are holding it near the end and the ball is 'orbiting' in a 2m radius circle.
- Now keep the ball going round at a steady speed, moving your arm and hand as little as possible.
- ? Is the ball pushing or pulling on the thread? (The thread is straight and slightly taut, so the ball is pulling on it.)
- ? Is the ball pulling inwards or outwards? (It is pulling outwards.)
- ? If you let the thread go, would the ball still keep going round in a circle? (No: it would fly off.)
- Get the ball going round at a steady speed, then suddenly release the thread.

? What happens? (The ball flies off, more or less in a straight line, and falls to the ground.)
? What was keeping the ball moving in a circle? (The pull of the thread.)
? In which direction was the pulling force acting? (Inwards, towards the centre of the circle.)
? Why does the Earth stay in orbit round the Sun? (There must be a force which prevents it from flying off into space.)
? What do you think the force is, and in which direction does it act ? (The Sun's gravity, pulling the Earth inwards, towards the Sun.)

The ball on the thread was 'orbiting' every few seconds. The Earth orbits round the Sun once a year (*18.4). As the earth moves round the Sun it also spins, about 365 times each year. The time to complete a spin is called a day (i.e. 24 hours).

Activity 18.2.2

Modelling day and night

Equipment: Mounted terrestrial globe, diameter at least 30cm, which can revolve at 23.5° tilt; overhead projector (OHP); stand for globe which brings its centre level with the OHP projection mirror; pieces of thin wire 5mm long; Blu-tack.

- If possible, work with curtains or blinds drawn. (Note that when experimenting with and observing the model shadow-stick, children will need to work close the globe in small groups.)
- Set up the globe and OHP as shown in Fig. 18.1, about 3m apart. It is important to make sure that the centre of the globe and the projection mirror of the OHP are exactly level.

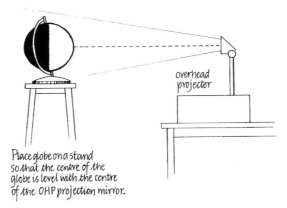

Place globe on a stand so that the centre of the globe is level with the centre of the OHP projection mirror.

Figure 18.1 Modelling day and night

? How much of the globe is in light and how much in shadow? (Half and half.)
? Imagine you were living on this globe, and that the OHP is your sun. In which part of the 24 hours would people in the light be? (Day-time.) In which part would people in shadow be? (Night-time.)

- Find where you live on the globe. Turn the globe so that where you live is right on the boundary between light and shadow.

To simulate day and night we need to find out which way to turn (more properly, spin) the globe. Begin by looking at the North Pole. If you were in a space-station looking down at the North Pole, you would see Earth spinning slowly *counterclockwise*. (If you were looking down at the South Pole, it would appear to spin clockwise.)

- Make sure you know which way the Earth spins, then turn the globe a little in that direction.
? Did your place on the globe move into shadow or into light? What time of day would it be when that happened in the real world? (If your home moves into shadow, it is evening; if into light, it is morning.)
- Turn the globe so that where you live faces directly towards the projector beam.
? In the real world, with light coming from the Sun, what time would it be now? (Mid-day or noon.)
- Now move the globe round slowly, making sure you move it the right way. Move it round one complete turn, watching what happens to the place where you live.
? What changes would people on your model world have experienced as the globe turned? (They would have gone into shadow [night-time] and back into the light [daytime] again.)
? In the real world, how long does it take for the Earth to make one complete turn? (24 hours; usually called a day.)
- Turn the globe so that where you live on the globe is at 'mid-day', i.e. facing directly into the light-beam. Fasten a short piece of thin wire upright where you live, with a small piece of Blu-tack. Look at its shadow and notice in which direction it falls. (If you live in temperate latitudes a wire 5 or even 4mm will be long enough. If you live nearer the equator, a longer wire may be needed.)
? In which direction is the shadow? (It points north if you live in the Northern Hemisphere, e.g. in Britain or the USA; but south if you live in the Southern Hemisphere, e.g. Australia, New Zealand or South Africa.)
- Now turn the globe (the right way!) so that the 'mid-day' on your model world turns to 'afternoon' and then 'evening'. Watch what happens to the shadow.
? How does the shadow change? (It becomes longer and changes direction, pointing more and more towards the east.)
? Why does the shadow change direction and length? (Because the angle at which light from the OHP strikes the globe changes as the globe is moved.)

This last point is very significant because it can be used to make the connection between the model and what the children experience in reality. The model shows what happens to shadows as the globe is turned, and we see the same pattern of change on Earth. The significance of the model for children's learning is that it can begin to establish the idea that it is the Earth's movement in relation to the Sun which brings about night and day, although to us on Earth it is likely to appear to be the other way round. It will be very useful to return to this model during the next activity.

Activity 18.2.3

Patterns of sun-shadows

What appears to us as a movement of the Sun across the sky during the day is in reality caused by the spin of the Earth. Observations using a model shadow-stick on a globe (Activity 18.2.2) are a particularly useful introduction to this difficult idea, which can then be developed by making observations of real sun-shadows.

Equipment and materials: For making sundial: 50 × 50cm board (e.g. blockboard or MDF, 18mm thick); cotton reel, pencil stub about 6cm long; hot-melt glue and glue-gun. For using sundial: sheets of paper cut to fit on base-board; Blu-tack; fluid-filled compass ('Silva' type); pencil; watch or clock.

- Make a basic sundial as shown in Fig. 18.2. The exact length of pencil needed for the gnomon will depend where in the world you live. In north temperate regions about 4cm is usually suitable; but in lower latitudes a longer one may be better.

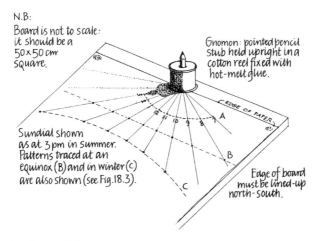

Figure 18.2   A simple sundial

- Work on a clear, sunny day when little or no cloud is forecast. It is usually best to work outdoors. Set up the sundial as early as possible in a level place, which will remain in sunlight all day and where it will not be in anybody's way.
- Place the compass exactly on the edge of the base-board; turn the sundial so that the cotton-reel is towards the south and the sides lie exactly north-south (Fig. 18.2).
- Fasten a sheet of paper with Blu-tack, parallel to the edges of the base-board and touching the cotton-reel. Write the date in one corner.
- Mark the shadow of the tip of the gnomon on the paper and write the time beside it. Continue to do this throughout the day. Recording on the hour and half-hour gives a record which is easy to interpret and a record at noon (mid-day) is particularly useful.
- At the end of the day's recording, before you remove the paper from the board, carefully rule lines between the bottom of the gnomon (i.e. the centre of the cotton-reel) and each of the shadow-marks. This will produce a pattern of radiat-

ing lines which can be compared with patterns recorded at different times of the year.

● *Keep all your records safely!* Carry on recording when you can throughout the year and compare your records to see how the pattern of sun-shadows changes.

? Look at a day's shadow record. When is the shadow longest? (Early and late in the day.) When is it shortest? (Noon; but be aware of time adjustments in summer, such as daylight saving.)

? What does the record show about the 'height' (elevation) of the sun? (It is highest at noon, lowest at sunrise and sunset.)

? How can sun-shadows be used to tell the time? (With a sundial. However, a simple sundial is only approximately correct through most of the year and making an accurate sundial is very complex.)

At this point it is very helpful to return to the model of day and night used in Activity 18.2.2, in order to show the similarity between the shadows seen on the model and those recorded in reality, and to reinforce the point that it is the Earth's movement (spin) in relation to the Sun which causes change in the direction and angle of sunlight during the day.

● If you have records available, compare the sun-shadow patterns recorded at different times of the year. In particular, compare the shadows recorded in winter and summer at the same times of day (Fig. 18.3).

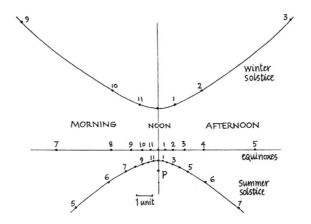

Patterns of sun-shadows cast by a vertical pin
1 unit high at point P. Each point shows the length and
direction of the shadows on four days in the year
at Leicester, England
(Based on a scale drawing by David Brown, British Sundial Society)

Figure 18.3   Patterns of sun-shadows

? What differences do you notice?

In temperate latitudes the shadow at any time of day is much longer in winter than in summer, because light from the Sun strikes the Earth at a shallower angle. Differences of this kind are responsible for the seasons, (see Activity 18.4.1). The patterns traced out by the shadows are also markedly different; but notice that at the equinox the shadow of a sundial always follows a straight line.

? Can you see anything in the shadow-patterns which is constant throughout the year? (The most obvious feature is the *direction* of the shadow at noon.)

In the Northern Hemisphere (outside the tropics), a sun-shadow always points due north at noon, so the Sun always appears to be to the south of the observer. In the Southern Hemisphere this is reversed: the shadow points south and the Sun is seen as being due north. What is less obvious is that the direction of the shadow is approximately the same at any particular time of day. For every hour that passes, the sun-shadow changes direction by 15° (i.e. 360 ÷ 24), so that, for example, at 3p.m. the shadow is always 45° east of its noon position.

18.3: The Earth and the Moon

The Earth has only one satellite, the Moon, which is unusual in that it is very large in relation to its planet, having a diameter nearly one quarter that of the Earth and about one sixth of its mass. The Moon is in orbit round the Earth and completes one revolution in about 28 days, a period known as the lunar month. In relation to the Earth the Moon's orbit is approximately circular, but its actual path through space is *not* circular because, as it moves round the Earth, the Earth is itself moving round the sun (*18.3).

The Moon is not always visible at night, but if it is, its appearance changes during any lunar month in a regular and predictable way. These changes are known as the phases of the Moon. Because the Moon is not a light source we see the part of its surface which is being illuminated by sunlight which is then reflected to Earth. The relationship between the Sun, Earth and Moon is a complex, three-dimensional one, but the simple model suggested here should enable children to understand the changes in the Moon's appearance which they are likely to observe.

Activity 18.3.1

Modelling phases of the Moon

Equipment: Play-ball 15–20cm diameter, painted half black and half white; adhesive tape; 30cm thin, stiff wire; stick or cane.

- Suspend the ball from one end of the stick by the wire. Fasten the wire to the ball at the boundary of the black and white halves.
- Work in a room or hall so that one person can move around the others in a circle. If there is more than one window, draw the curtains over all but the most brightly-lit one.
- Hold the stick so that the model moon hangs with the white half facing the window.
? What does the window represent? (The Sun.)
? What does the white half of the ball represent? (The half of the Moon illuminated by the Sun.)

- Keeping the 'moon' facing the same way all the time (i.e. white half facing the window), move in a circle round the people in the middle of the room.
? What do the people represent? (Observers on Earth.)
? Does the amount of the Moon illuminated by the Sun change? (No: as in the model, half is always in light.)
? If half the Moon is always in light and half in shadow, why are there changes in what observers see? (Because, as the model shows, the angles between the Earth, Moon and Sun are changing all the time.)

The changes in the appearance of the Moon are called its phases. It completes one orbit of the Earth in about 28 days; this is a lunar month.

18.4: The Earth, the Sun and energy input

The Earth moves round the Sun in an orbit which is like the edge of a huge, imaginary disc (the plane of the ecliptic). This is also the direction from which light travels to the Earth from the Sun. As the Earth travels round in its orbit it spins, but the axis of its spin (an imaginary line through the North and South Poles) is tilted at an angle of 23.5° to the ecliptic. Terrestrial globes are usually mounted in a bracket so that when placed on a table, which represents the plane of the ecliptic, they revolve at the correct angle of tilt.

Children (and adults) often believe, mistakenly, that the tropics are generally warmer than temperate or high latitudes because they are 'nearer the Sun'. The difference is in reality one of energy input, which children can model in the classroom.

Activity 18.4.1

Modelling energy input to the earth

Equipment: Mounted terrestrial globe, diameter at least 30cm, which can revolve at 23.5° tilt; overhead projector (OHP); stand for globe which brings its centre level with the OHP projection mirror; thin, stiff wire; pliers; board-marker or stick about 1cm diameter.

- Set up the globe and OHP as in Fig. 18.1. The centre of the globe should be level with the projection mirror of the OHP.
- By twisting thin wire round a board-marker or stick, make a wire ring about 1cm diameter, with a handle.
- To start observations, place the globe so that the bracket is at right angles to the light. (This places the globe as the Earth is at an equinox).
- Find where you live on the globe. Turn the globe so that it would be mid-day at your home (see Activity 18.2.2). Hold the wire ring 1cm from the globe, at right angles to the light, so that where you live is in the centre of the shadow cast by the ring. *Keeping the ring at right angles to the light* (Fig. 18.4), move it 'north' and 'south' so that its shadow moves towards the poles and the equator. Watch to see what happens to the size and shape of the shadow ring.
? How does the shadow ring change as the ball is moved towards and away from the poles? (Near the equator the shadow is circular. As the ring is moved towards

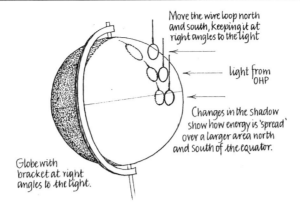

Move the wire loop north
and south, keeping it at
right angles to the light

light from
OHP

Changes in the shadow
show how energy is 'spread'
over a larger area north
and south of the equator.

Globe with
bracket at right
angles to the light.

Figure 18.4   Modelling energy input to the Earth

the poles the shadow becomes longer in the north-south direction and changes
shape to an ellipse.)
? Where in the sky would the Sun appear to be if you were on the equator and it was
mid-day? (Exactly overhead.) Where would the Sun appear to be if you were near
the North Pole? (Due south, very low in the sky.)

The wire ring models the way light energy from the Sun reaches different parts of the
Earth at different rates. The ring represents a certain amount of radiant energy
(Activity 12.3.5) reaching the Earth each second. Where the shadow of the ring is a
circle, i.e. when the Sun is directly overhead at the equator, the *rate* of energy input is
high because that amount of energy is transferred to as small an area as possible. If
the same amount (area) of light energy strikes the Earth at a shallow angle near the
poles, the *rate* of energy input (and therefore heating) is much lower because the
energy is spread out, as it were, over a much larger area (Fig. 18.4). This helps to
explain why the tropics are much hotter for most of the year than temperate regions.

Seasons
As the Earth turns in its orbit, the direction in which its imaginary axis points does
not change, so that in the Northern Hemisphere it is always seen as pointing to the
Pole Star. The constant tilt and orientation, coupled with its movement in orbit,
means that the angle at which light from the Sun strikes any part of the Earth at mid-
day is constantly changing throughout the year. The difference between winter and
summer, shown in Fig. 18.5, is too complex to model in the classroom, but museums
may have working models and there are good animations available on CD-ROM.

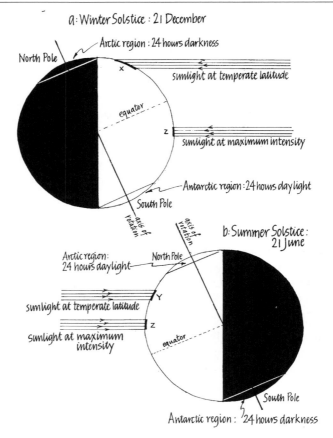

Figure 18.5   The tilt of the Earth and the seasons

Index